About the Author

Andy is a senior editor at IDW Publishing, overseeing *G.I. Joe* and *Star Trek* comics, among others. Andy is also the owner and operator of Comics Experience (www.comicsexperience.com), an education-based business dedicated to helping comic book writer and artist hopefuls fulfill their dreams. Most of his classes meet in New York or California. There is a distance-learning option for the writing course. Check out the website above to see if any of the courses or consulting are right for you. Andy's freelance writing has been published by Marvel Comics, Th3rd World Studios, Markosia and BOOM! Studios.

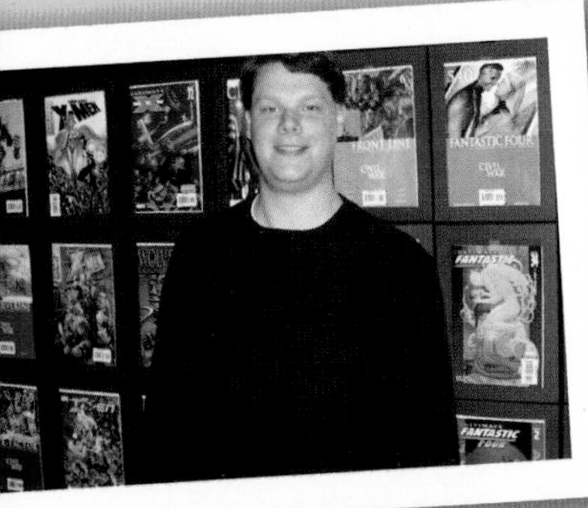

Andy has been editing comics since 2002 when he started as an assistant editor under Tom Brevoort in the "Marvel Heroes" line of books for Marvel Entertainment. There, he lent his talents to everything from *The Fantastic Four* to *The Avengers*. He developed *Madrox* and later *X-Factor* with writer Peter David and artist Pablo Raimondi. Andy spearheaded the twenty-five-part, galaxy spanning space saga called *Annihilation* with a wealth of writers and artists. When he decided to leave Marvel, he was an integral part of the *X-Men* editorial team. His favorite projects there were *Secret War*, *Madrox*, *Alias*, *Civil War*, *The New Avengers*, *Young Avengers*, *Ms. Marvel*, *Annihilation*, *The Pulse*, *Defenders*, *Union Jack*, *X-Factor* and *X-Men*.

Before coming to comics, Andy designed and taught two college courses for Webster University in St. Louis on comic book storytelling. Much of what is contained in this book has been tried and tested out on his oh-so-unlucky guinea pigs—ahem—students.

Andy is happy to have the good fortune to work in such a creative and fun industry, and to call many of his collaborators friends as well as colleagues. He lives in San Diego with his wife, Alix, and their son, Cale.

Acknowledgments

This book would not exist without the help and inspiration of Peter David, who invited me to write a guest spot in his book on writing for comics. Thanks for the opportunity, Peter. He introduced me to Pam Wissman at IMPACT Books, who massaged this project into existence and delivered it into the watchful care of editors Mona Michael and Kelly Messerly. Thanks also to Matt Bialy and Suzanne Lucas for working out all that contract mumbo jumbo.

Thanks to Carol Platt and Dan Buckley at Marvel Comics for allowing so much artwork to be used for this book, to Marco Chechetto for allowing the use of art from *The Courier* in the book and on the cover, and to John Romita Jr. for permission to use *The Gray Area* in the book and on the cover. John, you're the best in the business.

Thanks to all the contributors, especially those who wrote pieces for the book and gave interviews: Art Adams, Neal Adams, John Byrne, C.B. Cebulski, Chris Eliopoulos, David Finch, Gene Ha, Klaus Janson, Karl Kesel, Mike Perkins, Khoi Pham, Walt Simonson and Chris Sotomayor. Thanks to Frank D'Angelo for his assistance with the interviews.

Thank you to everyone who donated art files (without them, this book wouldn't look nearly so pretty): Gabriele Dell'Otto, Justin Ponsor, Laura Martin, Laura Villari, Mike Perkins, Pete Pantazis, June Chung, Brian Michael Bendis, Ed Brubaker, Tom DeFalco, Geoff Johns, José Villarrubia, Brian Reber, Chris Sotomayor, Jim Cheung, Bill Crabtree Frank D'Armata and many, many more.

My deepest thanks to the people who taught me nearly everything I know about comics over the last few years, especially Tom Brevoort, Michael Higgins and Klaus Janson. This book and my own career would not have been possible without the three of you.

CONTENTS

How Comics Are Unique

Prose has the written word. Photography captures a moment in time. Radio brings us sound. Film breathes life into movement and brings it together with sound. And comics…what do they do that's different?

Comics are the most powerful medium on the planet. Comics can have one author–as writer and artist–one single mind and talent that creates the whole package. Only written prose shares this with comics. No other medium can so directly transmit the author's ideas and images into the mind of the receiver. Unlike the novel, comics transmit the images from the author's mind without translating them into descriptive phrases. In a novel, I have to describe the dark, wet, dreary forest with the sticky, muddy ground and hollow-eyed owls, but in comics I just draw exactly what my mind sees and show it directly to you, the reader. Even with photography, the photographer rarely makes up the landscape and so requires many outside elements to bring his photo to life. In television and film–forget about it–actors, directors, writers, producers, editors and cinematographers–everybody gets his piece of the message.

The canvas size and shape can change in comics. Sure, with film, you can have widescreen or a square image, and with paintings and photography you can literally adjust your canvas size and shape, but with comics, the size and shape of the canvas can change from moment to moment. Once a film starts off in letterbox format, that's where it stays. The painter's canvas doesn't change before your eyes. Once it's done, it's set in stone. The comic panel (sometimes called the *frame* or *window*) can change from page to page–from panel to panel, in fact.

Unlike in film and television, there is no special effects budget. Your budget cap in comics is the imagination. Blowing up a planet costs a lot of money to put on film effectively, but in comics, it's the cost of the art board, a pencil, and the time and effort. A summer blockbuster in a comic costs the same as a romantic comedy or noir detective story or Greek tragedy. The playing field is equal. We all work with twenty-two blank pages and our own wits.

The song says that if you can make it in New York, you can make it anywhere, but I believe that if you can make it in comics, there's no point in going anywhere else. There is no other medium that can bring the message any closer to your audience. Communicating and telling a story effectively in comics is as close to projecting thoughts directly into someone's mind as you're ever going to get.

But there's a catch (isn't there always?). The author of the comic is also the producer, the writer, the director, the cinematographer, the editor, the actors, the art director, the costume designer, the lighting technician, the cameraman and the marketing genius. You have to do it all and you've got to do it well.

Insider Comics Terms

Art board The surface comics are drawn on. There is specific comic book art board called Bristol board that is made for comics to be printed at the usual size. The boards, made specifically for comics, include blue-lined information. They have places for the title of the book, issue number, page number, your name, and the name of the inker. In addition to the elements at the top, they also include technical lines and information that is very valuable to the artist. Because the markings are in blue, they will not be picked up by a scanner set to scan in bitmap, so the board can mark clearly where your copy safe and trim lines are without you having to worry about those measurements showing up on the final printed comic book.

Bitmap A type of scanning that assigns only one of two values to any given pixel: black or white. The blue line on the art board is light enough to be considered white by the scanner.

Bleed The bleed area on a page is everything that is outside of the copy safe and extends past the trim lines. This area can contain artwork, but it is called "bleed" because it will bleed off of the final page after it is cut.

Camera The reader's view in a panel. This term is borrowed from filmmaking because the focus of the panels acts like a camera, zooming in for close-ups, pulling back or panning. Panel descriptions are often done in camera angles.

Caption Captions contain copy. They can be any shape desired, usually a rectangle of some kind, and they typically sit on top of the artwork, like a word balloon. A caption can be any kind of narration, be it first person, omniscient or any other narrative device.

Copy Any and all written language that appears on the final comic book page. It can be written in word balloons, thought balloons, captions, sound effects or it can be free-floating.

Copy safe Copy safe is an invisible (to the reader) border that sits inside the trim lines in which it is deemed safe to place dialogue and important action. Upon printing a comic book, it is common for printing press plates to shift slightly, allowing the content of a page to shift in any direction on the page. Using the copy safe area correctly should prevent any important action or dialogue from being cut off the page even if the plates slip.

Crop marks Printer marks that show where the final page will be cut off.

Double-page spread Two facing pages joined by an overlapping element and intended to be read across the fold of the book. The story on a spread is read as if the two pages were one single page: One reads from the upper left to the upper right corner, moving over the fold or spine of the book. When the reader reaches the top right corner of the right page, he moves back to the left side of the left page and reads from left to right again until the entire spread is complete.

DPI Dots per inch. A scanner can be set to scan for different amounts of DPI. The higher the number (400dpi is normal for comic book printing), the larger the computer file becomes and the clearer the image is.

Facing pages Two pages that are visible at the same time. They are read as two independent pages despite the fact that they are both visible.

FTP A computer server that allows fast uploading and downloading of large files by multiple users.

Page One side of a sheet of paper from the fold in the middle out to one edge. It is read from top left to bottom right (although Japanese manga comics are read from top right to bottom left). It is usually comprised of more than one panel, but it can be one panel only.

Panel A single confined image within a page. Panels are the building blocks for comic book storytelling.

Scanning Using a device that scans an entire art board and makes a digital file of the artwork in your computer.

Sound effects Onomatopoeia words that indicate a noise of some kind relating to the panel in which they appear. They are typically not contained in a box or bubble. The BANG from a gunshot is a sound effect and would not be contained in a caption box.

Stat panel A repeated panel that can be copied and pasted digitally.

Thought balloon The same as a word balloon except that its edges and pointer are made to look like a puffy cloud. The cloud indicates that the dialogue contained inside is not spoken, but rather is the character's inner monologue.

TIFF File format preferred for colorists to work from.

Trim The second and outer invisible (to the reader) border on every page. The trim lines depict where the image should be cut (at least if the plates don't slip upon printing). Anything on the outside of the trim lines will be trimmed off the page after printing.

Word balloon When a character speaks, it is normal that his dialogue will fit into a (usually) white balloon with a black outline. This balloon will also have a short pointer extending from it toward the speaker, indicating to whom the dialogue should be attributed.

So you want to be a comic book storyteller. What does that mean?

Boiled down, it's fairly simple. It means you have a job to do and that job is to tell the story. If you're writing, drawing or writing and drawing, it doesn't matter, your job is to tell a story and to do so effectively and in an entertaining way.

You have two priorities:

1 Communicate clearly to the reader.

2 Entertain the reader.

Nothing else matters.

COMMUNICATION: THE FIRST PRIORITY

Writers have to make sure that there is never a moment when the artist reading your script wonders what location he's in, which characters are in the scene and who is talking with whom. Every descriptive line should communicate information that propels the characters through the story. Every line of dialogue must communicate one thing on the surface, and another thing beneath the surface—subtext is a necessity. For example, in *The Empire Strikes Back*, Han Solo is about to be put to death and the princess says to him, "I love you." Solo's response is, "I know." The audience knows that what "I know" *really* means is "I love you, too." That's subtext. It's the meaning beneath the words.

Writers have to know why characters have conversations in the locations they're in. That location carries meaning. Are they in an office? Outside in the daylight? In a parking garage? Every decision carries a message.

Artists have to make sure that all the clarity the writer puts into the script makes it to the final page. If something is confusing to them in the script, it's their job to make sure that it's clear as day on the final drawn page.

If the panel descriptions leave artists room to add their own touches to the page, they have to do so knowing the impact their decisions carry. If they draw one of the two speakers in the conversation from an extreme low angle, they must do so knowing the effect that this camera angle carries. That speaker will appear large and strong. Should the figure appear this way? Perhaps, but perhaps not.

Showing Emotions

On this page by John Romita Jr., all actions flow properly. Before the two men can break into the building, they must unlock the window—the reader then feels surprised along with the characters to find that their foes are waiting for them.

***The Gray Area* #1, page 25: ©2005 John Romita, Jr. and Glen Brunswick. Used with permission.**

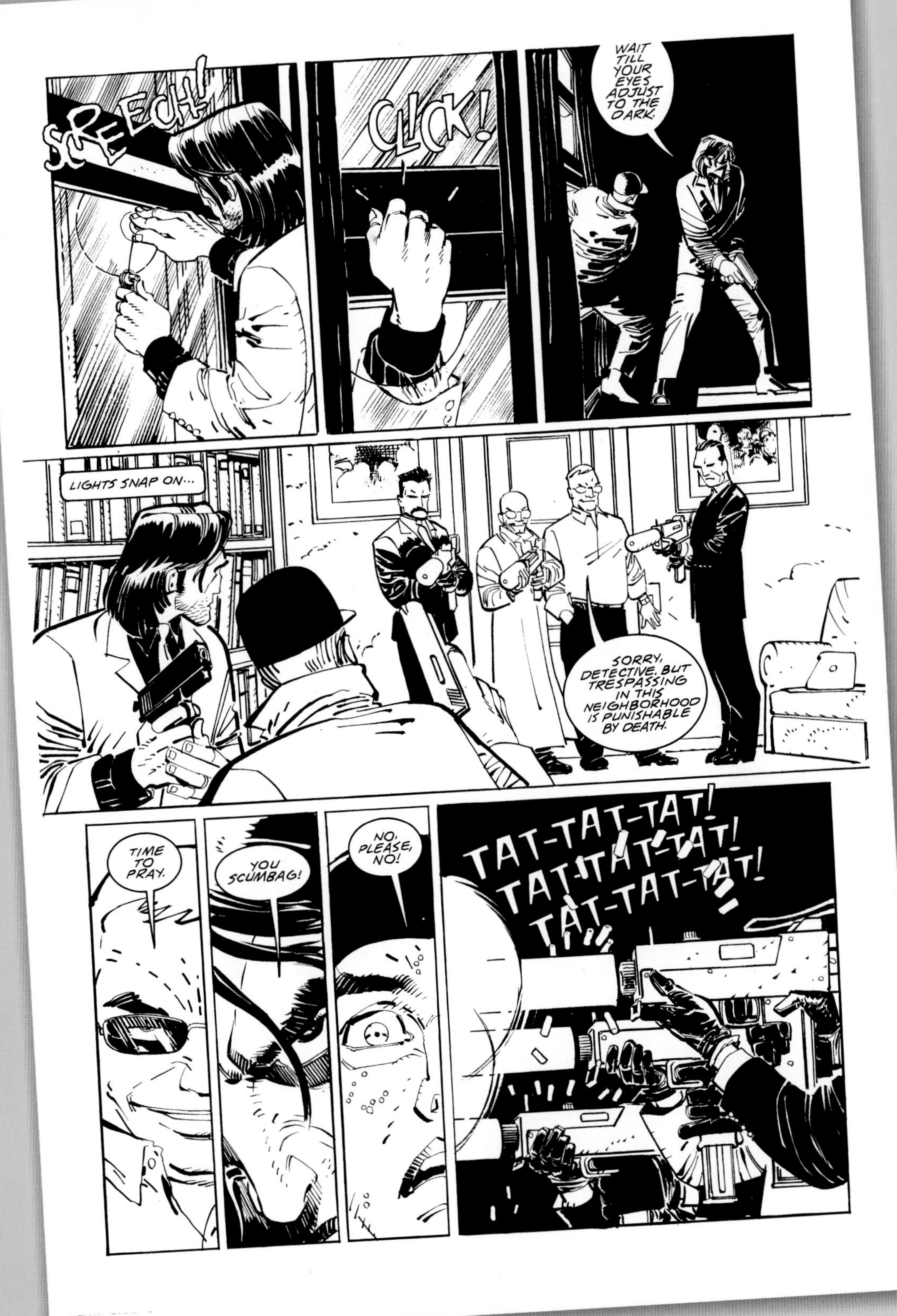
SCREECH!
CLICK!
WAIT TILL YOUR EYES ADJUST TO THE DARK.
LIGHTS SNAP ON...
SORRY, DETECTIVE, BUT TRESPASSING IN THIS NEIGHBORHOOD IS PUNISHABLE BY DEATH.
TIME TO PRAY.
YOU SCUMBAG!
NO, PLEASE, NO!
TAT-TAT-TAT-TAT!
TAT-TAT-TAT-TAT!
TAT-TAT-TAT-TAT!

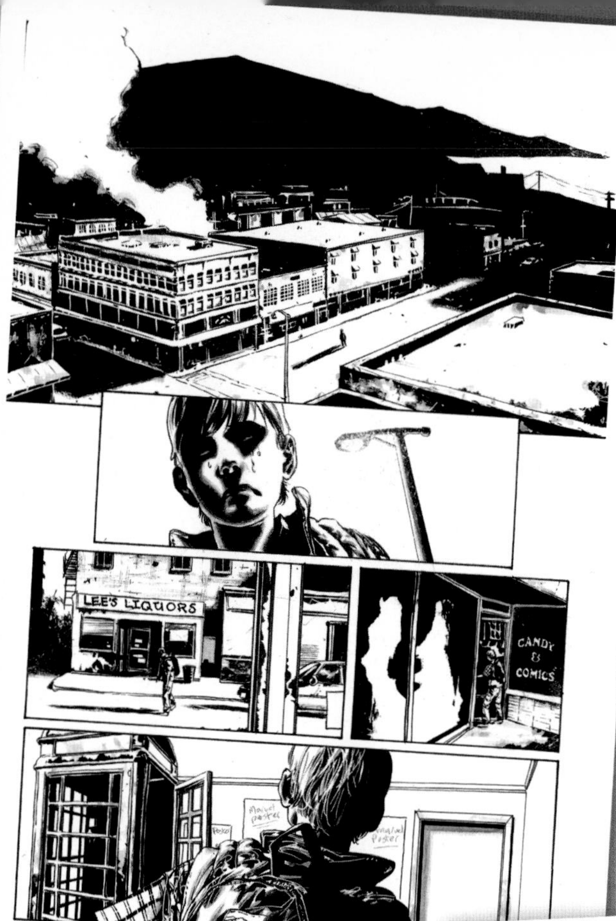

Sometimes, It's Necessary to Establish Everything

Establishing shots are generally necessary in transitioning from one scene to the next. In this page, artist Mitch Breitweiser begins with a location establishing shot to give the reader a clear indication of where this scene takes place. In the second panel, notice the telephone pole behind the young man, again, establishing that he's outside instead of inside the buildings shown.

***Drax the Destroyer* #3, page 13: ©2008 Marvel Characters, Inc. Used with permission.**

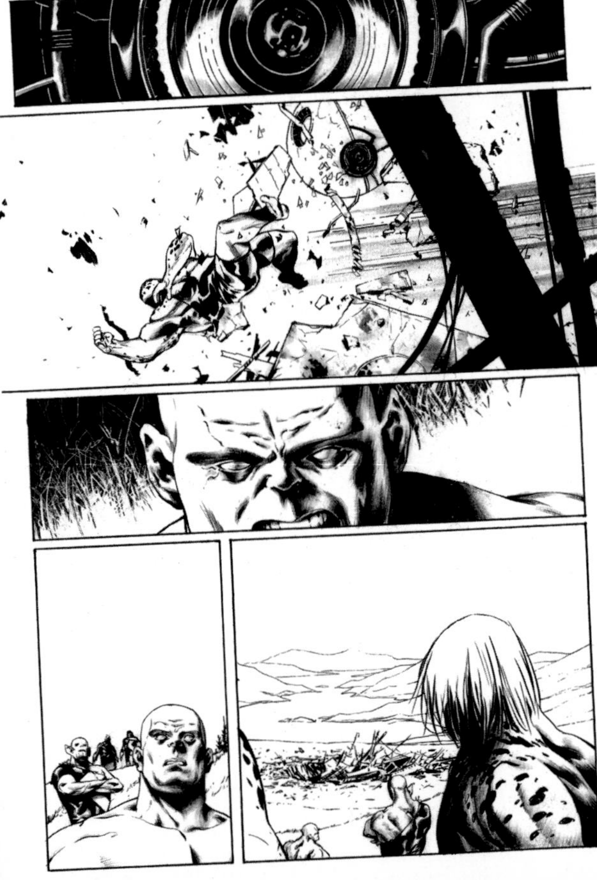

Sometimes, the Emotion Is More Important

In another page of Mitch's, an establishing shot wasn't called for. Instead, it was decided to go in for a close-up to accentuate the confusion caused by sudden action and then catch up the reader later on the page. That's what was done here. The reader should be confused until panel 4, where Mitch pulls the camera back to establish the scene.

***Drax the Destroyer* #1, page 16: ©2008 Marvel Characters, Inc. Used with permission.**

ENTERTAIN: THE SECOND PRIORITY

The second function of a storyteller is to entertain. Obviously, all comic readers would like to be entertained, but here's the only rule: Never put entertainment before communication. Communicate the information that needs to come across, and then make it entertaining. Placing emphasis on entertaining rather than telling leads to failure.

I'm sure you can recall a time where you saw an amazing splash page that blew you away with how beautiful it was, but it also left you wondering how it related to the panels surrounding it. When this happens, the reader is pulled out of the story and the illusion is shattered.

Once the information—the storytelling—is down, writers and artists have to figure out how to communicate it in the most entertaining way possible. There is always a dramatic and appropriate way to illustrate a scene. It's a fine line to balance on, and knowing how far to push comes with practice.

It Starts With Story

Always tell the story first, and then entertain. You'll know the story is good when simply telling it is entertaining.

Do Nothing Lightly

Every decision made carries information and impact to the reader. So make every decision carefully.

SCRIPTS 1

Think of comics like a movie. How many great movies have terrible scripts? Oh, sure, there are stupid movies with stupid screenplays that I love, but they're guilty pleasures. I wasn't upset when *Transporter 2* was "overlooked" by the Academy Awards. I loved the movie, but it isn't a high point for the filmmaking craft.

Great films start with great scripts—*Saving Private Ryan*, *The Departed*, *Fight Club*, *Thelma & Louise*, and a hundred others. And these scripts are great for many reasons, but one of the fundamentals is that the screenwriter understands how film works. There's a lot of trick photography in *Fight Club*, but the screenwriter and the director understand that these ideas can work in film.

It's the same thing for comics. Sometimes, when I work with a writer for the first time, I wind up saying, "he gets it." That means that the writer understands how comics work, what to describe and what to leave out, and how balloons will flow on a page and through panels. This is often something that is just hardwired into a writer's brain.

But it's not impossible to develop "comics awareness" as a skill. It's not easy, though. Writing a good script for comics is extremely difficult. With film, the writer leaves an awful lot up to the director and the director isn't obligated to stick to the script. This is not the case in comics. In comics, the writer tells the artist a story and lays it out in detail. The artist does have leeway, but the artist's job, in most cases, is to clarify and intensify what the writer has written.

Writer's Tools

Typically, a writer needs a computer with some kind of writing software on it. There is no standard software for writing comics. Microsoft Word, WordPerfect, Final Draft, or any number of writing programs are acceptable—just make sure that when you're doing work-for-hire, the people you're writing for can open your files.

Email is essential. Email is how most script notes are given and discussion about scenes takes place.

Comics is a collaborative art form; the writer and the artist have equal value and equal input in the final product. Great scripts are clear, concise and engaging. But they also have clear turning points and well-established characters.

TURNING POINTS

In all good and dramatic scenes there is at least one turning point, a change that propels the scene and the plot forward.

Imagine a scene in which Batman and Superman are talking and they decide that in order to track down the Joker, they're going to split up. The scene's events play out like this: Batman sits in his Batcave; Superman flies in and lands. The two talk, decide to split up, and Superman leaves while Batman drives away in the Batmobile. It's a scene insofar as a conversation occurs and a decision is made about how to go about tracking down the Joker. But nothing dramatic occurs.

Now imagine it this way: Batman sits brooding in the Batcave, having nearly given up his search for the Joker. Superman flies into the cave and lands, suggesting ways to track down the villain. Batman has tried them all and grows irritated at Superman's suggestions. Batman knows the Joker will strike again and the guilt of not finding him nearly breaks Batman's spirit. He lashes out at Superman, who is taken aback. Batman's nearly hopeless. Superman stands, taking a punch to the chest from Batman. The two stand next to each other. Superman puts his hand on Batman's shoulder and says, "We'll find him. It's what we do." Batman steps back and straightens his back. "Yes, it's what we do." Superman suggests using his superpowers under Batman's direction—essentially offering to become a tool for Batman to use—which inspires a new plan. Batman tells Superman to take flight over the city while he goes in his car to implement the plan. The two heroes leave the Batcave, Batman in the Batmobile and Superman in the air.

The plot events of the scene haven't changed. I've fleshed them out more and given more detail. At the beginning of the scene, Batman has exhausted all avenues at his disposal to find the Joker. He's ready to give up (not that he would, because he's Batman and he doesn't do that). At the end, Batman has a new plan and hope of finding the Joker. So somewhere between the beginning and the end of the scene, something happened that turned the scene from one of hopelessness to one of hopefulness. That "something" is the turning point. Are you beginning to see how difficult finding a scene is?

The turning point occurs when Superman gives those few words of hope to Batman and it jolts Batman back to his senses. This is a full scene that moves the plot forward and has a turning point, which means there is drama.

IDENTIFYING TURNING POINTS

- A scene starts off negative and ends more upbeat.
- A scene starts off with a positive feeling and ends with a negative feeling.

Multiple Turning Points

- Sometimes a scene can have more than one turning point: A scene can start positive, turn negative and then turn back to positive.
- It is possible for a scene to start positive and turn to super positive, or to start negative and turn to super negative.

ESTABLISH CHARACTER

But that's not all that makes a good scene. In order for it to truly work, Superman and Batman need to be established.

- Who are they?
- What can they do?
- Why are they working together?
- What is their relationship to each other?
- Why in the world is Batman sitting in a cave?
- Who is the Joker?
- Why must he be found?

In the course of the whole story, these things need to be established. That doesn't mean that someone blurts out all of this information in a series of boring word balloons. Most of the other elements of the story have probably been established prior to this scene, but if this is the only scene, all this information needs to be in it.

A good scene has answers to all these questions and gives some insight into the characters as well.

The first version serves only to get from point A to point B. But the reworked version has some punch to it. It's a scene worth reading on its own. It tells you something about these two characters—that Batman is the driven obsessive type and prone to darker emotions and that Superman is the optimistic hero. This isn't new information to fans of the characters, but it still says something about them.

Artist Sample Scripts

Artists looking for sample scripts to show their work need those samples to have all the ingredients of a great script, but also to give them an opportunity to show off how they've mastered everything from extreme close-ups to establishing shots, and from landscapes to cityscapes. They need to find scripts written for an artist. A script needs:

- A full scene, at least one page long.
- A scene that has a turning point and is not just a conversation between two people.

iNSidER PROFiLE

John Romita Jr.

JOHN ROMITA JR. started his pencilling career in 1977 and never looked back. Training under his father, John Romita Sr., offered him the best comics training probably of anyone in the business. His father, a great influence on John both as an artist and as a human being, is one of the fathers of modern superhero comics. John Jr. grew up with someone who had already mastered the field, and as such, learned early on how to tell a story. His runs on *Daredevil*, *The Uncanny X-Men* and *The Amazing Spider-Man* mark high points for all three titles, and he remains a hard-working, disciplined penciller at the top of his field. He also created *The Gray Area* with writer Glen Brunswick and allowed me to print much of that art in this book.

OCCUPATION: Cartoonist/penciller

DATE OF BIRTH: August 17, 1956

FIRST PUBLISHED WORK: *The Amazing Spider-Man Annual* #11, "Chaos at the Coffee Bean" (1977)

INFLUENCES: In the comics industry, my father, John Buscema and Jack Kirby. From outside of comics, there's a whole book of illustrators.

LONGEST RUN ON A BOOK: *The Amazing Spider-Man*

BEST KNOWN FOR: Spider-Man

FAVORITE CHARACTER WORKED ON: My favorite character, overall, would be Spider-Man. But my favorite character to draw is probably Daredevil.

DREAM PROJECT: Let's see, I worked on Spider-Man with my father. If I was to start the business again I'd say that's a dream project. From this point, if I have to choose a dream project, I think it would be to work with Frank Miller on *Daredevil* again.

MOST PERSONAL WORK: The 9/11 Spider-Man issue, *The Amazing Spider-Man* #36.

ART TRAINING: Degree in advertising illustration from SUNY Farmingdale. That training was fantastic. It covered everything from advertising to classic illustration to anatomy to fine arts. On the job training I worked as a production assistant at Marvel in the late 1970s.

BEST ADVICE RECEIVED WHEN STARTING OUT: My father gave me the best career advice. He said, "There's always somebody bigger, stronger, smarter and faster, so keep your feet on the ground." I think that's why I've been able to at least pay the mortgage this long without struggling. I get to a point where I think I've done a good job, and then it still isn't good enough, 'cause there's always somebody doing a better job somewhere.

MORE INGREDIENTS for Great Scripts

Here are some more ingredients necessary for good scripts.

DESCRIPTIONS

Descriptions should be easy to read: They don't need to be overly detailed. The more clear the writing, usually, the shorter the panel description. Descriptions should tell the artist only what's important for the story. Artists must be able to count on the fact that if it's included, it's important. For example, a full description of a room full of tapestries may not seem like much, but it may be an important detail if, say, in a later scene the tapestries are set on fire.

PANEL COUNT

There are exceptions, but normally, keeping the panel count low (no more than five panels) is key to telling good stories. If there are six or more panels, the layout must be kept simple (see page 42). Artwork needs space to breathe and to shine. Too many panels means that no matter how the page is laid out, it'll feel cluttered. The more panels, the more difficult it becomes to lead the reader's eye.

DIFFERENT SHOTS

It's important that scripts give different kinds of shots to draw. Too many similar shots in a row is boring and repetitive. We want establishing shots, medium shots, close-ups, action shots and point-of-view shots. When I'm doing portfolio reviews, I find that most folks just want to draw splash pages. Strong splash pages are very important for expressing big actions or important events.

ONE ACTION PER PANEL

There is only one action per panel. Multiple figures can appear in a panel, but there should only be one driving action per panel. Again, there are exceptions to every rule, but in a five-panel page, there's not room for more than one important action in each panel.

Writers should not provide descriptions with more than one action in a panel for the same character. The great *Batman* editor, Denny O'Neil, once described to me this panel: Batman crashes through the window, rolls across the floor, punches the Joker in the jaw, unties the hostage and cracks open a beer from the fridge. Now that's quite the panel! Obviously, it's impossible to depict all of these actions because they are all the same character and each panel selects one sliver of time. An artist might take that panel description and create one very dramatic image: Batman crashes through the window.

Sample Script Tip: Make Sure You've Got a Variety of Things to Draw

A sample script should provide several different kinds of objects. It should have scenes with wildlife and plant life as well as city scenes. It should have men, women and children in it—maybe some animals—but also cars, buildings and machinery. As a writer, you want to show off your descriptive skills. If you're an artist, you want to show that you can draw more than just a handful of things. In order to be a comic artist, you've got to be a Renaissance man.

EMOTION in SCRIPTS

There are two kinds of emotions in comics: the emotion in a scene or story, and the emotions of individual characters.

STORIES AND SCENES

An entire story can have an emotion, and the scenes that make up that story can have emotions. The writer usually gives clues in the art direction to tell the artist what emotion portions of the story should convey. The artist looks for descriptions of the environment, what the characters are going through, the scene's turning point, whether the environment changes slightly at the turning point. Maybe the sun comes up and starts to shine light on our characters if the turning point is upbeat and the scene takes place in the early morning. These are the kinds of decisions that the artist can make that will add to the subtext and inform the reader on an almost subconscious level.

CHARACTERS

Characters must undergo emotional development—often called *character development*. What are the characters passionate about? In the scene on page 13, Batman doubts himself. And Superman is surprised; he's probably never seen his friend so distraught. An artist depicting that scene has to sift through the language, find that emotional content and pull it to the surface—dramatizing it as effectively and clearly as he can.

Go for the gut. For example, Batman is distraught. Maybe he is seated, his head slightly bowed. Perhaps the only light source is directly above him, casting long shadows down on his face. Or perhaps, in a fit of rage, he's thrown everything off the table in front of him. These are the things that the artist can decide if the writer hasn't already. Artists must find what works for them and what works best for the composition of the page as a whole. They must dig into the character's emotional core.

Writers on Layouts: Approach With Caution

Often, when working with freshman writers, I have to ask them to take out the layout designs they suggest because they won't work on the page.

Many writers don't understand, for example, that stacking panels one on top of the other on the left side of the page creates a problem. The reader won't know to go from the top panel to the one below it, or to the panel to the right of it. It's a jam that should always be avoided. (See chapter two.)

SCRIPT INTERPRETATION

With all things, there is a certain amount of leeway. Artists working from scripts, even their own, don't always need to do exactly what is written. For example, a suspenseful scene in which a police detective walks up to a house and opens the door to discover a robber at a table full of money holding a gun at the detective—that's probably three panels, but could be as many as seven.

OPTION 1

Panel 1: The detective walks from his car to the house.

Panel 2: The detective opens the house door.

Panel 3: Reverse angle, over the robber's shoulder as he points a gun at the now surprised detective.

OPTION 2 WITH INTERPRETATION

The artist may expand on this and pencil small panels of the following to help build suspense:

Panel 1: The detective opens his car door.

Panel 2: The robber, inside, looks up.

Panel 3: The detective is at the house door.

Panel 4: The robber lunges for his gun, which is sitting on a table full of money.

Panel 5: The detective begins to open the door to the house.

Panel 6: The detective's face looks surprised.

Panel 7: The robber is twisting his body to point his gun at the detective.

The artist has expanded the scene to add more suspense and drama to the action. Nicely done, Mr. Artist. As long as this hasn't gotten in the way of the pacing of the book as a whole, it was probably a good move.

HOW MUCH INTERPRETATION?

So how much leeway does the artist have? If you are the writer, editor and publisher, as well as the artist, then you've got all the leeway you want. But if you are working with an editor, you should check with him before you make any significant changes. As a general rule, you shouldn't make changes to a script unless there is a problem. If there is a problem, look for the easiest solution to that problem and let people know of any changes so they can be approved by everyone involved (remember, it's a collaborative project)—this also may include tweaking the lettering script so there is no confusion when pages get handed to the letterer. As a courtesy, I would also touch base with the writer. Perhaps the writer will have another idea that is even better than your revision.

DON'T WORK IN A VACUUM

I've worked with several artists who take great liberties with the script because they have gotten bored with the material given to them. This definitely warrants a call to the editor or writer. It may be that there is a very real problem with the script that needs to be addressed. Sometimes, the artist—who often spends the most time with a script, slaving over it day after day—has insights that both the writer and the editor have missed. On the other hand, some artists simply get bored because they have a short attention span. In these cases, it's still important to come up with a strategy to keep the artist interested in the story.

SOME RULES OF THUMB

The best rule of thumb is this: If the artist's changes clarify the storytelling or tell the story using fewer panels, it's okay. If an action needs an extra panel, and it can be added without spilling over onto the next page, it's probably a good idea. But artists shouldn't be changing the events of the stories.

I once approved a page of layouts with five panels for an artist. When the artist turned in the page, it had become a twelve-panel page. I looked at what he had added—no new events, no new characters, just stressing more dialogue beats. He didn't make a single change that altered the intent of the story. All his changes were fine with me.

A word of caution about artists reducing the number of panels: While reducing panels can be good, it is only if the actions are clear. But here is the truth: Most artists cut panels when they are crunched for time and it usually ends up removing important information. Cutting panels usually decreases the clarity of the action. The reader will miss a step in the chain of events and the story begins to break down because of it. Younger writers have a tendency to put too many panels in their scripts, and younger artists have a tendency to take too many out. It's a constant tug-of-war.

Communicate

Whether you're a writer, penciller, inker, colorist or letterer, if you have an idea, share it. Remember, comics can be a wonderful, collaborative art form.

Making a Sample Script

Any sample script you write or illustrate should have at least one character showing some real emotion.

I've worked with writers who put a lot of detail into their scripts and have very specific ideas about how events should play out on the page. The most attentive writers put in every detail—the kind of shot, the camera angle, the position of all figures, facial expressions, even color schemes and character motivations. Sometimes, as an editor, these are difficult scripts to read. By the time I get through all the description, I've forgotten what happened in the panel before it!

Other writers, such as Tom DeFalco in the sample on page 23, leave most of the storytelling up to the artist. I'm talking about the two extremes. You'll notice that the Geoff Johns and Ed Brubaker scripts on the following pages sit happily someplace in the middle. But Tom's scripts may give the artist four pages in one paragraph saying only that there is a fight, who is involved, and what the outcome needs to be to flow into the following scene.

Writers like Tom DeFalco have few complaints with their artists. They leave a lot open to the artist and invite contributions. But there are few artists who make the most of the freedom that Tom allows in his scripts. On the flip side, often what a writer sees in his mind's eye won't actually play properly on the page. For example, if a writer lists five characters from left to right for the shot (we'll call them A, B, C, D and E) but then has them all speak in the following order: C, A, D, E, C, D, A, the panel simply won't work. Can you imagine the crazy balloon tails in this panel? They'd cross all over each other.

In the case above, it is appropriate for the artist to diverge from the script—to make changes in the way the story plays out. We're all human. Writers make mistakes, artists make mistakes, and yes, even editors make mistakes. In each link of the chain, we have opportunities to catch mistakes and adjust so that they don't make it to the final product. As an editor, I appreciate a phone call or email before a member of my creative team makes changes. There are times when something isn't supposed to make perfect sense and it plays a role in the story down the line—so if an artist makes a particular adjustment without contacting the editor or the writer, it can foul up the works down the line.

So the question is: When is it okay to diverge from the script? This always—always—goes back to the two priorities. Clarity of story, followed by entertainment.

When faced with a plot-style script like Tom DeFalco's, the artist is taking on part of the plotting. Those decisions determine how an action sequence plays out over four pages. To effectively create an engaging scene requires not only clear storytelling, but a flair for the dramatic—communication and entertainment all at once. The script will be clear, but it needs interpretation. If it's just panel after panel of them punching, it gets old fast, and the reader's not entertained. The artist has to make decisions about how the events play out and get from point A to point B. In these cases, look to the characters. What makes Black Tarantula a formidable villain to Spider-Girl? What is Spider-Girl afraid of? Does she have a chance to beat him one-on-one? The answers to these questions help decide staging. Perhaps Spider-Girl attempts to take on the Black Tarantula head-on but fails. He's too powerful for her, so she tries to catch him in a spiderweb from a distance, but he tears her webs apart. Perhaps Black Tarantula counterattacks, smashing the wall Spider-Girl is clinging onto, causing her to fall. Even action sequences come from character. And all of these decisions help clarify character motivation and relative power levels, as well as entertain.

If a writer provides a five-panel page to draw and says that the first panel is the biggest, but the artist feels the fourth panel is the most important or most splashy image, the artist will want to speak with the editor or writer. These are the kinds of decisions that fit into an uncomfortable gray area. There may be good reasons for the scripts to play out in a specific manner. I've had a penciller delete whole panels claiming he could combine them with other panels and communicate the whole story. It turned out he was just lazy and the story suffered incredibly because it was missing important beats—sometimes repeated panels with no dialogue—but important nonetheless.

Ultimately, if the artist is thinking of making a change or adding something to a script, he should consider why he wants to do so. If the answer is because it is cooler, then it's a good idea only if the clarity of the story is unaffected or improved by the change. If the answer is because what the script is asking for is not clear and the adjustment will help the reader follow the story, that might be fine. Artists have to train their minds to think in this way. If the artist has found a more entertaining way to communicate the intended message, he's not out of bounds to suggest it to the editor and/or writer to see what he says.

Almost everyone I know in comics is open to input from others and, in fact, welcomes it. It's one of the big reasons I enjoy working in comics. The idea as I see it is to always look at the finish line. If a suggested change will make the final story better, I don't care who it comes from. I've had letterers suggest dialogue changes that improved the flow of the page and therefore improved the final story.

INSIDER VOICE

John Romita Jr. on Taking License With a Script

I take license with the scripts and I do what I think works better so that it's understandable. And writers aren't always perfect, just like artists aren't always perfect. But writers can't always count for choreography being in perfect order.

There's a lot of wiggle room in how a script is presented to an artist. Look at Tom DeFalco's script on the next page. It's just a plot. He hasn't broken it down into panels. That's the easiest form of script to write, but the hardest to illustrate. It also happens to be Tom DeFalco and Ron Frenz's preferred method of working. As with writing, there's a huge spectrum of pencilling styles as well.

THINK VISUALLY

It's time to get to the nitty-gritty. Comics do not have sound. It is not a tactile medium for the most part, it's not a scratch-and-sniff thing you're going for. And, please, tell me you're not eating your comics. So, that's four of the five senses that are not impacted by comics. That only leaves the one: sight. Comics is a visual medium.

What does that mean at this early stage of the book you're reading? It means I'm going to stress to you that everything the writers, pencillers, editors, colorists, letterers and production folks do is aimed at the final visual aspect of the comic book.

Artists

Choose one of the sample scripts provided here, and take a shot at sketching them out into panels. Or try them all!

Writers

Examine the styles of these different scripts. Using the rough scene sketched out on page 13, write your own scripts using these styles.

Tom DeFalco
Amazing Spider-Girl #1
"Whatever Happened To The Daughter of Spider-Man?"
Plot for 22 pages
Submitted: July 10, 2006
Revised: July 14, 2006
Our theme: Good people have to stand up to evil or it will thrive.

Page 1
We open the first issue of our amazing web-stunner as a well-endowed, small waisted, Image-style version of **Spider-Girl** stands in the center of the page in a dramatic this-is-my-costume shot as she confronts a horde of heavily-armed thugs. (While the page will have the appropriate over-the-top dialogue, it will also have a caption that will basically ask, "What the heck is this nonsense?")

Page 2
Undaunted by overwhelming odds, we have a three-panel multiple image sequence as Image-Spider activates her web-shooters, causing them to immediately morph--

--growing larger and larger--

--until they've been transformed into a giant-sized Bill Sienkiewicz Elektra-style super gun.

Sometime later, after the crooks have been subdued, a grateful Spider-Man (or mayor) thanks Image-Spider for protecting the city--

--And says goodbye to her as she boards a starship bound for Planet Spider.

(While the above is happening, the captions will continue with snarky comments/questions and defensive answers. Also, all of the above underlined description has occurred on a comic book page.)

Back in "reality", an astounded **Mayday Parker** (she of the snarky comments/questions) is holding the comic book pages as she talks to **Jimmy Yama** (he of the defensive answers) and the artist. (Ron, give this guy a distinctive look because he's going to be May's future boyfriend. All I know about him now is that he's a little shy, a withdrawn, very serious about his art and does not have blond hair) In this panel, Mayday is amazed that Jimmy would write this nonsense…especially because he knows the real Spider-Girl. After introducing May to his artist, Jimmy justifies his work because he wants his comic to appeal to real comic book readers.

After handing the pages back, Mayday shakes her head (more with amusement than disgust) as she walks away from Jimmy and the artist while wishing them the best of luck. (Hey, they're going to need it. Everybody knows a comic about a Spider-Girl will never sell.)

Page 3
(Story Title/Credits/Indicia) As Mayday walks toward the reader, a dramatic image of the real **Spider-Girl** will hover above her. Meanwhile, her captions/narration will give her origin/backstory in broad strokes and introduce her to any new readers we may pick up. (Over this page and dribbling into the next one, we'll tell the readers who she is, what her powers are, that she had a super-hero career, but "retired" a few months ago because of the stress her spider-life was putting on her family. We'll explain that she recently fought one of her dad's old enemies and then later was involved in a battle to save the planet--a battle that took a pretty vicious toll--and left Mayday verrrrrrrry shaken. She definitely needed a "break" after helping to save the world from Galactus Also, beginning here--and extending throughout the entire book--Mayday will be asking herself whatever happened to the daughter of Spider-Man? Does she still have her sense of responsibility? Does she enjoy her new "normal" life too much to give it up? Did she quit for her mother or herself? Does she still want to be Spider-Girl?)

Pages 4-5
As Mayday enters **Midtown High**, her captions/narration explain that she's been using that break to make some serious changes as she prepares for her junior year of high school.

We'll see one of those changes as Mayday walks past a wall poster that has a picture of her on it, along with a slogan that says something like **PARKER IS PERFECT FOR STUDENT COUNCIL.** (Yes, she's running.)

We see another change when **Eugene Hardy/Thompson** greets her.

Eugene attempts to give her a kiss and put a possessive arm around her--

--But she deftly avoids both his attempts. (While Mayday likes Eugene, she's not sure that she's **reallllllly** into him.)

Just then an excited **Courtney** and **Davida** enter the scene, carrying one of Mayday's campaign posters.

It has been defaced. (LOSER or QUITTER is written across her face.)

Even as a stunned Mayday looks at the poster, two other teenage girls make catty comments. We'll call them **Lindsay** and **Hillary** for now. Lindsay is a definitive "Mean Girl" who is running against Mayday for student council and thinks the "Quitter" comment may have something to do with May's rep for "disappearing" whenever the going gets tough. Hillary is basically Lindsay's second-in-command, her lap dog.

Courtney, of course, immediately gets in Lindsay's face and tells her to back off. Lindsay responds by hitting blow the belt with a comment about the fact that Court's boyfriend moved to New Jersey to get away from her.

Mayday steps between them to play peacemaker, reminding Courtney that they're due at St. Andrews…where they regularly volunteer.

As they go, Eugene reminds Mayday that the gang is gathering at the coffee shop tonight and he's expecting her to be there.

THE AVENGERS #65 (#476)
The Red Zone: Part I
"Panic Attack"
Geoff Johns (555) 555-5555
REVISED October 18th, 2002

PAGE ONE.
RECAP PAGE.
New headshots of our team in this issue, 7 members: Captain America, The Vision, She-Hulk, Scarlet Witch, Warbird, Jack-of-Hearts and Ant-Man.

*The text should be white on black.

1. Trusted by the public, and recognized as a world power themselves by the United Nations, they are the Earth's Mightiest Heroes, united together to protect us from any threat imaginable. They are THE AVENGERS!

2. Their leader, Captain America, has made it his mission to instill as much trust among the members of the Avengers in one another as the public has in the team itself. With the abundance of alpha personalities involved, and their diverse backgrounds, this is not an easy task.

MEMBER PROFILE: The Vision

4. Originally built in the 1930's, this synthezoid was the first artificial intelligence created. Decades later, the android was found and rebuilt, eventually joining the Earth's Mightiest Heroes.

5. In addition to strength, endurance and flight, the Vision is capable of altering his density – to become ethereal like a ghost or as hard as diamond. He feels his true power, however, is to experience human emotions. Something he continues to struggle with.

PAGES TWO AND THREE.
A spread of Mount Rushmore.

A sunny afternoon, not a cloud in the sky. We follow a young boy's hand, maybe 5 or 6 years old, up pointing at Mount Rushmore. His name is Paul. Brought here by his parents for a summer trip from Chicago. Now that his father got laid off, they have the time. We can just see his hand coming in from the left corner of the spread…pointing up at the Memorial.

It's a spectacular view from the Borglum Terrace, lush green trees all around. A clear shot to the American icon. The faces of Washington, Jefferson, Lincoln and Roosevelt looking out at the country. But there's something strange…

Bubbling just over the tip of Jefferson is a thick red fog. Just a think line of it now, wafting in the wind.

1. BANNER: Mount Rushmore, South Dakota.

2. CAPTION: 1:39pm.

3. PAUL (OFF-PANEL): What's THAT?

CAPTAIN AMERICA

Number One

Note to Letterer: "Location Caps" means big typeset words right over the artwork, not in a caption box. I generally want them to begin in the upper left-hand corner of the panel.

PAGE ONE

1–An establishing shot of a barbed wire fence line around the edge of a rocky mountainous terrain, someplace that looks like you'd hide a secret facility inside the canyons beyond the fence line. It's a hot day.

LOCATION CAPS: FIVE YEARS AGO -- RUSSIA, NEAR THE KAZAKHSTAN BORDER

2–Inside the high walls of the canyon, two soldiers in Soviet-like uniforms drag a partially conscious Red Guardian (the Russian version of Cap) between them. They're walking into the area where the secret facility, like a military base, basically, is. The Red Guardian's knees drag in the dirt.

SOLDIER: < We caught this one trying to breach the perimeter fence to the north, General Lukin.>

RED GUARDIAN(struggling): < …uhhh… what is…?>

3–The soldiers throw him to the ground at the feet of two men, both wearing military boots, but two different styles – because one is the Red Skull's feet, and the other a Soviet General's.

SOLDIER: <The neural blasters took him down just as expected.>

RED GUARDIAN: …uhnn…

4–Now we see the two of them, General Aleksander Lukin, a man in his early 60s, who looks tough and mean as hell, like someone who's lived a long hard life (make him really memorable, like a streak of grey across one temple or something like that), and the Red Skull, standing with his arms crossed, smiling. Lukin is looking down at the man at his feet (who we don't see), and frowning slightly. Behind them we can see some ram-shackle buildings, barracks and other things like that. This is an old base from the 60s, probably.

GENERAL: Forgive the interruption, Herr Skull… This will only take a moment and then we can get to our business.

SKULL: Don't apologize, General… I'm always happy to wait when entertainment is provided.

5–Lukin scowls, not looking at the Skull.

GENERAL: Keep your satisfaction to yourself, sadist.

GENERAL(linked): What I do here, I take no joy in.

CAPTAIN AMERICA #1–2nd draft–pg. 1

PAGE TWO

1–The general kneels down and helps the dazed superhero onto his knees. The Red Guardian looks like he's got no fight left in him, but he spits out brave words anyway.

GENERAL: <So, even after the fall, the Red Room still produces men such as yourself? I would have thought that time was long passed.>

GENERAL(linked): <Did they tell you what happened to your predecessors, Red Guardian?>

RED GUARDIAN(struggling): <…General Aleksander Lukin… under the authority of President Yeltzin …>

2–Close on the Red Guardian, sweating under his mask, maybe some blood trickling from his nose.

RED GUARDIAN(struggling): <… you are hereby… under arrest… For abandoning your post… For theft of government… secrets… and weapons…>

RED GUARDIAN(struggling): <…and for crimes of treason against Mother Russia…>

3–Looking past the Red Guardian, from behind his head and shoulders, up to the General, who is pulling out a pistol and frowning sadly.

GENERAL: <Mother Russia?>

GENERAL(linked): <I'm sorry to tell you that I am all that is left of the true Mother Russia, boy…>

4–Pull back for this one, like a wide thin full figure panel. The Red Guardian on his knees, the General aiming his gun at the Guardian's head and firing. Some soldiers and the Red Skull watching. Maybe we see the buildings behind them, with more guards around them, too.

SFX: Blam

5–The Red Guardian flops backwards onto the dirt, dead, the bullet-hole right between his eyes. The General looks down at him, his mouth tight, not smiling or frowning.

CAPTAIN AMERICA #1–2nd draft–pg. 2

INSIDER PROFILE

Gene Ha

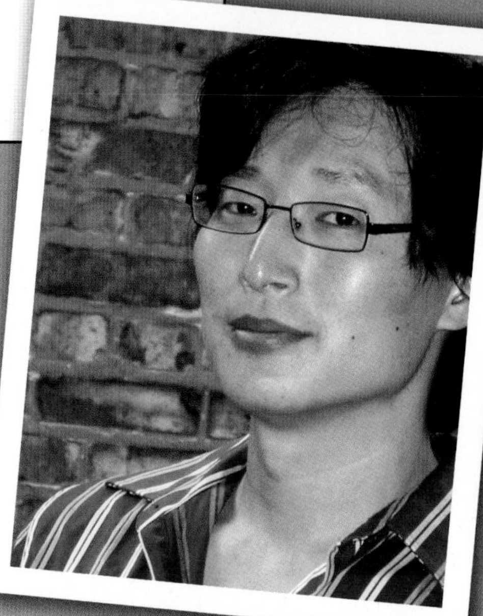

WEBSITE: http://geneha.com/

OCCUPATION: Comic book artist

DATE OF BIRTH: August 19, 1969

FIRST PUBLISHED WORK: *Green Lantern* #36, "The Ghost of Christmas Light" (1993)

INFLUENCES: Bill Sienkiewicz, Matt Wagner, John Byrne, Adam Hughes, Brian Bolland, Howard Chaykin, Barry Windsor-Smith, Mike Grell, Gene Colan

LONGEST RUN ON A BOOK: *Top 10* #1–12

BEST KNOWN FOR: *Top 10* and its prequel, *The Forty-Niners* for Wildstorm

FAVORITE CHARACTER WORKED ON: Toybox and Jeff Smax.

DREAM PROJECT: The two things I love are working with a great writer and working with friends. I've already worked with Alan Moore. I'm hoping to work on a few issues with Bill Willingham. At some point I'd like to work with my friend Lowell Francis, who currently works as a nonfiction editor.

MOST PERSONAL WORK: *Oktane*

ART TRAINING: Bachelor of Fine Arts, illustration focus from the Center for Creative Studies, Detroit, Michigan (now the College for Creative Studies)

ALL-TIME FAVORITE ARTIST: Diego Velázquez, a Spanish court painter

BEST ADVICE RECEIVED WHEN STARTING OUT: In my first few years I worked all the time and achieved a lot of early successes. My old art school chum Jim called up and asked how I was doing. I told him about how in demand I was. He asked me if I was happy. I realized I wasn't. It wasn't advice exactly, but it changed my life. I took more time to hang out with my friends and live life. I met Lisa a few years later. I've been happy ever since.

GENE HA is one of the greats of today's working artists. Those who understand what he brings to the table are in a hurry to work with him on anything they can. No one in comics creates images that look the way his do. He's a singular talent and a distinct voice in all the clutter on the comic racks. Some of the greatest comic creators of all time have bent over backwards to work with Gene because of his impeccable storytelling and dramatic, yet realistic, art style.

INSIDER VOICE

Gene Ha on Types of Scripts

I enjoy very bare-bones scripts best. I like surprising both the reader and the writer with how I present the story. Both James Robinson and Bill Willingham are good examples of writers who create rich, solidly built stories but leave most of the visual details to the artists.

It's still great fun doing a detailed script with a good writer, too. The longest script I ever got was Brad Meltzer's *Justice League of America* #11. He had very specific directions about the cinematography. It all made sense so it was a pleasure to draw.

2 PAGE LAYOUT and DESIGN

In the broadest terms, page layout and design is the composition of artistic elements on the page. When it comes to comics, we look at how the individual panels are arranged, shaped and positioned in relationship with each other. Ease on the reader is important. The order in which the reader should look at the panels must be intuitively obvious. The composition within each panel should lead the reader's eye gently into the next panel.

Laying out a page is not easy. To do it right takes time, study and a lot of attention to detail. This is the most often overlooked and rushed step of the artistic process. For that reason it's a good idea to do layout thumbnail sketches before moving forward. It helps to focus attention on the importance of the layout and design of each page. When this step is rushed or skipped altogether, the page layout can become a virtual train wreck—trapezoid or squeezed panels that were shaped in such twisted ways simply because the artist didn't do a thumbnail layout first.

Next time you swing by your comic shop, flip through the comics on the rack. The easiest way to identify an artist who did not bother thinking through the page design and layout before starting is to look at the top of the page and then glance to the bottom. If the panels at the top have appropriate space and flow nicely, but the panels toward the bottom are cramped and shoehorned into places or stacked on top of each other, there's a good chance the artist cut the layout stage out of his process.

In the following pages you'll learn a little more about the importance of page layout and scene design and how they help tell dynamic stories. Enjoy...

Penciller's Tools

The penciller uses several more tools than the writer. These include but are not limited to:

- Various pencils
- Blue line
- Drafting table
- Bristol board
- Light box

Splash Page Composition ➡

Note how Art composed this splash page so the reader's eye naturally flows from top-left to bottom-right, focusing the attention on the skull that the ape has found. The ape is looking at it, the sea monster's whole body curves the reader's eye into it, and the woman's body frames it.

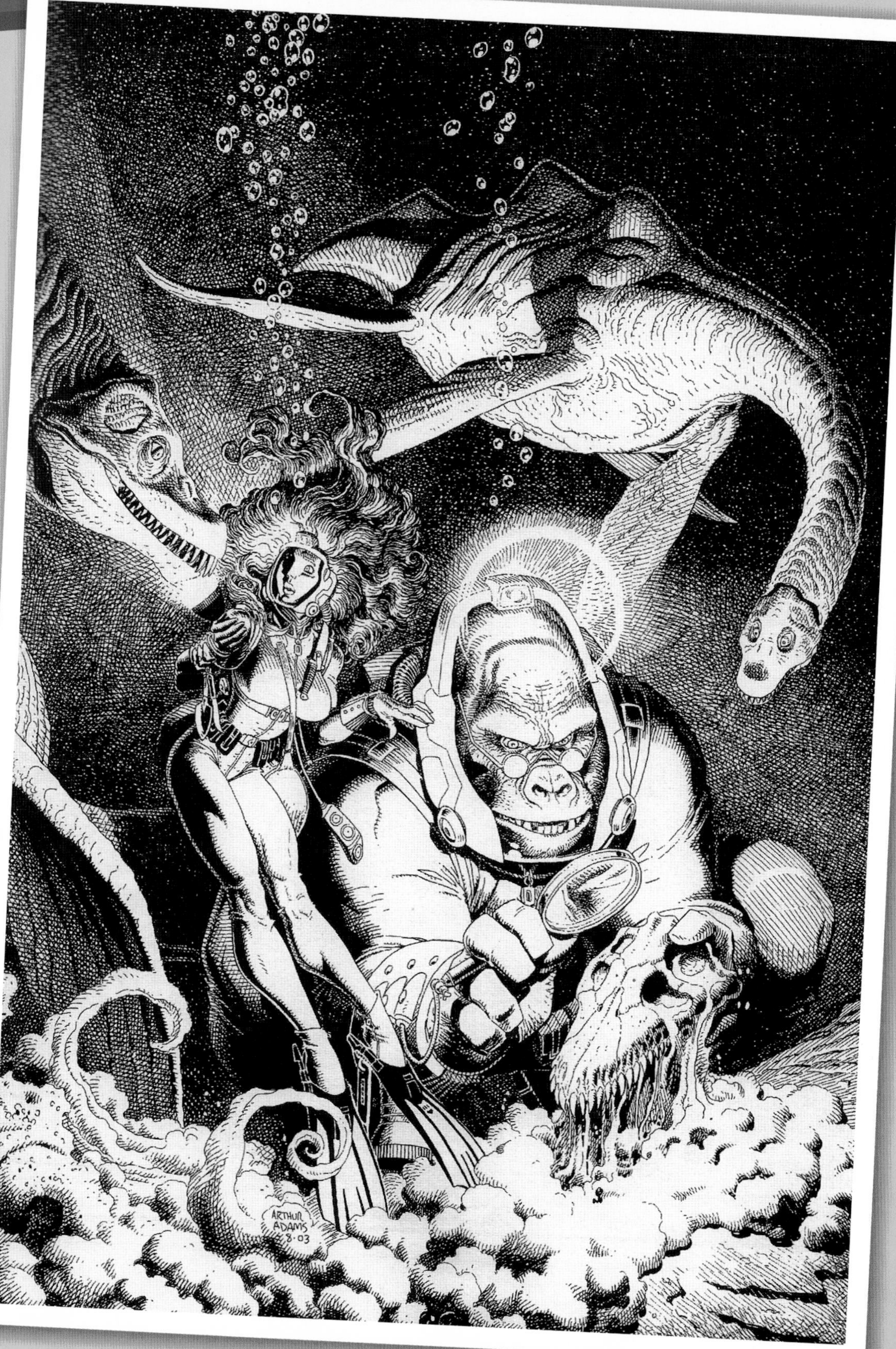
ARTHUR
ADAMS
8.03

iNSidER PROFiLE

Neal Adams

WEBSITE: www.nealadams.com

OCCUPATION: Comic book artist

DATE OF BIRTH: June 15, 1941

FIRST PUBLISHED WORK: A cartoon that appeared in a teacher's publication while I was in high school, a gag. I forget the gag. I think I got ten dollars for it.

INFLUENCES: I love Stuart Immonen's stuff. I love Adam Hughes. I feel Chris Bachalo is great and there are people showing up every day. I don't have an all-time favorite artist. One of the people I look up to very, very much is Joe Kubert because he represents things that one might not easily understand outside of the fact that he's a terrific artist. He does wonderful work. He's easy to read and he has a standard for himself that's very good. He also has a tremendous work ethic, which he had to learn, just like the rest of us.

LONGEST RUN ON A BOOK: Golly, I don't know. Generally the runs I have on books are about ten issues. I felt that in doing that I was making whatever statement I had to make, whatever it was. It wasn't a conscious effort but basically I was able to do all the things I wanted to do in ten books.

BEST KNOWN FOR: Well, it's all according to who is talking because you could be talking about publishers, and I think I was best known for being a royal pain in the ass. By other people, probably showing a different way. I think I'm known for opening the doors.

FAVORITE CHARACTER WORKED ON: Whatever character I'm working on at the time is my favorite.

DREAM PROJECT: I'm interested in making films.

MOST PERSONAL WORK: *Superman vs. Muhammad Ali*, probably one of the best graphic novels ever done, even though I did it. It does everything I want to see in a graphic novel and it's a world beater in that the first response to "I'm gonna do Superman/Muhammad Ali" was for people to laugh. They said, "That's ridiculous; that's stupid." I thought it was a very important thing to do for the world. I think it made a statement for America, perhaps a statement we didn't deserve. And that was, "There are heroes in the black community, one of them is Muhammad Ali."

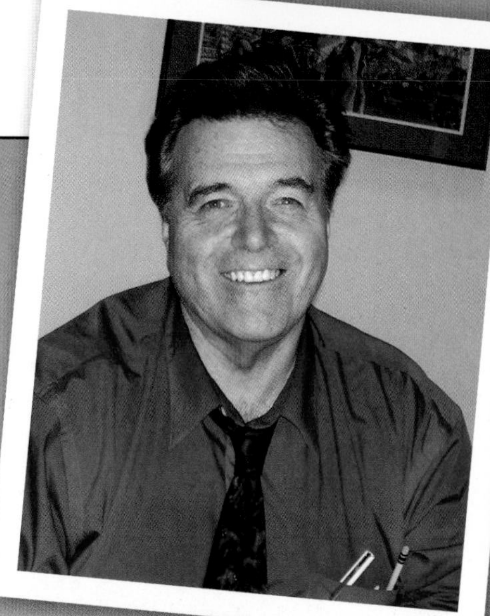

NEAL ADAMS is probably the most influential American comics artist living today. As he said, he tended to do relatively short runs on titles, and yet his *Batman, Green Lantern/Green Arrow* and *Avengers* runs are considered some of the most American comics ever produced. His dynamic art style broke the grid pattern on nearly every page and he moved his camera around to extreme positions, creating more energetic work. His attention to detail and realism, even in these fantasies, influenced several generations of artists who have followed. He lives in New York and is currently working on a secret comic book project.

ART TRAINING: I went to the School of Industrial Art, which was an art high school in New York. It was originally a vocational art school, and I went through high school. I didn't go on to college because I actually had to continue out of high school to work and I got work drawing pictures, and I was lucky enough to do that.

INSIDER VOICE

Neal Adams on How Page Layout and Design Changed and Why

When I came to comic books, it was right at the moment when they were doing cover sizes in what they called "twice-up"—the art was twice the size of the printed page—but the pages had been reduced in the period of time before that to 50 percent up, or 150 percent of the printed page. So you had the page at 150 percent page size. Before that I had originals from the previous ten years where the pages were 200 percent. So everybody worked at 200 percent. I did maybe one or two covers at 200 percent and then they went, "Why are we doing the covers at 200 percent and the pages at 150 percent?"

So they made covers at 150 percent, it worked out great, and that's what everybody does now. So you had a very interesting question: You're working at 150 percent, what does that do? At 200 percent your vision can only see a portion of the page, it can see maybe four panels or see only the top two tiers or the bottom two tiers. You can't see the whole page when you're working. So you can only see the typical Jack Kirby breakdown (Kirby frequently used a six-panel grid—see page 42). Working at 150 percent you can actually envision the whole page when you're looking at it. Now you have to ask the question: Am I drawing panels or am I drawing a page? At this size, you could contemplate the idea of designing a page. Before that, it wasn't so easy. You would design panels—panel, panel, panel, panel—and break them up slightly differently. But essentially you were drawing panels, and your compositions were in panel. Even when Frank Frazetta worked, and Al Williamson, all those guys at DC were drawing panels. Suddenly, your page was of a size where you could say, "Wait a second, maybe I could design a page."

Design with a different definition. Not designing panels, designing pages.

READ the ENTIRE SCRIPT FIRST

There's more to the thumbnail stage than laying out the panel order, sizes and shapes. Much is communicated to the reader through the set and lighting design. The script has something to say about these things.

Read the entire script first. Identify the theme, the setting, the tone, the emotions—all the details—and figure out what needs to be communicated and how best to do that.

Just about every scene begins with an establishing shot (see page 58), where the reader is immediately told where he is, who is there, and hints about what is happening.

What information beyond what's called for in the description can be communicated in the establishing shot? By reading the rest of the script, you may pick up important details such as time of day, location, surrounding buildings or parks. Do children live in the house? Is the owner out of town a lot? These facts can be shown in that establishing shot.

Let's say there's a house with a front porch, the lawn is overgrown, and there's a stash of rakes and shovels with cobwebs on them. The one-story house has a screen door and there are toy trucks to the side of the door. There's a row of similar houses in a line down the street and we can clearly see the sun high above in the background. Okay, now that is an establishing shot. A really good artist will indicate where the people inside the house are. Maybe we can see them through the window. From one panel, an establishing shot, can show the time and place—midday and the suburbs—this house in particular, that the owner either hasn't been home in a while or is a slob, that he probably doesn't have much money, that kids live in the house and that it is probably summer. By adding all of those elements, artists not only fulfill the requirement, but also bring the shot to life by adding much needed character.

INSIDER VOICE

John Romita Jr. on Talking Heads

I think the trick is to be imaginative. Try anything nonsequential. The dialogue is going to remain the same, but you don't have to have those two talking heads in the panel—a dripping faucet, a mouse in the corner, a bird on a ledge—anything that is different and yet gives you room for dialogue.

Setting design is the location, time of day and lighting (and color if it's a color comic). The most basic information about the location usually comes from the writer. If the writer doesn't provide the information, it's up to the penciller. First, the penciller must make sure that everything the writer indicates makes it onto the page and is communicated to the reader (unless something is purposefully being withheld from the reader for dramatic effect). But, since comics is a collaborative art form, artists must also build on what the writer provides.

The panel description may just say: establishing shot of a barn. An artist's job is to bring that statement to life and engage the reader. In one form or another, every panel on the page is an establishing shot—sometimes a re-establishing shot. Every panel should establish new information.

TALKING HEADS ARE OKAY

Talking-heads scenes are not intrinsically boring. They are if there is no drama in them and if the artist doesn't bring anything new from panel to panel. Some of the most entertaining scenes I've read in comics have been talking-heads scenes. Kevin Maguire creates fantastic expressions that communicate more than the dialogue balloons next to them. Michael Gaydos, by using repeated images and zooming in and out with the camera, creates very real drama with his conversation scenes—often using full body images and body movement to generate subtext.

DESIGN COMPLEMENTS SCENE INTENT

Every scene has a heart. It could be a suspenseful, romantic, lighthearted, horrific, adventurous scene. Once an artist figures out what the scene is about, he determines how to stage it—what setting design will best complement the intent of the scene. The more straightforward the genre, the easier to determine the set design. For example, horror scenes usually are dark, lit from below or directly above, have little color, and the camera is zoomed in tight, giving the reader no peripheral vision and a sense that an attack can occur from any side at any time. That said, it shouldn't fall into clichés. The reader's expectations can be used to surprise him. A romantic scene begun in the way I just described may provide a clever turn when it is revealed to the reader that there was no danger. On the other hand, it may just come out of left field and not work. It's a gamble.

SETTING QUESTIONS

Once an artist finishes reading the script or scene, he has to ask himself several questions about the setting. The most basic are:

- Indoors or out?
- Time of day?
- How many people are in the scene?
- What is the mood?
- What are the characters wearing?

- Is there anything previously established about these characters that needs to show up in this scene? Any identifying marks? Bruises? Torn clothes?
- Whose property are we on? Given that, what kind of property would he or she own?
- Is the cast supposed to be isolated?
- Is there ambient noise and commotion?

Many of these questions will not be answered by the script—though no doubt some will be. Either way, the artist has to figure it out. Not every detail will necessarily make it onto the page, but if the artist knows the answers, it will make the page consistent. Many artists don't establish, even in their own minds, where the lights are in a room. The artist will change camera angles and shadows will move from one side of a person's face to the other. It's not always obvious to the untrained eye, but if not done properly, it is confusing.

Setting design is not something to be bulldozed through so you can "get to the action." When used properly, setting design communicates valuable information and adds subtext and character to the cast and the comic.

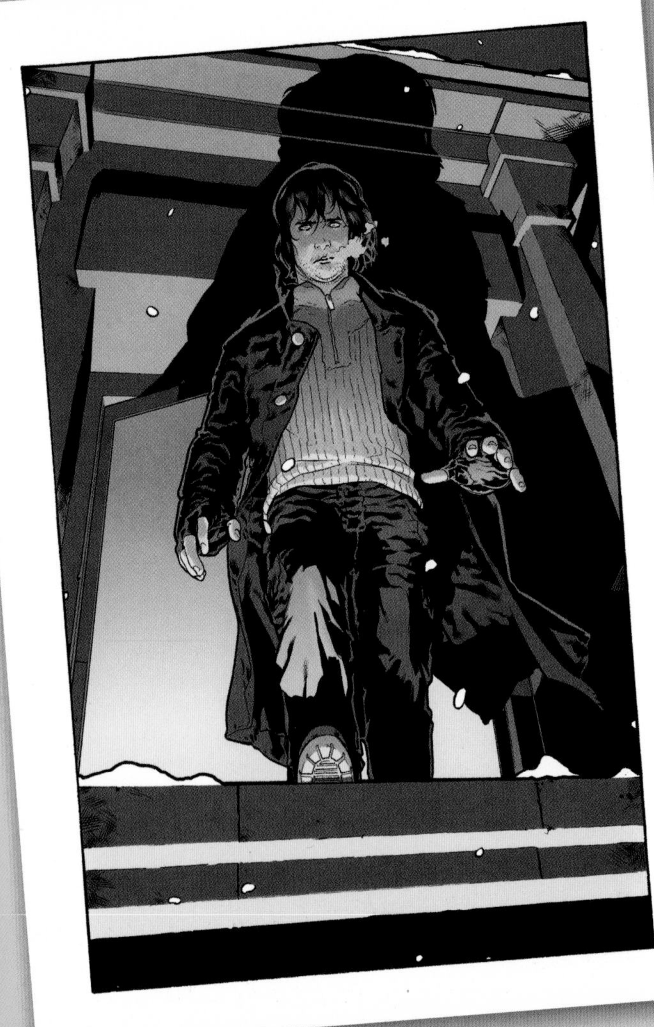

Establishing Suicide

In the opening page of *X-Factor* #1, artist Ryan Sook is supposed to communicate that Rictor is about to commit suicide by jumping out a window. To do this without showing the whole building, he picked the moment in which Rictor steps onto the ledge. The snow falling tells the reader he's now outside and the low camera angle looking up indicates that he is elevated, as does the light coming from below casting a shadow above him. Little details complete the scene.

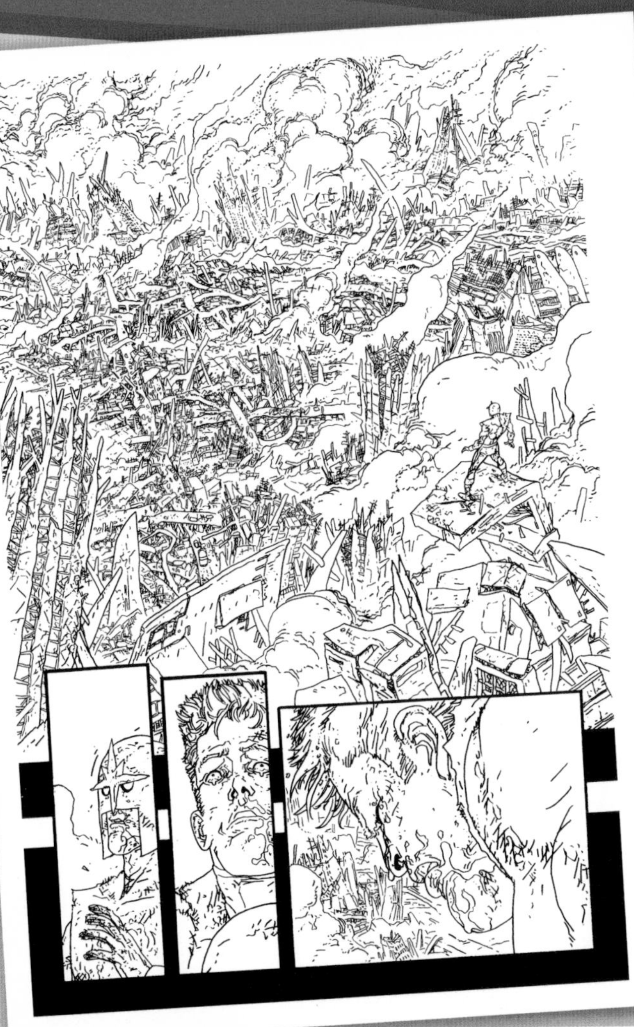

Devastation

Here, artist Scott Kolins hands out basic and impactful information. The world has been destroyed. To do this, he needed to elevate the camera to get the appropriate distance in the shot and scatter rubble across the whole scene.

***Annihilation: Prologue*, page 34: ©2008 Marvel Characters, Inc. Used with permission.**

INSIDER VOICE

Gene Ha on Reading Nonfiction

Most of the nonfiction reading I do is online. I do a lot of Internet searches for comics reference. One of the joys of a good script are all the new settings and details. A typical challenge is drawing a Roman Empire that never fell. What do Roman Imperial televisions and soft drinks look like?

iNSidER PROFiLE

David Finch

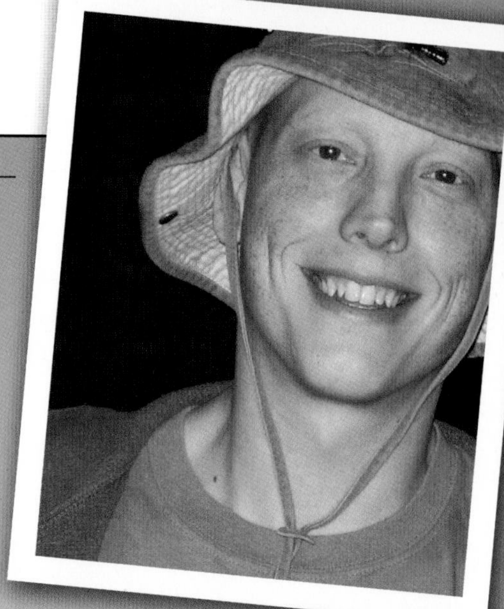

WEBSITE: www.dfinchartist.com

OCCUPATION: Penciller

DATE OF BIRTH: May 19, 1972

FIRST PUBLISHED WORK: *Cyberforce* #6 backgrounds

INFLUENCES: Marc Silvestri, Jim Lee, Frank Frazetta, Mike Mignola, Simon Bisley, Kevin Nowlan, Adam Kubert, Travis Charest, Dale Keown

LONGEST RUN ON A BOOK: Fifteen issues each of *The New Avengers*, *Ultimate X-Men* and *Cyberforce*

BEST KNOWN FOR: *The New Avengers*

FAVORITE CHARACTER WORKED ON: Moon Knight

DREAM PROJECT: Getting on a regular series of *Wolverine*

MOST PERSONAL WORK: *Ascension*

ART TRAINING: George Bridgman's *Complete Guide to Drawing From Life*, *How to Draw Comics the Marvel Way* and a lot of on-the-job training at Top Cow.

ALL-TIME FAVORITE ARTIST: Mary Cassatt

BEST ADVICE RECEIVED WHEN STARTING OUT: It was from Kyle Hotz and he told me to draw everything in Bridgman's *Complete Guide to Drawing From Life*...close the book and then draw everything again.

DAVID FINCH is arguably the most popular artist in comics today. His work has propelled many Marvel characters to the top of the sales charts. His hyper-heroic characters inspire courage and his villains chill the blood. He commits to entertaining readers on every panel of every page. His approach differs from some others on this list, because he will decide to go for a "money shot" at times instead of something more mundane that will communicate clearly. He debates with himself in these cases but is always sure to fill in any missing gaps along the way.

Characters need to have a well-thought-out and defined look. In comics—at least the ones I tend to make—that means a costume of some sort. The best costumes are the simplest ones. Very few complex costumes become classics. Superman has a big red "S" on his chest. Batman has a bat on his chest; Spider-Man a spider. Okay, those are the easy ones. So how does one design a costume for a guy named Wolverine? Or a woman named Rogue? Or Jean Grey? And should the costumes change?

RULES OF COSTUMING

There are several different answers and opinions on all of these questions. Original graphic novels tend not to have to worry about superhero costumes all the time. It's different for almost every character. There are, however, a couple general rules.

Distinguish Character

This is especially true when characters are compared to one another. Even the Fantastic Four, who have the same costume, look distinct. One's a woman, one's an orange monster, one man has blond hair and the other has brown hair with white at the temples—and the blond one is usually covered from head to toe in fire. The reason characters must look so distinct is so it is easy for the reader to tell them apart and quickly identify them. In the beginning of color comics in America, the superheroes were put in brightly colored costumes because the printing plates on the printing presses would get so hot they'd bend and blur the images—often the only way to tell characters apart was by what color the smudge on the page was. Over time, it became a part of the superhero genre that superheroes would wear these amazingly bright costumes, but the original necessity for it was simple character identification.

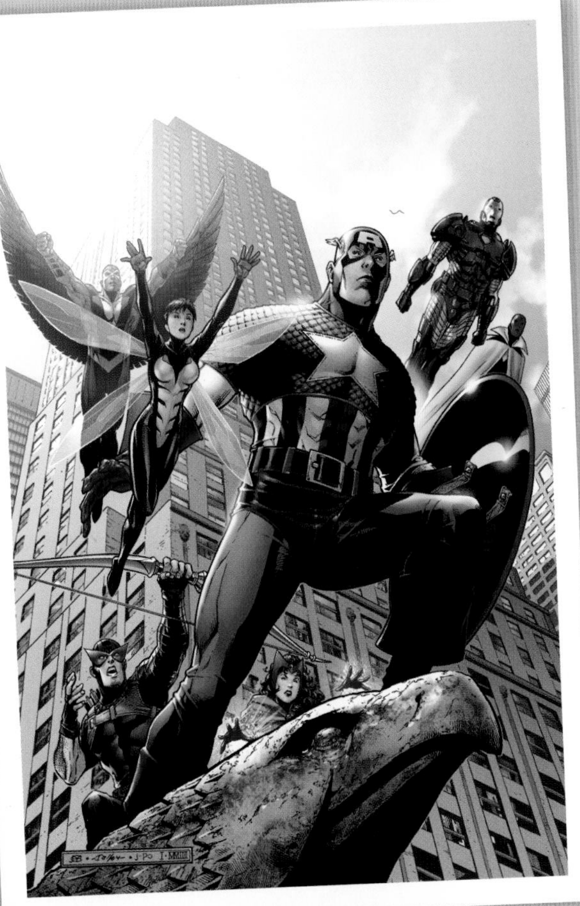

Costumes Can Distinguish Characters
Look at the Avengers. Every member has a different color scheme and theme to his costume. In Jim Cheung's image, Captain America clearly appears patriotic; the Wasp's yellow and black costume suggests her namesake; the reddish brown and winged costume clearly belongs to a guy called the Falcon; and the metal suit belongs to Iron Man.

***The Avengers* #82, cover: ©2008 Marvel Characters, Inc. Used with permission.**

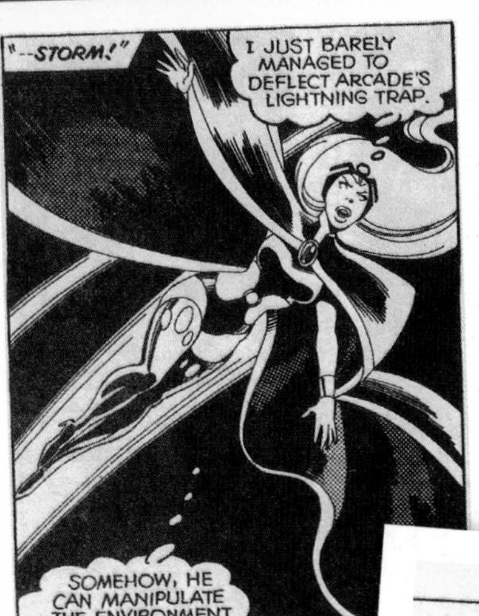

Reveal Character

The reason that some costume changes in superheroes stick and others don't is because of what they say (or don't say) about the character who is changing costume. In the 1980s, the X-Men character Storm changed her look dramatically. She went from having long flowing robes and a cape with straight hair to having no cape, leather pants, a leather sleeveless jacket with spikes and a mohawk. It was jarring, but it also came from Storm's character. Some twenty years later, this is considered a high point in the character's history.

Think of characters as actors. The Godfather should never be seen in anything but a tux or suit. Tyler Durden from *Fight Club* wouldn't wear khaki pants and a polo shirt. The clothes help to make the illusion of the fictional character complete. They help the reader forget he's reading a story and encourage him to fully embrace the illusion.

Costumes Can Reveal Character

Over the previous several issues, Storm's ideals changed. She believed a firmer stance needed to be taken against her enemies and she decided she'd look the part. Storm, before was done by John Byrne; Storm, after was done by Paul Smith.

INSIDER VOICE

David Finch on Character

I like characters that get bloody and dirty. I like the sort of characters that look good with holes all over their costumes.

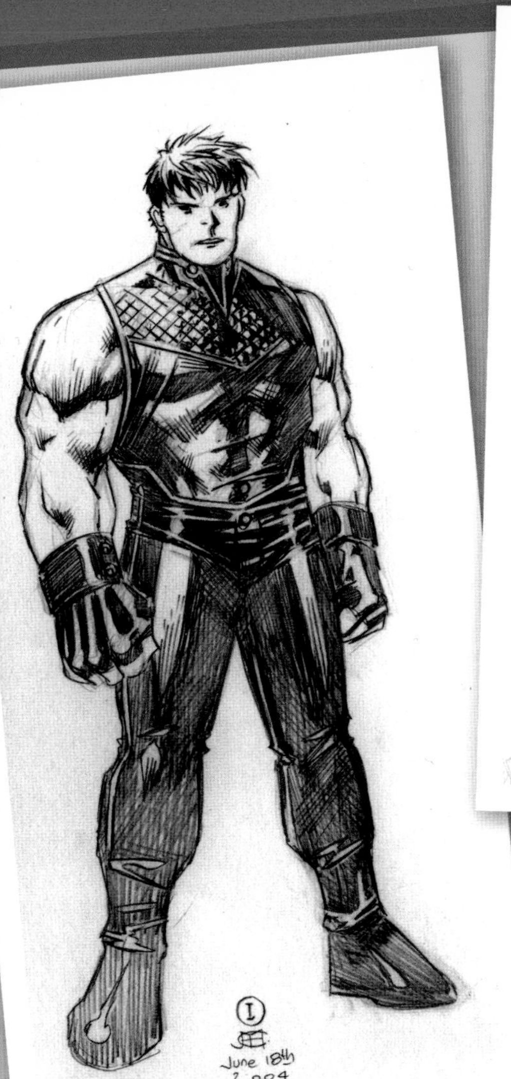

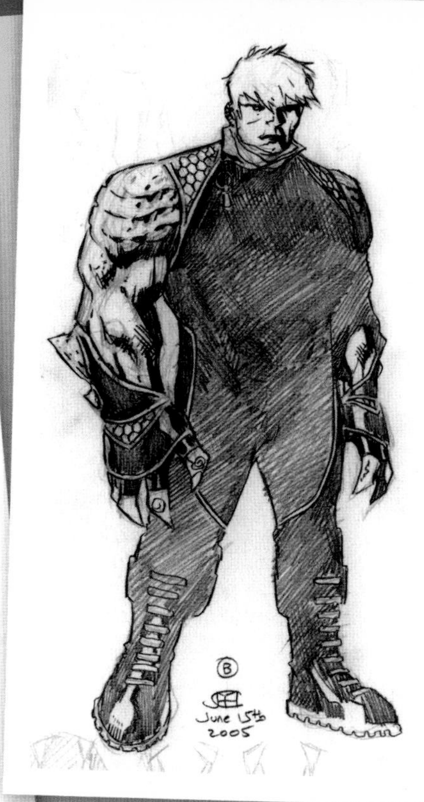

Design for Character

Jim Cheung designed the look for all the Young Avengers. Here we see two attempts at Hulkling, trying to get the masculine form of the character but also hint at who he is inside as well.

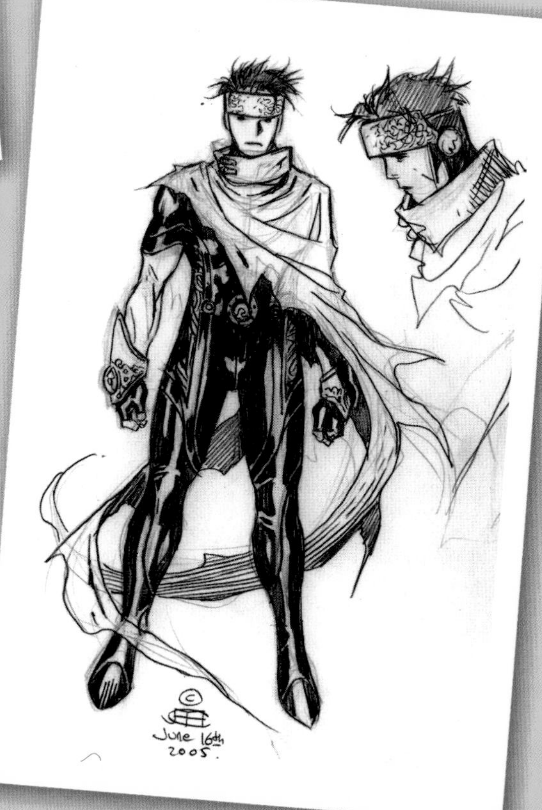

Design for Character Again ➡

Here is another of Jim's designs, this time for Wiccan. He casts spells but is also trying to be young and fit in, so a slightly modern take on the classic sorcerer look was needed.

THE COURIER

ANDY SCHMIDT - MARCO CHECCHETTO

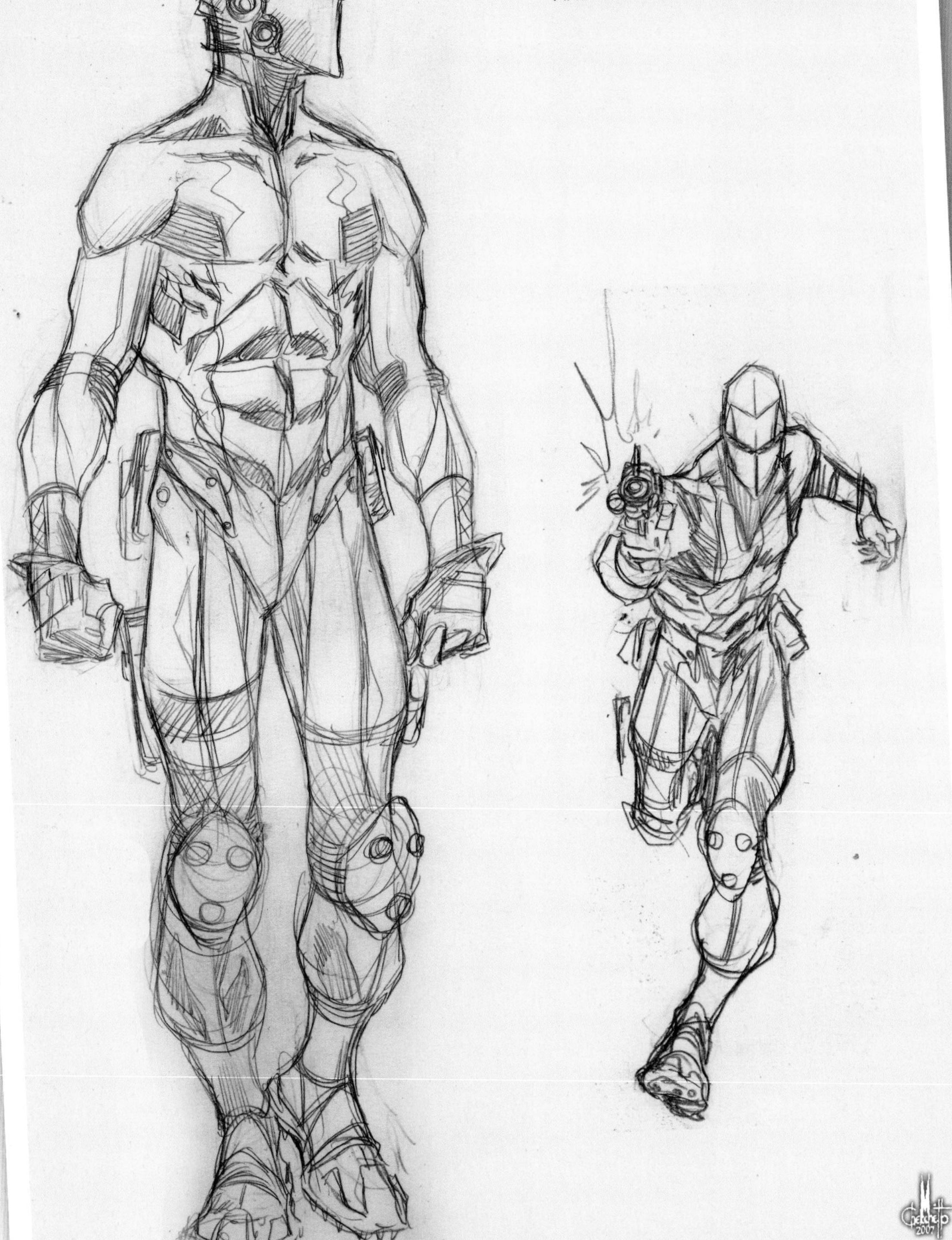

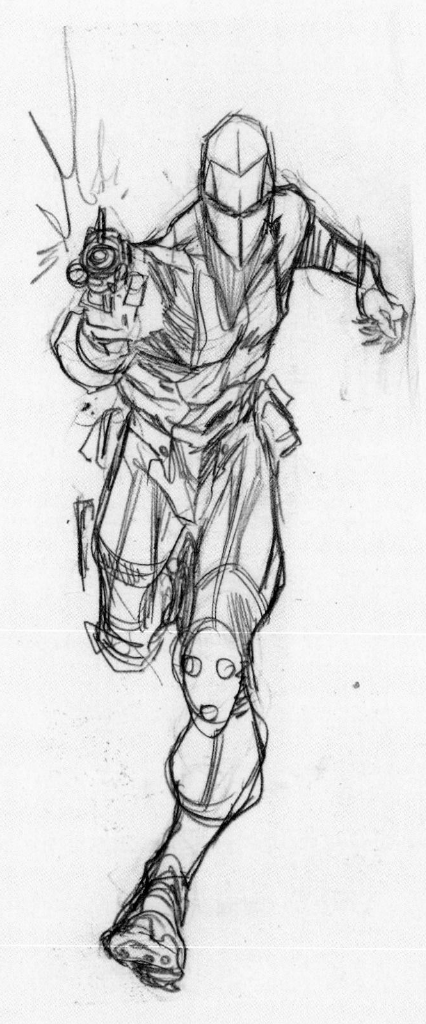

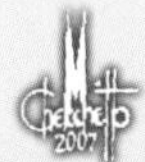

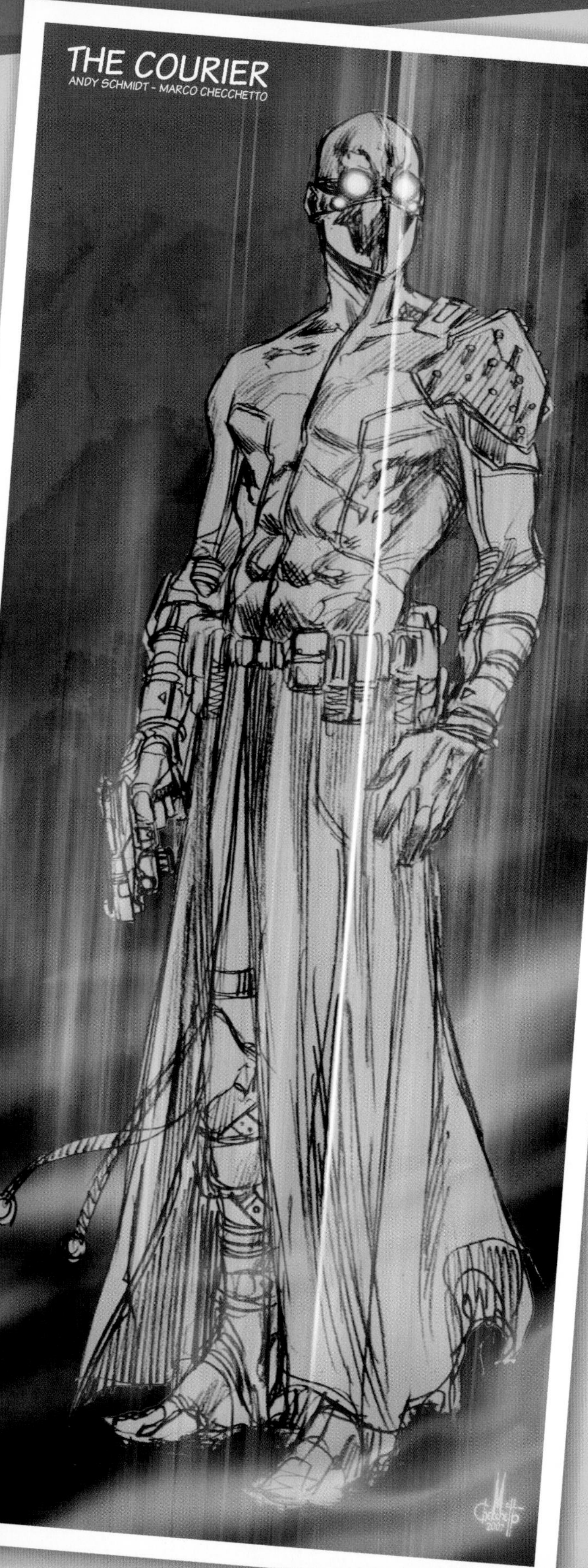

Science-Fiction Costumes

Here are two designs by Marco Chechetto for *The Courier* (a project he and I are working on at this writing). In the first design, the character has functional apparel, a visor that has infrared vision, gadgets on the belt and a costume that hides his heat signature. But the character is very quick and agile, so I asked Marco to add the flowing gown to the design so it could billow in the wind and twist and turn to show the fluidity and speed of his movements.

The Courier: ©2008 Andy Schmidt and Marco Chechetto

INSIDER VOICE

Gene Ha on Education

I honestly can't think of a class I took that hasn't become useful in my career. Once, when drawing a wraparound perspective, I used trigonometry to calculate the warped perspective lines.

PANELS

Once the setting is defined and characters are decked out in costumes that reflect their personalities, planning of the panel layouts begins. They begin as small thumbnail sketches on separate pieces of paper.

At its core, there are only two different kinds of panel layouts: grid and freeform. All page designs fall into either category.

GRID

The grid is the most basic page layout and it's exactly what it sounds like. The panels are arranged in a grid, meaning that all are the same size and shape. If you split a page in half vertically or horizontally, you have the most simple grid. Split it again and you have the four-panel grid, with four panels of the same size and shape. The six-panel grid was Jack Kirby's preferred design for years. Typically it has three rows with two panels each. Any way you chop the page so all panels have equal size and shape, you've got a grid.

The benefit to the grid is that it requires little thought from the artist. The grid acts like a television screen. The artist knows the shape of each panel and puts all of the action within its boundaries. The reader knows on instinct what the proper panel order is. Sounds like half the work is already done? That's because it is.

Ten-Panel Grid
While I don't recommend putting ten panels on a page, if you do, you're better off with a grid than going freeform (see page 44). Here, Kevin Maguire split the page once vertically and four times horizontally. Note all the panel sizes and shapes are equal.

***Defenders* #1, page 5: ©2008 Marvel Characters, Inc. Used with permission.**

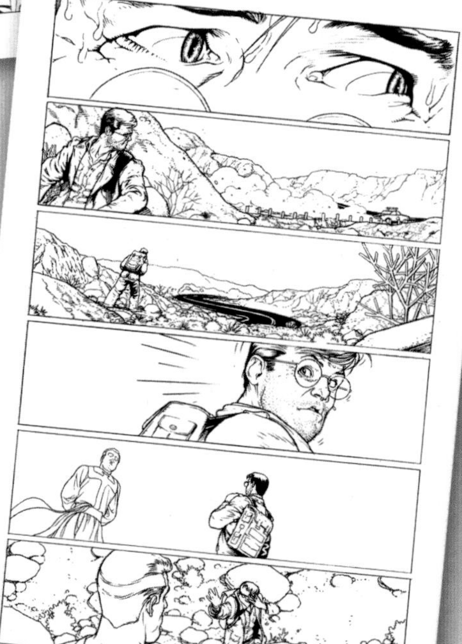

Widescreen Grid
Although the page is not split vertically, it's still a grid with equal sized and shaped panels that stretch across the width of the page. This particular layout became very popular in the late 1990s and early 2000s.

***Defenders* #1, page 7: ©2008 Marvel Characters, Inc. Used with permission.**

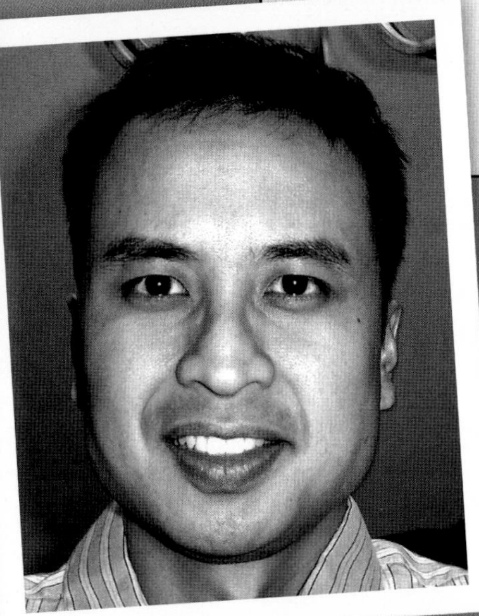

KHOI PHAM is a self-taught penciller from outside Philadelphia. While working as a lawyer, he spent his evenings absorbing everything he could about comics art from books and instructional videos. When he felt he was ready, he took the leap and submitted samples to various publishers. It wasn't long after that and enjoying the convention circuit that Khoi started getting regular work, which culminated in his working on several issues of Marvel's *X-Factor* and an exclusive contract from the company. His most recent work can be seen in the pages of Marvel's *Mighty Avengers*.

iNSidER PROFiLE

Khoi Pham

NAME: Khoi Pham

OCCUPATION: Comic book illustrator

DATE OF BIRTH: August 10, 1973

FIRST PUBLISHED WORK: Marvel's *What If? Spider-Man: The Other*

INFLUENCES: John Romita Jr., Travis Charest, Leinil Yu, Barry Windsor-Smith, Walt Simonson, David Mazzucchelli, Jim Lee

LONGEST RUN ON A BOOK: Present run on *Mighty Avengers*

BEST KNOWN FOR: *Incredible Hercules* and *X-Factor*

FAVORITE CHARACTER WORKED ON: Ares

DREAM PROJECT: Just drawing comics for Marvel is a dream enough.

MOST PERSONAL WORK: Haven't had the experience, yet.

ART TRAINING: Self-taught.

BEST ADVICE RECEIVED WHEN STARTING OUT: Chris Matthews of *Hardball* fame said in a graduation speech, "If you want to play a game, go to where it's played and find a way to get in." I read it on the Internet.

FREEFORM

Freeform is defined by a negative. Anything that is not a grid layout is automatically a freeform layout. The page can be a six-panel grid except that instead of two panels on the last row, it's one long panel—that makes it a freeform layout. The layout can get insane without parallel lines on any of the borders or no strict panel borders at all—shapes form the borders.

There is no safety net with freeform. Unlike with the grid, it is not always intuitively obvious in what order one reads the panels. The temptation to try different techniques to see if they work increases when using freeform. The artist is more likely to make mistakes. Don't get me wrong—just because panels are ordered in grid formation doesn't mean the page is perfect every time. But the grid is a kind of safety net, and freeform is like jumping on that trapeze knowing that if you slip, you fall to the concrete floor.

Freeform does, of course, have its advantages. Freeform allows for more dynamic storytelling. By shifting around panel size and shape, it is easier to emphasize a particular panel. If the fifth panel on the page is the one with the most important action, you can blow that panel up to a third or even a half of a page, with surrounding panels reduced in size accordingly.

In freeform, the panel size and shape carry meaning. In the grid, they do not. A thin, tall shape to a panel indicates something to the reader, a series of widescreen shots indicates something else, circular panels mean something else, and rounded corners on panels indicate something else again. All these things carry messages to the reader. Artists must be careful (or at least aware) of what messages they are

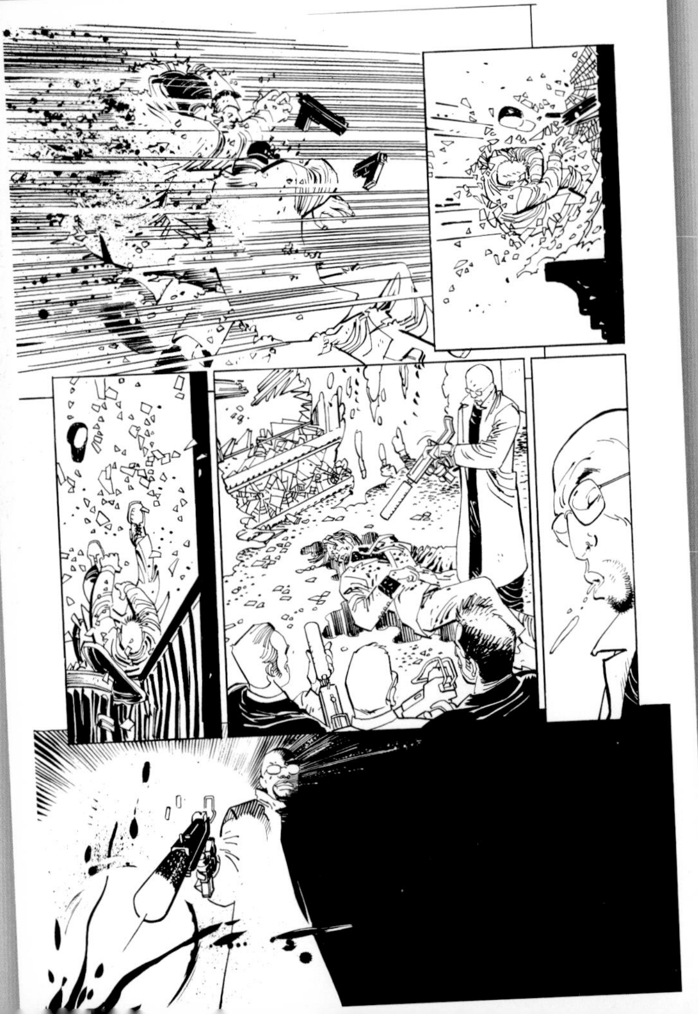

Borderless Panels

In John Romita Jr.'s page of *The Gray Area*, he also uses different sizes and shapes to communicate. Panel 5 is a tall, thin panel, approximating a short amount of time, just long enough for the character to make a sideways glance, but perhaps not long enough see what's coming. The final two panels don't have a border. The shadows from panel 6 bleed into a completely black area—effectively the seventh panel on the page, a panel of darkness, indicating death. The fact that the panels connect in the art suggests that the action of the first panel is the reason for the darkness in the second.

***The Gray Area* #1, page 26: ©2005 John Romita Jr. and Glen Brunswick. Used with permission.**

sending by way of the layout. Ron Frenz, the penciller on *Spider-Girl*, always puts an extra-thick border around his establishing shots and bleeds the top of the panel off the top of the page. It's an effective technique. Once the reader has seen the device a couple of times, he knows that panels bleeding off the top of the page indicate a change of scene. It's a simple device, but would lose its effectiveness and meaning if Ron used it for anything other than establishing a new scene. With freeform, artists have the ability to create their own visual language.

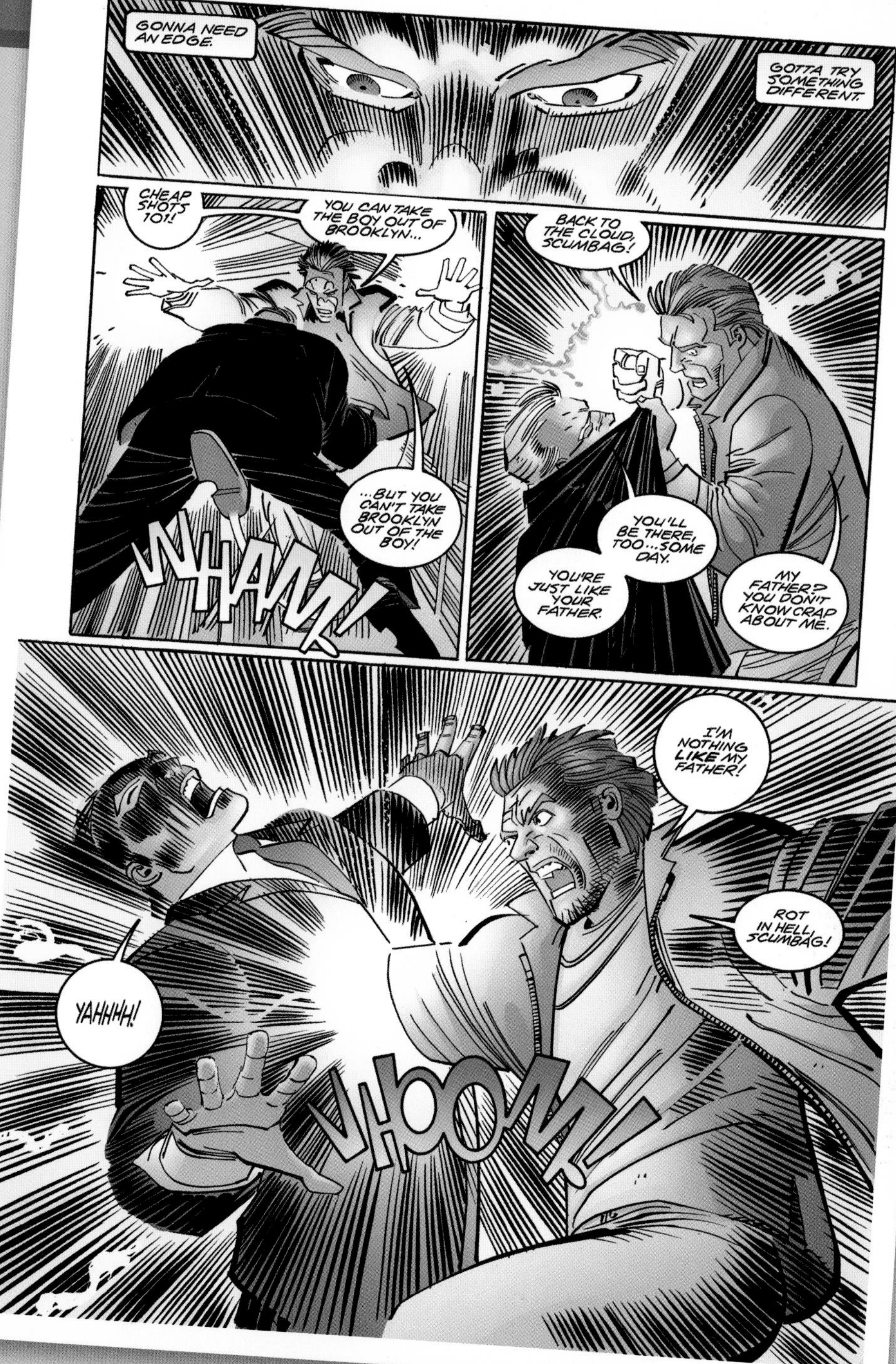

Freeform That Looks Like a Grid

Here, John Romita Jr. used similar rectangular shapes so that the page reads like a grid page. But in order to emphasize one panel over the other, he gave it twice as much room. What's good about this is that it incorporates the advantage of the grid—always knowing what order to read panels in—with the creative freedom of freeform.

***The Gray Area* #3, page 26: ©2005 John Romita Jr. and Glen Brunswick. Used with permission.**

FREEFORM and the THREE-TIER STRUCTURE

American comics are built on the three-tier structure. A tier structure simply means that the panels lay on the same horizontal and vertical lines. It's orderly. It makes for a much cleaner and more intuitive reading experience and allows emphasis to be placed within the structure. For example, in a six-panel page in which the fourth panel is the most important and deserves the most space, the first three panels might be in a row along the top, the fourth panel may be much larger with its own tier, and the last two may sit on a third and smaller tier. This gives the dominant image a proper amount of space while still providing clear panel order.

The design, even though not the simple grid (see page 42), still puts the emphasis on what is going on inside the panels rather than the arrangement of the panels. The fact that the fourth panel on this imaginary page is the largest carries a message—that's the most important panel on the page. The reader understands that and isn't thrown off by every panel sitting on its own tier or some panels bleeding off the side of the page and others not. Layouts should be simple—there is no prize for complexity.

DOMINANT PANEL

As in the scenario above, it is often the case that the artist or the writer chooses one panel to be dominant on the page. In comics, space on the page is directly proportionate to the importance of the image. Your average panel is one-fifth or one-sixth of the page. A sequence of panels that is meant to build up to a big moment may be a combination of smaller panels that, together, take up one-third or more of the page. One panel that is clearly important or shocking can be as large as a double-page spread. The main dangers creators face when choosing dominant panels is accidentally downplaying other key information on the page or cramming the other panels awkwardly around the dominant panel. Also, the artist must choose dominant panels wisely, making sure they really are the most important images and not just their favorites. Not every page has a dominant panel. Some pages have several panels that have equal importance. There are times when you have a dominant panel on the page but you might wish to hide it. The reader automatically knows that something important happens in the panel as soon as he glances at the page—and usually sees what that event is. To keep the surprise for the reader, the artist should refrain from using the freeform technique and use some form of grid—this way, the reader doesn't automatically read ahead.

The gutter is the area on the page between panels. Usually, gutters are empty white space that separates each panel from the other panels on the page. Gutters have several functions:

- Gutters simply make a page look clean. Pages with overlapping panels or panels that butt up against one another can quickly become cluttered. These tools can be useful, but gutters will often save the day, keeping pages looking neat and tidy.
- Gutters separate the events of each panel from the events of the next panel—indicating that some measure of time has passed between them. Each panel captures a moment in time. Gutters help the reader's mind realize that time has passed between two panels and understand that there is an inherent connection between the two panels. Think of it like an old slide show. Every time the slide show presenter clicks the button, one slide disappears, leaving the screen blank for a second before the replacing picture appears. The gutter is like that blank screen. It allows the mind to put the first image away and prepare for new information. The gutters perform the same function. You can see it in all of the grid examples in this chapter.
- Gutters give readers a clear structure to follow. If the gutters are parallel and perpendicular to each other and are straight all the way across the page, it looks good and it's easy for the reader to follow.

GUTTER COLORS

White gutters work best because, as with everything in comics, to do something different carries meaning. Some colorists prefer black gutters for comics with darker tones. Straight black works as well as white gutters because they don't stick out in the reader's mind and don't interfere with the storytelling. On occasion, different colored gutters can be useful to denote different locations. When working on the *Madrox* limited series, the colorist, Brian Reber, colored the gutters differently for scenes that took place in different locations—white gutters for Chicago and black gutters for New York. It was a simple device, and it helped clarify—probably subconsciously—where each scene was taking place.

LEADING the EYE

Composition is about leading the eye through the art and back to the focal point. One of the main tools comics artists use to direct the viewers' eyes to the focal point is line—both literal (those you can see) and invisible (those that are implied).

FOCAL POINT

A focal point is easy to see on any panel once it is drawn. It is the place within each panel to which the reader's eye is most drawn. Confusing panels often have competing focal points. Most of the time, every panel should have only one focal point. This does not mean that there can be only one element in a panel. A character in the foreground with a massive cityscape in the background would work well. The character is the dominant focal point and the background is just that—a background.

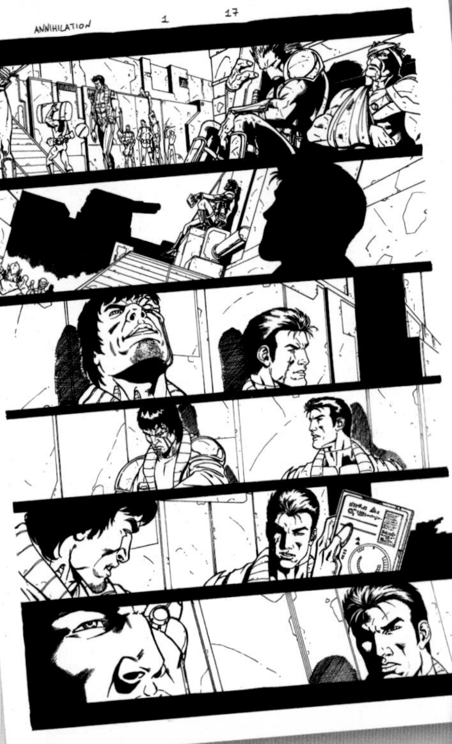

Shifting the Focus ↑
On this page, Andrea Di Vito is working on a grid and therefore must shift the focal point position in each panel so that it doesn't repeat and the reader's eye moves more fluidly. From top to bottom you can see the focal points positioned like so: Establishing shot is centered, then right of center in panel 2, center, left of center, right of center, left of center.

***Annihilation* #1, page 17: ©2008 Marvel Characters, Inc. Used with permission.**

FOCAL POINT POSITIONING

Positioning of the focal point depends on the shape of the panel.

- **Horizontal panels** have three basic places the focal point can go: left of center, dead center, and right of center.
- **Vertical panels** are the same; the focal point can only be above center, dead center, or below center.

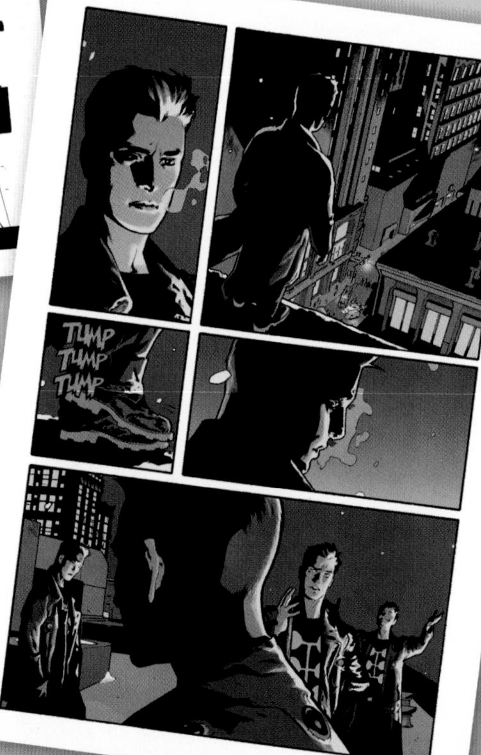

- **Square panels** are much trickier because there are more places to put the focal point. The options are: dead center, above or below center, to the left or right of center, upper left corner, upper right corner, lower right corner, or lower left corner. The many options can be good or bad, depending on the strength of the layout artist.

BAD BOUNCE POTENTIAL

A bad bounce occurs when focal points from adjacent panels compete with each other, or lead the eye in the wrong direction, or bump up next to one another.

← Leading the Eye

Ryan Sook's page for *X-Factor* #1 does a good job of leading the reader's eye. Panel 1 creates an invisible line following the character's line of sight that leads directly to panel 2. Panel 2's buildings and lighting effect draw the eye down and slightly to the left, back in the direction of panel 3 on the second tier. The position of the foot in panel 3 again points to the right toward panel 4. The head in panel 4 is looking over his shoulder and off panel straight back at the reader, leading the reader in the direction of panel 5 on the third tier.

***X-Factor* #1, page 2: ©2008 Marvel Characters, Inc. Used with permission.**

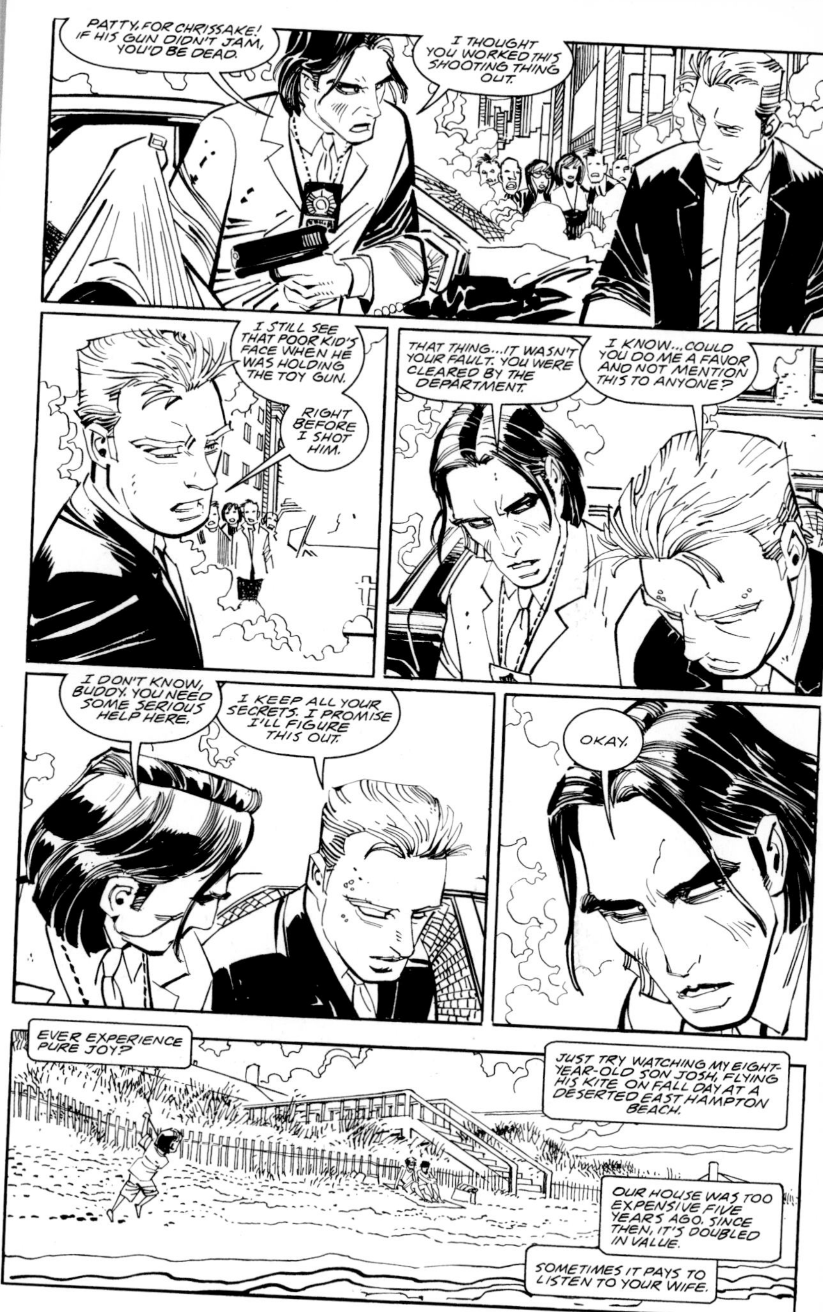

Imaginary Lines

There are seven examples of line of sight moving the reader intentionally on this page. Sometimes the lines lead to focal points and sometimes toward the next panel. See if you can find them all.

***The Gray Area* #1, page 11: ©2005 John Romita Jr. and Glen Brunswick. Used with permission.**

A certain amount of space is needed between focal points in different panels. Also, focal point positions shouldn't be repeated inside adjacent panels (two horizontal panels on top of one another should not both have a focal point to the right of center, for instance). Of course, sometimes these rules are broken—if the artist is going for a particular effect, like a repeated image or zooming in or out on the same set of figures—but these instances are the exception.

Focal points should bounce around from panel to panel, but not randomly. The focal point draws the eye. How and where the reader's eye is guided greatly affects the ease or difficulty of the reader's experience with the comic. As much as possible, the reader's instinct should guide his eye. If the reader has to stop reading to figure out which panel to read next, he will be confused or pulled out of the story.

USING LINE TO DIRECT THE EYE

When imagining a five-panel layout with two characters talking, you probably imagine the character on the right facing left (toward the center of the page) and the character on the left facing right (toward the center of the page also). This is not random. Our minds insert certain lines or directions into our perceptions. Artists use these lines to direct the reader's eye: A background element such as a slanted roof can create a line; the way a figure is positioned, if it forms a shape that points in one direction, can form a line.

LINE OF SIGHT

The most common line used is the line of sight. (See page 67 for more on line of sight.) As humans, we know how the eyes work, so we will follow a character's line of sight instinctively. The reader will follow each character's line of sight from the character's head, across the page, to see what he is looking at. In the next panel, the reader's eye is bounced back in the opposite direction once he sees the second character facing back toward the first.

You don't believe me? Try imagining the same page layout but with the characters' heads facing off to the sides of the pages instead of facing toward the center of the page. In the first panel, the figure's head is placed to the right of center and is facing off to the right. Okay, if this is the case, I'm never going to make it to panel 2 because the first character's line of sight has bounced me out of the panel and off the page. It interrupts the flow completely.

INSIDER VOICE

Gene Ha on Webcomics

I have a huge amount of admiration for the young webcomics and indie comics artists working today. I love the energy and wit of *Scary Go Round*, by John Allison (www.scarygoround.com). The constant invention in the *Scott Pilgrim* books blows my mind. When Scott's defeated opponent exploded and turned into coins (à la Super Mario Bros.) I knew Bryan Lee O'Malley was an important new talent.

And yes, like everything else, people break these rules.

Look at the examples here, then pick up your own comics and notice the focal points and lines that lead your eye around the panels. You'll notice if the composition is lacking in these areas because you'll have to think about which panel to read next. If the composition is done properly, you may not notice because you won't have to think about where your eye moves at all—it'll just move seemingly on its own.

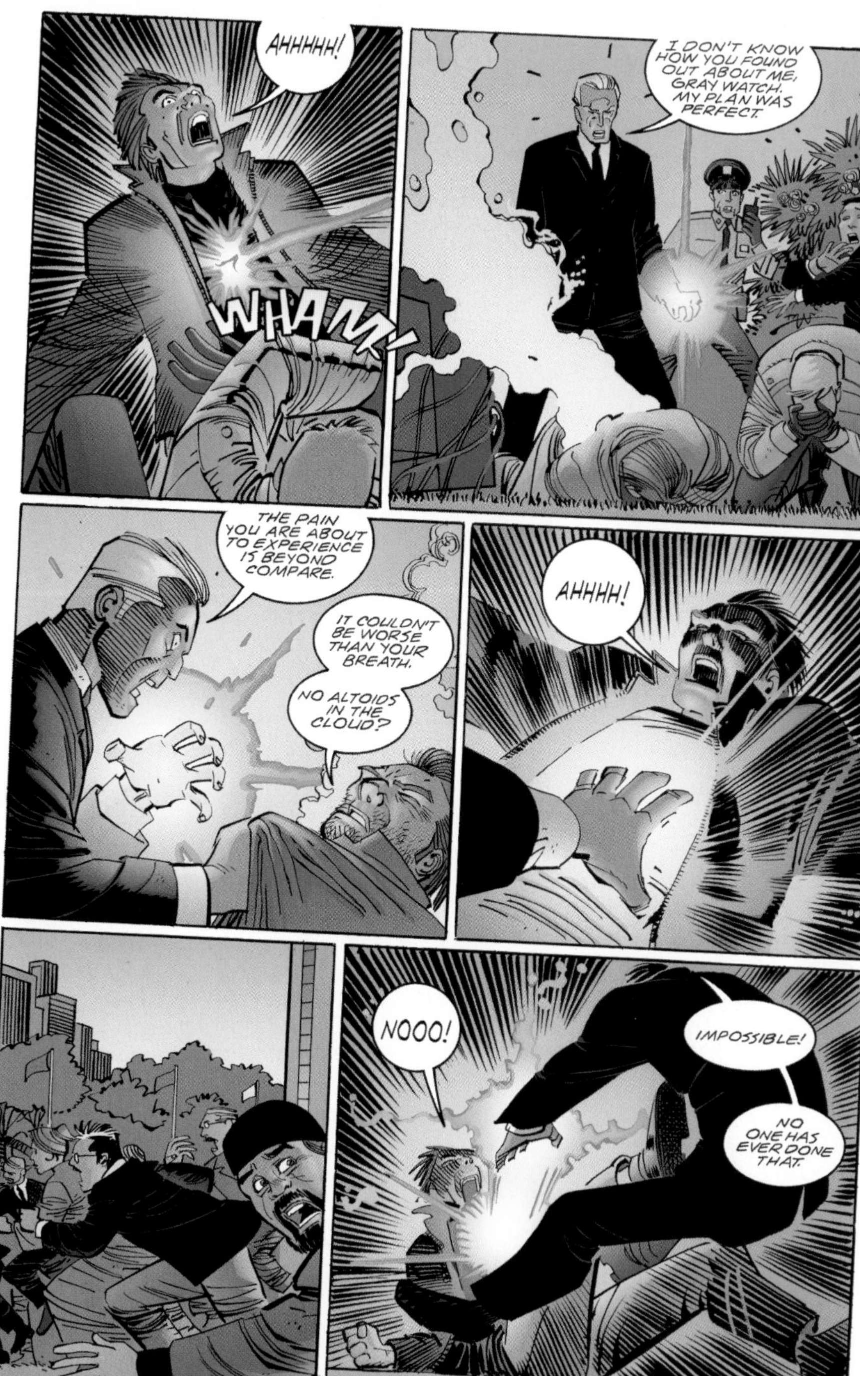

Literal Lines

This page from *The Gray Area* offers several examples of lines literally leading the eye to the panel's focal point.

PANEL ORDER

The American eye is trained to read from left to right and from top to bottom—and in that order. This comes from how we read prose. We start at the top left and go to the right. When our eye reaches the end at the right, we go down and back to the left. This is the same way comics panels are arranged on the page.

Of course, the writer also tells the artist in what order the panels should be read. In scripts, panels are labeled by number. A problem may occur when an artist uses freeform layouts rather than a simple grid layout—it's no longer guaranteed that the reader will know what order to read the panels in. Since freeform is currently a more widely used layout choice than grid, here are a few tips to keep in mind.

KEEP PANELS ON THE SAME TIER

Panels grouped on the same tier (along the same horizontal and vertical lines) will be read together. If the panel on the left is lower than the panel on the right, it becomes difficult to know for sure which panel to read first. When each panel on the page sits on a different tier, the reading order becomes drastically difficult to decipher. Even freeform layouts need to be as simple as possible. Tricks and nuances in the layout are likely to confuse the reader.

DON'T STACK ON THE LEFT

As our eyes are trained to read from left to right and then from top to bottom, stacking panels on top of one another on the right side of the page is no problem. Imagine a layout that has one tall panel that occupies half of the page along the left, from top to bottom. And the right side of the page has four panels on top of one another. Because we start at the top left, we will read the entire first panel along the left side of the page before moving to the top right panel. Since we can't move farther to the right, our eye moves down and to the left (back toward the first panel). Since we've already read the first panel, our eye simply drops straight down to the panel directly underneath the top right panel. This is also why we would drop to the third panel on the right and then to the bottom panel on the right.

Now imagine the same layout but flipped so that the four panels stacked on top of each other are on the left side of the page and the long panel covers the right half of the page. This layout is problematic. After reading the top left panel, our instinct is to continue to the right into the large panel. Usually, that would be panel 2, but it sits on the same tier as the last panel on the page, so it should also be the last panel on the page. The question is, do we read the large panel on the right second in the panel order, or do we continue down the left panels and read the large panel on the right last? It's not clear and there is no intuitive answer. The only way to know for sure is to read the page and find out when you get to the end whether or not you read it in the proper order. The rule is, don't stack panels on the left side of the page.

BREAKING THE PANEL BORDER

It's perfectly fine for figures or objects to break through borders of single panels as long as the object or person doesn't overlap another panel—unless the panel it overlaps is the next panel to be read. If a figure breaks through the panel border at the bottom left and moves down into the panel beneath it, that's fine if the panel beneath it is the next panel in the reading order. If, on the other hand, the top left panel is panel 1 and there is a panel just to the right of it (panel 2) and the panel below it is panel 3, there's a problem. The person or object breaking the panel border creates a line that will lead the reader's eye into whatever panel it extends into. If it extends into a different panel in the reading order, the reader is brought out of the story and is forced to decide, not intuit, which panel he should read next. The illusion breaks and the reader is catapulted out of the story.

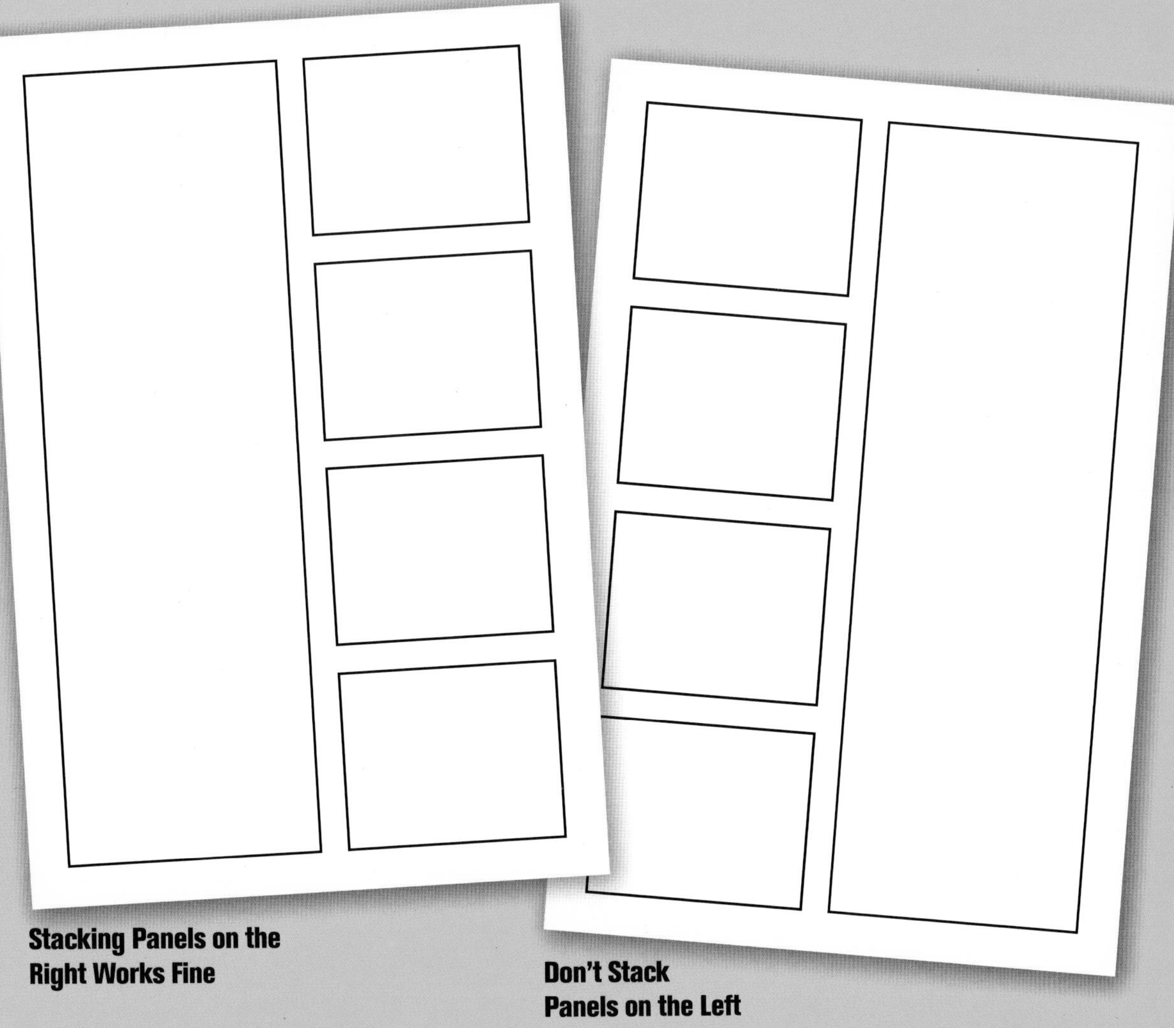

Stacking Panels on the Right Works Fine

Don't Stack Panels on the Left

The IMPORTANCE of DEAD SPACE

Many artists try to put every detail imaginable into every panel of every page. I appreciate the work that goes into these jam-packed pages, but they can be overwhelming. Once pages are laid out and figures are positioned in the panels with appropriate composition to help lead the reader's eye, pencilling of the pages begins. At this point artists need to remember the importance of dead space. Dead space is any area on the page that is not filled with pencils, an open area with a (usually) flat color or that is left white. The human eye and brain can process a lot of information, but they do need to rest. Dead space gives the reader's eye a chance to rest and process the information it's taking in. Gutters fill a similar function.

How much dead space is necessary? That's up for debate. If you are a George Pérez fan, you probably think you don't need much dead space. If you're a Jae Lee fan or a John Cassaday fan, you probably like a fair

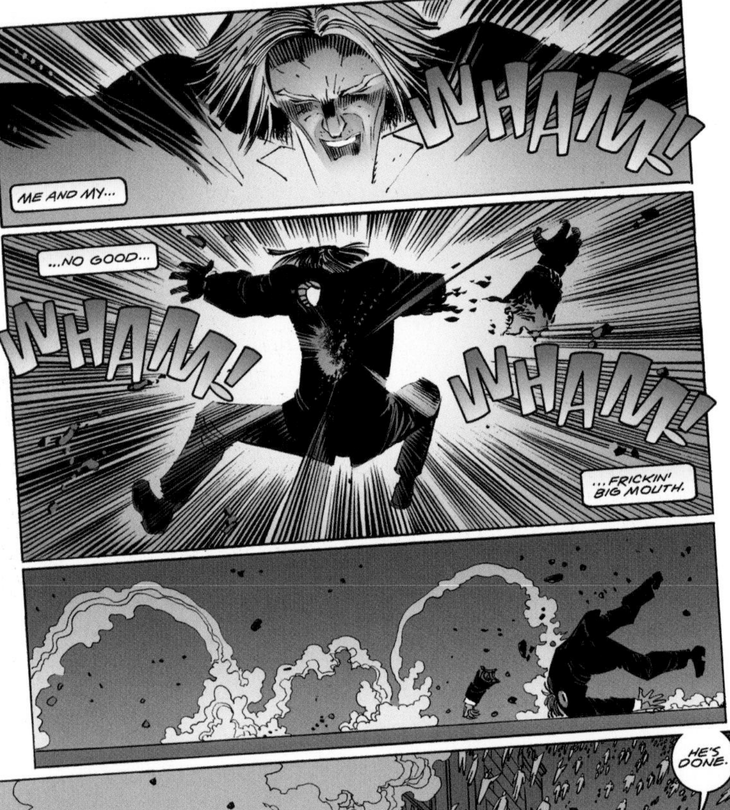

Dead Space in Found Objects

In this example by John Romita Jr., we've got an action scene that is broken up in panel 3 by using dead space to convey how far the character traveled or rolled across the ground. It gives the reader a place to rest. In panel 4, the smoke coming off the main character surrounds him with dead space, thus making him the focal point for the panel.

***The Gray Area* #3, page 1: ©2005 John Romita Jr. and Glen Brunswick. Used with permission.**

amount more. It's up to the taste of the individual reader. Growing up, I loved George Pérez's art—by far my favorite artist for years. As I got older, I started to enjoy a more open page. I'm still a fan of Pérez's work and his style is appropriate on many projects. Jae Lee's style is also appropriate for many different kinds of stories, but I'd rarely consider them both for the same gig.

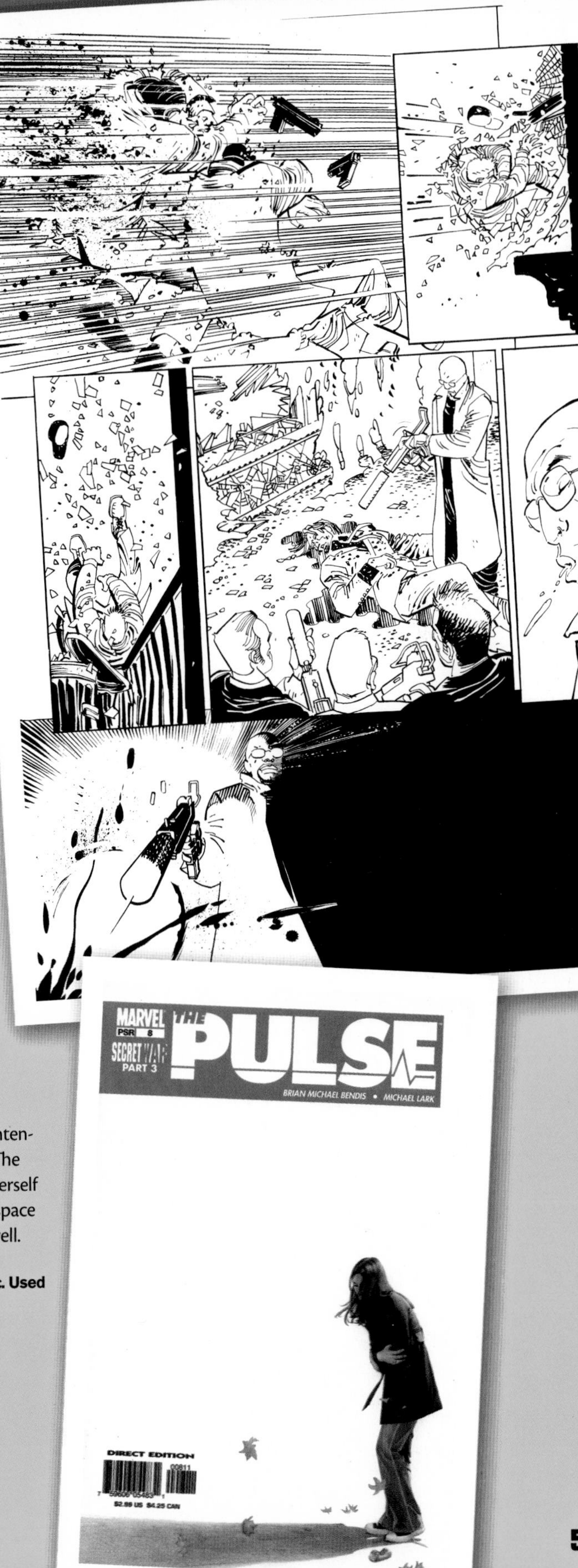

Dead Space in Action

In the final panel on this page, the black dead space acts as a period at the end of a sentence. That's it, the scene is over and the character is dead.

***The Gray Area* #1, page 26: ©2005 John Romita Jr. and Glen Brunswick. Used with permission.**

Dead Space as Content

On this cover to *The Pulse*, artist Mike Mayhew intentionally left 80 percent of the cover a flat white. The story for the issue is about Jessica Jones finding herself increasingly alone in the world. The use of dead space on the cover conveys a sense of loneliness very well.

***The Pulse* #8, cover: ©2008 Marvel Characters, Inc. Used with permission.**

3 SPACE RELATIONSHIPS

Have you ever read a comic book that was all close-ups of people talking or yelling at each other? Or a comic that jumps from scene to scene without establishing shots? I'm sure we all have—even the most seasoned pros sometimes forget to call for establishing shots. And what does an establishing shot establish? It often gives the reader a time and location. But its primary function is to set up the scene to come. That establishing shot tells the reader how many characters are involved in the scene, what objects are involved, and where everyone and everything is in relation to each other. That's what we'll discuss in this chapter—objects and characters and how they relate to each other.

Establishing Relationships

In this full-page establishing splash, artist Mike Perkins gives the reader a very clear location, London's Tower Bridge, and picks an aerial view so that the reader can see all of the players on the stage and where they are located. This creates a mental map in the reader's mind that will carry the reader through the rest of the action sequence without having to pull back out for multiple long shots throughout the scene.

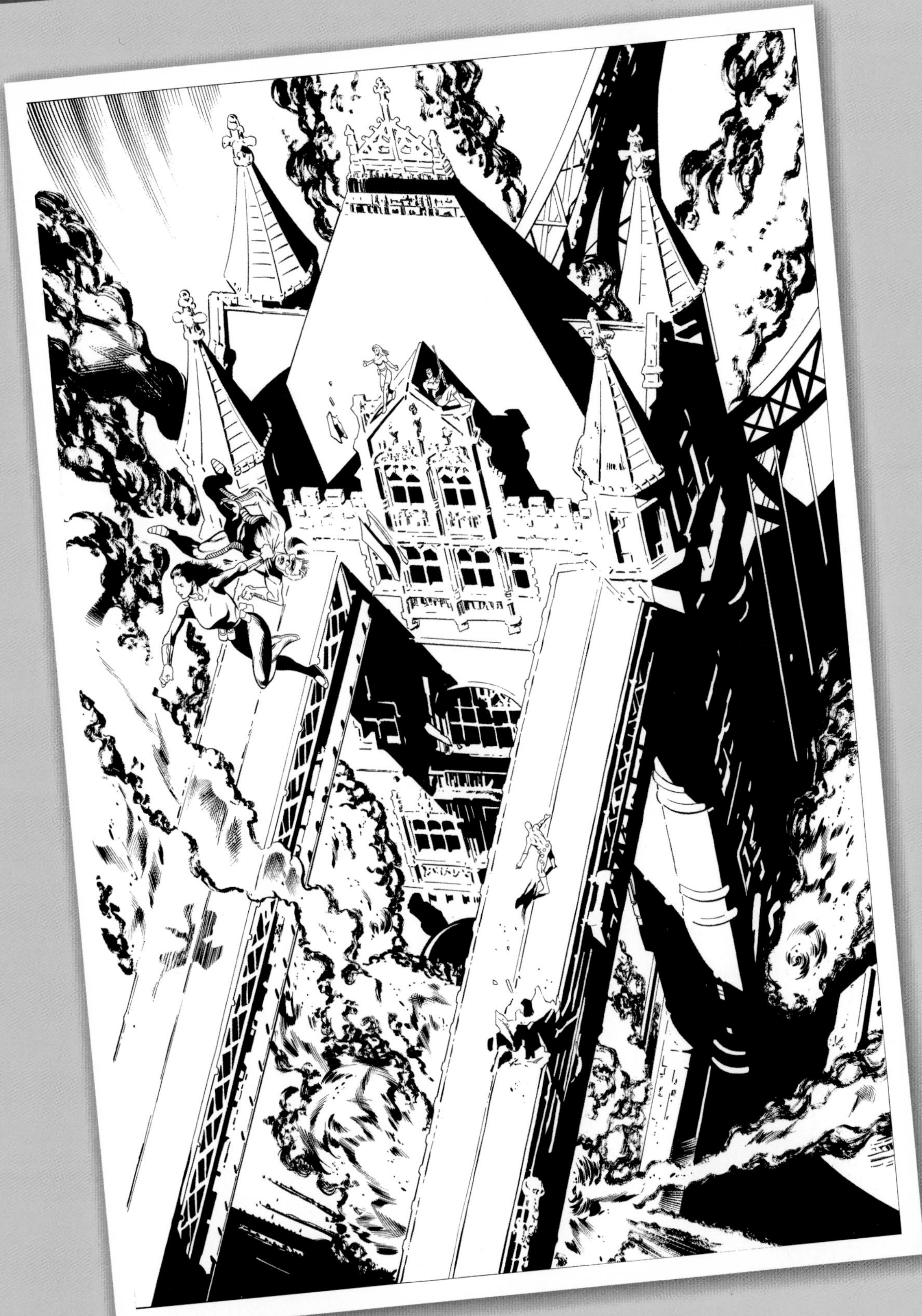

ESTABLISHING SHOTS COMMUNICATE

There are two quick reasons why I'll stress establishing shots: First, a scene is made much clearer with one establishing shot (sometimes more than one is necessary); and second, most artists hate drawing them. I've been told by many artists that establishing shots are boring, so they don't want to draw them. Yeah, okay, that may be true, but it doesn't have to be.

Here are a couple of exciting establishing shots: The opening sequence from *Star Wars*. We see a shot of outer space and then—zoom—comes the rebel ship and then—zoom—comes the huge Imperial Star Destroyer. That's an establishing shot—it establishes that we're in outer space, that a small ship is being pursued and fired upon by a larger ship. I know everything I need to know before cutting inside and meeting the characters—and that's one heck of a way to open a movie. Another good example is in *Terminator 2: Judgment Day*. The film shows a pile of human skulls and a metal foot slams down on one of them, crushing it. The camera pulls back and up and reveals a huge landscape covered with human corpses and reveals an army of machines murdering everyone in their path. I know instantly that the human race is being wiped out, and it's machines that are doing it.

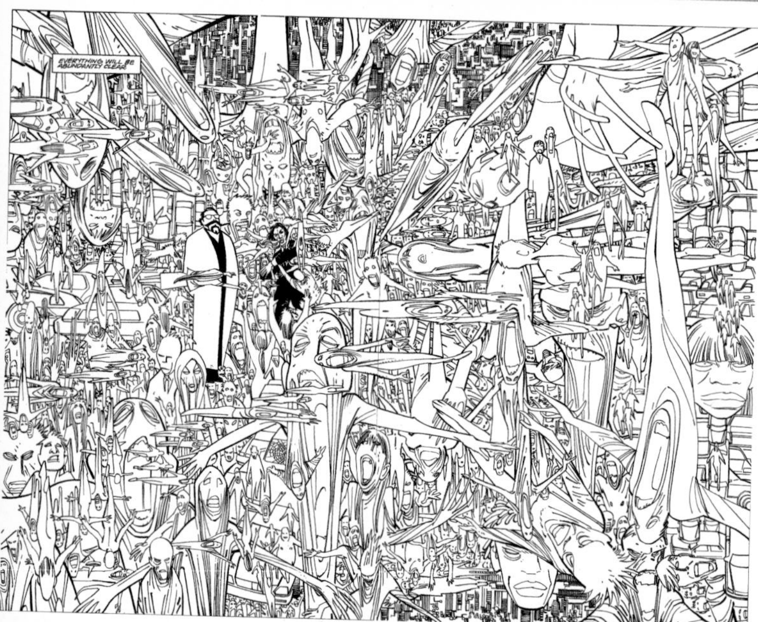

Spatial Relationships Gone Mad!

In John Romita Jr.'s double-page spread establishing shot of the afterlife, the reader follows the main character, in the black suit, into the world after death. This is the reader and the lead character's introduction, and John has established that all these people and things are moving in different directions and overcrowding each other. The laws of physics do not apply here, and this is communicated by the relationships between the characters. Note how crowded the lead character is. By establishing such close proximity to the character, a good sense of claustrophobia is created—all from the spatial relationships.

***The Gray Area* #1, pages 30–31: ©2005 John Romita Jr. and Glen Brunswick. Used with permission.**

Both examples establish locations of people and objects, as well as the conflict in the scene. In the first, a smaller ship is pursued by an enormous ship. In the second, man is fighting for his survival against the superior machines. These establishing shots communicate the maximum amount of information in the least amount of space—and for that reason, they entertain as well as communicate.

Space relationships enable effective communication of story. Beginning with an entertaining establishing shot is one way artists enhance scripts.

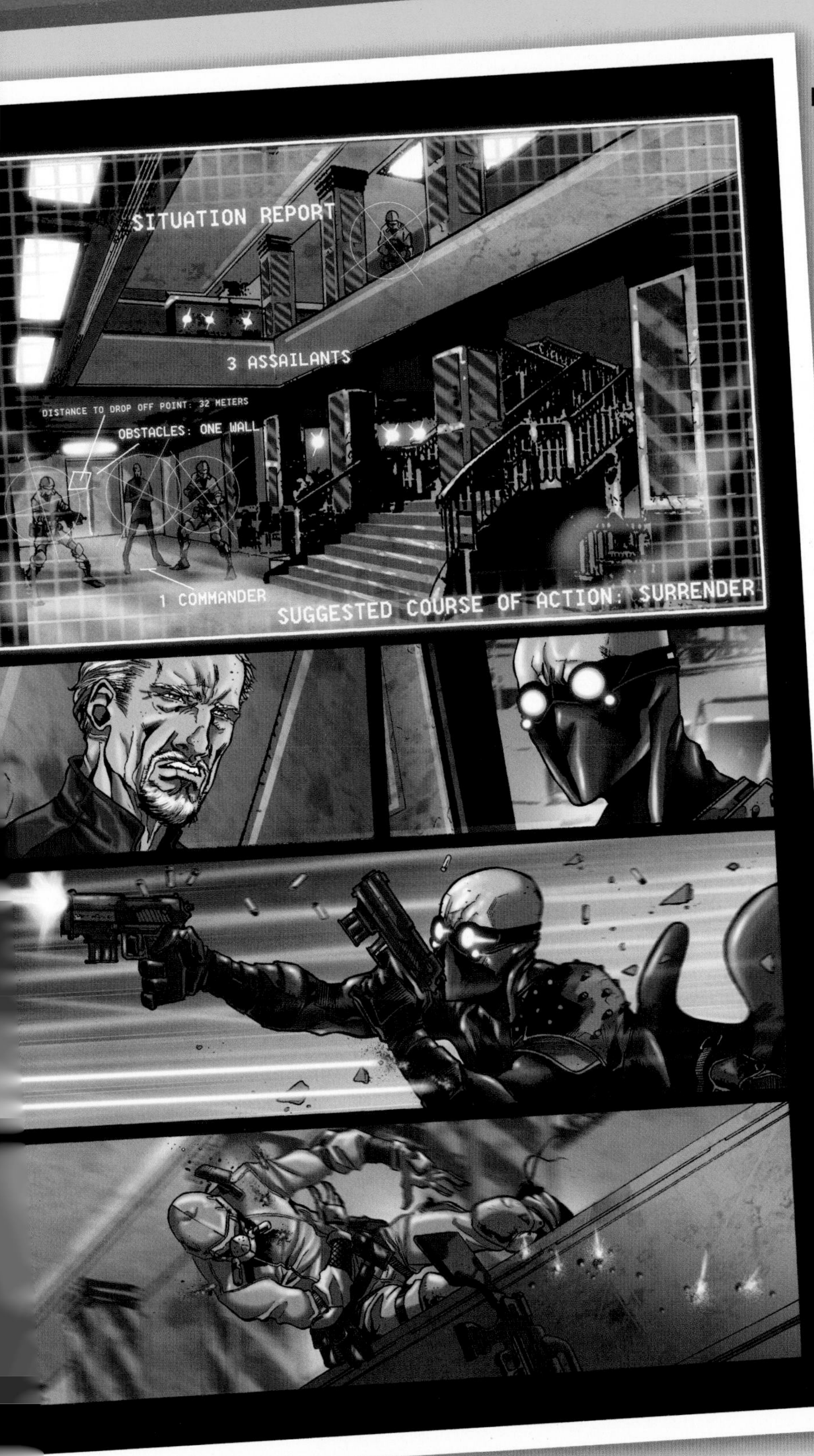

Layering Information

In the first panel of this page from *The Courier*, Marco Chechetto layers information over the shot. The scene is set: several assailants, one leader, and a hallway to go through to get past them. But by using the Courier's point of view, Marco put a digital readout that outright explains the situation. What makes it fun is the last digital display that reads: "Suggested course of action: Surrender." When the Courier moves to action three panels later, Marco has not only established where all the Courier's enemies are, but what kind of character he is as well. The last panel on the page shows an enemy falling off a balcony. By referring back to panel 1, the reader easily identifies which enemy this is and where he is located.

***The Courier* #1, page 3: ©2008 Andy Schmidt and Marco Chechetto.**

Establishing people in places requires at least one object or marker to determine where the characters are in relation to their environment. The reader needs to be able to tell where everyone is in close-ups.

This can be difficult. Say you're looking at a scene with three men talking in the desert. The artist has only the ground to establish them to. But that doesn't help the reader. The bland ground of the desert won't tell him who is facing which direction.

However, if the sun or moon is placed low to the horizon, it becomes an indicator. Each close-up on one of these three guys shows the celestial object in the background behind a character indicating that he hasn't moved since the opening shot.

So, with these three characters standing still in the scene, one character appears with the moon over his left shoulder, the second character has the moon over his right shoulder, and the third character doesn't have the moon behind him at all, signifying that he is facing the moon and the other two characters. This one object provides enough of a reference point to figure out who is speaking in each panel even without seeing the characters' faces clearly.

If a scene opens on an exterior shot of a building and then cuts inside, it is still necessary to establish people in the environment. John Romita Jr. and I sat with a young artist a few weeks ago. The artist's first page showed the exterior of a house in the suburbs, then cut inside, introducing the lovely family who live in it. The house looked great, and the people inside looked good, too. John's suggestion was to place one of the inhabitants in the exterior shot—he recommended that we should see the speaker through a window, perhaps. Upon looking at the rest of the scene, John saw that it was Christmastime and that the scene takes place around the Christmas tree. John suggested that the Christmas tree should be in the window instead of a speaker. This way, when the artist cut inside the house, he would always have that Christmas tree as a reference point to use. If the tree is in the shot, the reader knows what room the characters are in and where they are in relation to the window. Either the person or the tree will work. The point is to have a link—a marker or indicator—from one shot to the next to provide spatial context for the reader.

The bottom line is that the environment must continually establish where characters are in relation to each other and their surroundings.

When dealing with multiple characters in a scene, it's important to clearly establish where they are in relation to each other. From the script, artists have to first determine how many characters are in the scene and where they should be positioned. If the scene has six guys in a drug deal talking with one buyer, then the establishing shot should show six guys on one side and one guy facing them on the other. Is it a casual conversation? If so, then a character or two might be reclined or leaning on something. Every choice an artist makes about blocking people in relation to other people in a scene carries a message to the reader.

BLOCKING

Blocking is a term that comes from theater and that I use. In theater, it's the positions and movements the director gives the actors. In comics, the artist is the director. Blocking helps me to differentiate page layout and design from the actions or people and placement of objects within the panels. In comics, artists block out the scene in their minds, if not on paper, before they get started. They must consider how to establish which characters are close together. The more spread out the characters (which may be necessary due to the scripting of the scene), the more difficult it becomes to show where all the characters are. The easiest thing for an artist to do is place the camera angle up so that when the focus is on one person, there is a second person partially in the shot. That easily shows how far away from each other the two characters are.

Other options might be:

- An over-the-shoulder shot with the camera behind and slightly above one character's shoulder so the panel is partially framed by the character's one shoulder and part of his head in the extreme foreground. The primary focus of the shot would be the person that our framing character is looking at (usually someone speaking toward the camera). This establishes the two speakers' distance from one another.
- A long shot that shows all characters in a scene together—full body shots. This is particularly useful when establishing which characters are on which sides of the conversation, but it is not particularly good at establishing who each character is, since they will typically be fairly small in the frame.
- Placing one person in the extreme foreground, one in the middle ground and another in the background can be very useful if the scene calls for such an arrangement.

BLOCKING CLUES

- Facing characters are engaged in a conversation.
- Facing characters very close together probably means conflict or some kind of romantic tension.
- Characters all facing the same direction sends the message that they are on the same team.

- One character in the background looking at another character who is facing away from the background character is probably spying on the foreground character.
- A large distance between two characters may indicate distrust or some kind of business transaction.
- One character surrounded by a group of other characters may communicate that the center character is in danger, or perhaps being judged by the surrounding characters.

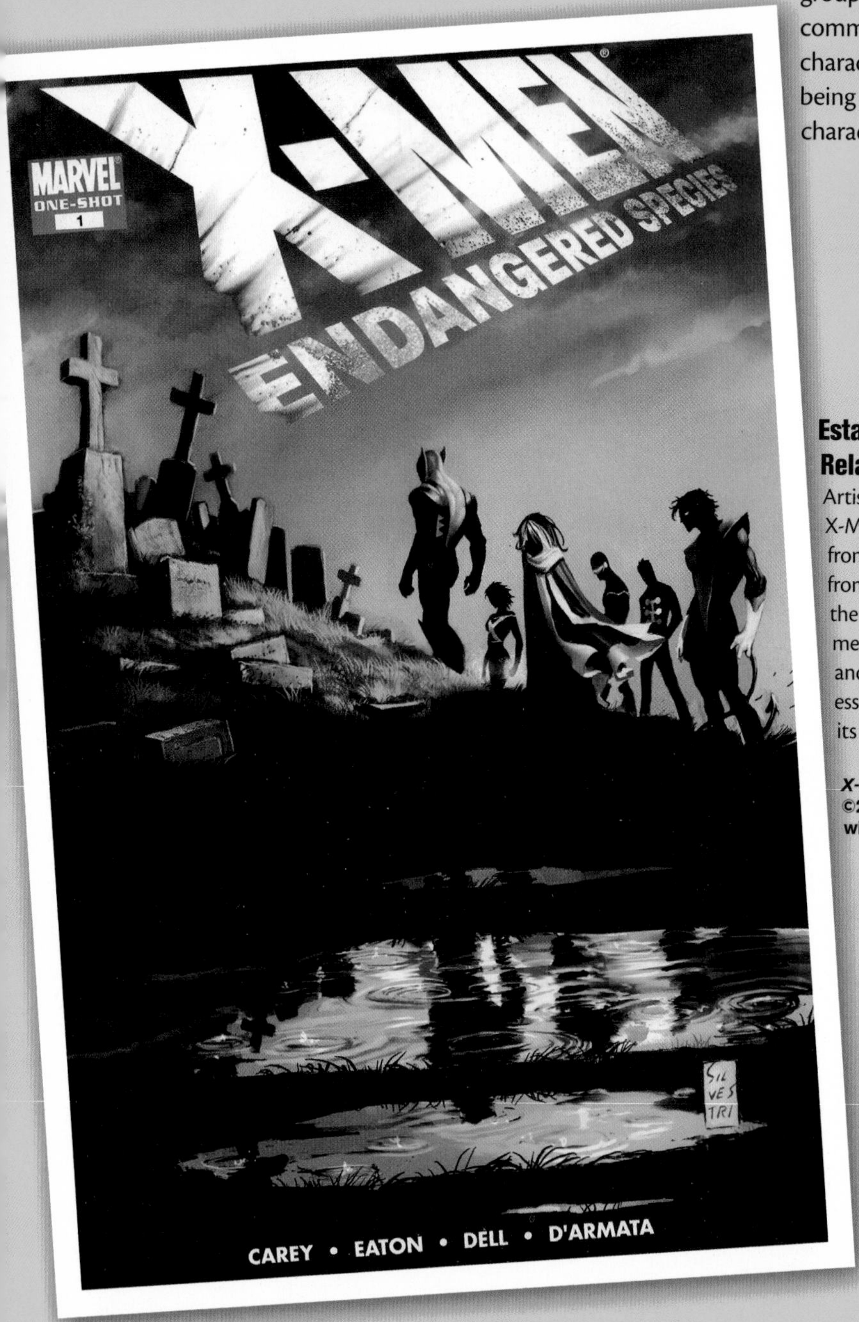

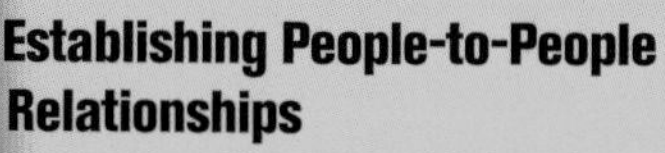

Establishing People-to-People Relationships

Artist Marc Silvestri establishes the X-Men characters at a safe distance from the graves but also spread apart from each other. Had he cropped out the graves, the piece would have lost meaning. Seeing both the characters and the graves in the same shot was essential for the piece to communicate its message effectively.

***X-Men: Endangered Species*, cover:**

Comics are a series of static or still images. There is no bobbing for us to look at and recognize. And a walking man doesn't actually move. So the trick to depicting movement in comics is just that—a trick. Artists create an illusion of movement. Here are a couple tricks of the trade.

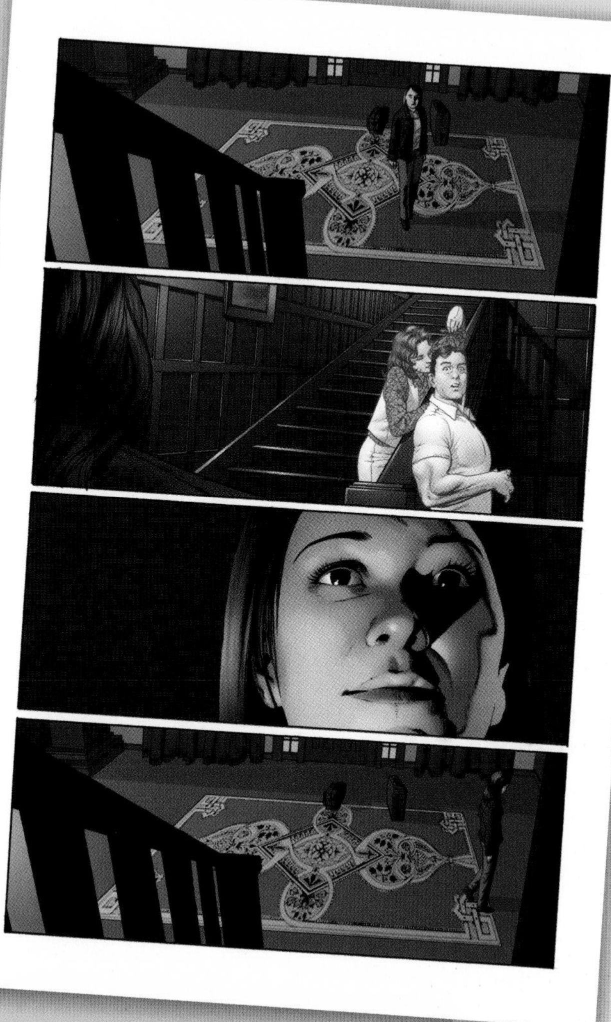

Landmarks

Landmarks involve a unique object or collection of objects placed in a position in the scene so it will often be seen. No matter how many characters are in the scene, the reader will always know where they are moving from and moving to based on their distance and direction from the landmark.

On John Cassaday's page of *Astonishing X-Men*, Kitty Pryde has just come home to the Xavier school. You'll notice the banister to the stairs in three of the four panels. The banister keeps the location firmly planted in the entry room. This becomes important in the last panel, in which Kitty decides to turn into another room. Because Cassaday continued to establish the location of the events, the reader understands without a thought where Kitty is within the mansion at all times.

Astonishing X-Men **#1, page 4: ©2008 Marvel Characters, Inc. Used with permission.**

Speed Lines

Classic speed lines denote movement by illustrating the path of an object in motion. This was used a lot in superhero comics, but has fallen somewhat out of fashion. They're simply a line or collection of lines drawn from the object in motion and tracing its path backwards from where it originated. Typically, the more speed lines, the faster the object is perceived to be traveling.

The classic tell for movement in superhero comics can be seen here on Ronan's hammer as he swings it down into his opponent's head.

***Annihilation* #5, page 19: ©2008 Marvel Characters, Inc. Used with permission.**

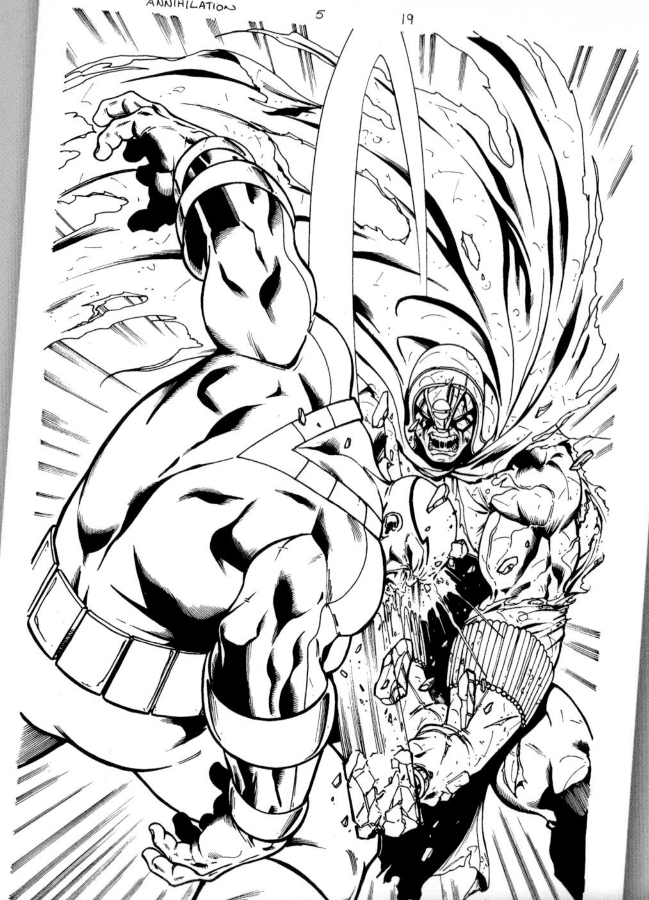

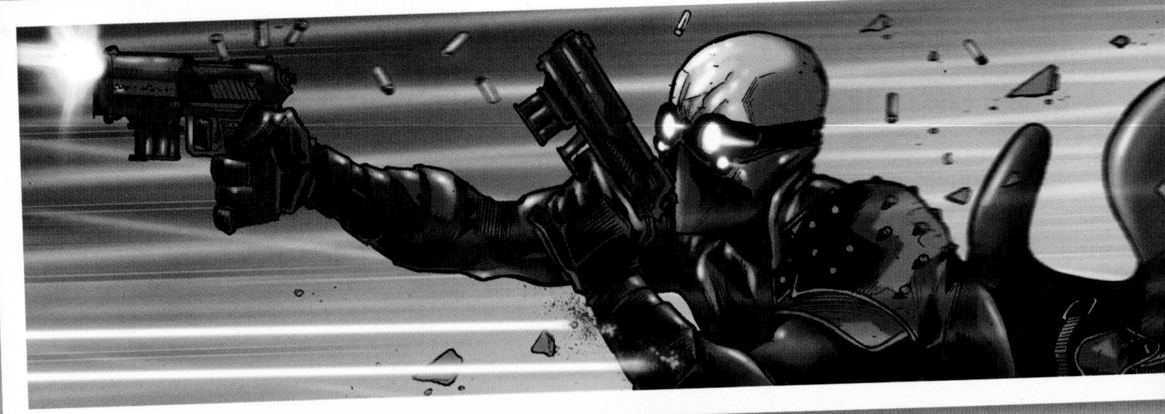

Speed Lines in Manga

In manga, speed lines have been used slightly differently. To show motion, an object or person in movement would be drawn very clearly and in focus but the entire background of the panel would be filled with speed lines, thus creating the illusion of the foreground figure traveling in the direction of the background speed lines.

In this panel, the figure is placed against a background comprised only of speed lines. This is a trick borrowed from manga. It provides a sense of motion without depicting anything actually moving.

***The Courier* #1, page 3: ©2008 Andy Schmidt and Marco Chechetto.**

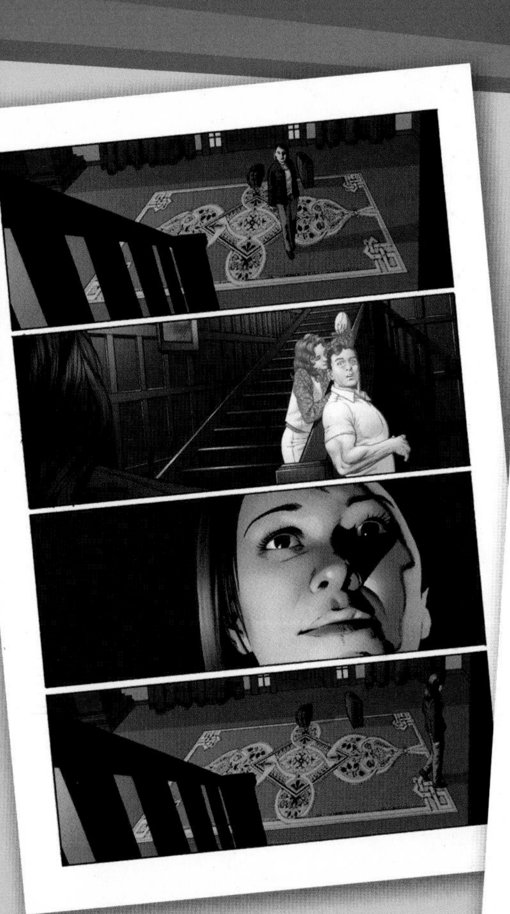

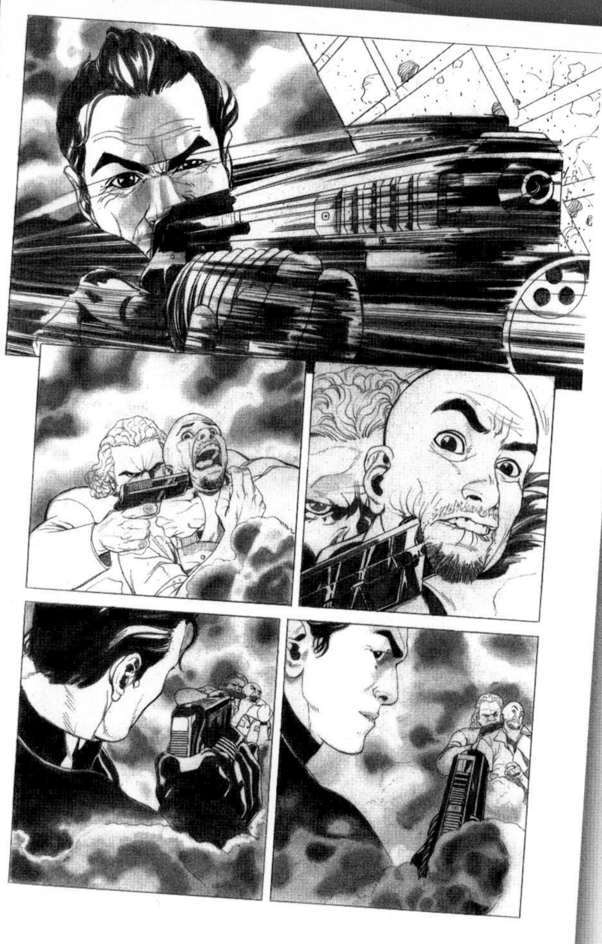

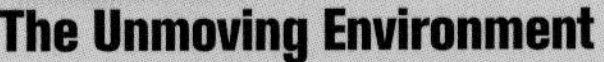

The Unmoving Environment

This is the most standard way to convey movement. It's just a series of panels, each with exactly the same background, as if the scene is being shot by a still camera. In each subsequent panel, the figure is placed in a different location within the panel. With a shot of an empty room, you may find a man opening the door to the room on the left side of the panel. In the second panel, the room will remain exactly the same but the door will be closed and the man will be placed in the center of the panel, probably in a walking position. In the final panel, the room remains the same, but the man is now placed on the far right leaning against the window, peering out at the streets below. Voilà! That man seems to have moved!

***Astonishing X-Men* #1, page 4: ©2008 Marvel Characters, Inc. Used with permission.**

Motion Blurs

Much like speed lines, motion blurs trace the path of a moving object. This is usually done by a colorist on the computer, but can be done with ink washes or gray tone pencils, too. In life, when an object is moving quickly, the human eye can't focus on the object so it appears blurred. Motion blur is just smudging the image. If the image is someone punching right at the camera, a motion blur might be effective if used only on the foreground fist. The face and the rest of the character's body should be sharply in focus. For the blur to be effective, something else must be stationary and in focus. I like the motion blur when used sparingly because it's a representational expression and feels more real than speed lines.

In the first panel here, artist Chris Cross rubbed the lead from his pencil across the gun barrel to create a motion blur similar to what one would see in a photo of something moving quickly. Since most people recognize the effect from a photo, it appears as though the gun barrel is in motion.

***Captain Marvel* #2, page 3: ©2008 Marvel Characters, Inc. Used with permission.**

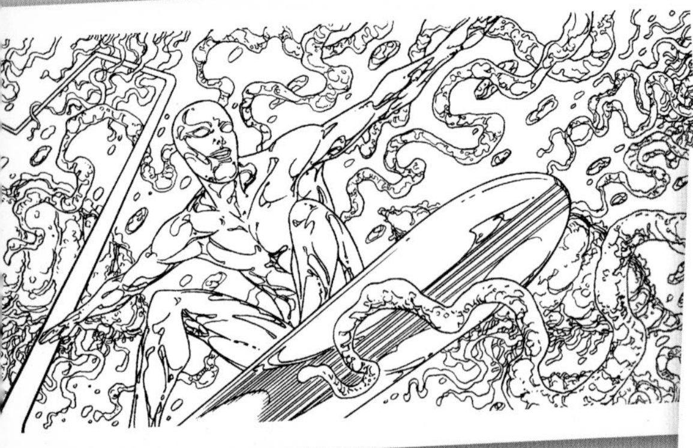

Figure Position

Conveying motion with a figure alone requires positioning the person in such a way that the reader recognizes it as walking, or running, or diving, etc. It's probably the most difficult way to convey motion in a comic. The reason is that readers are humans. We walk and run every day. We know exactly what it looks and feels like, so the artist is trying to re-create a sensation and image that an audience is extremely familiar with. All other tricks to approximate motion come from this. If all artists could convey motion simply in the figures, there would be no need for motion blurs, speed lines, or any of these other tricks.

In this panel by artist Scott Kolins, it's clear by the figure's posture that he is surfing and in motion. Even with this dynamic pose and exciting camera angle, it's still a tough illusion to convey, but Scott handles it well here.

***Annihilation: Prologue*, page 29: ©2006, 2008 Marvel Characters, Inc. Used with permission.**

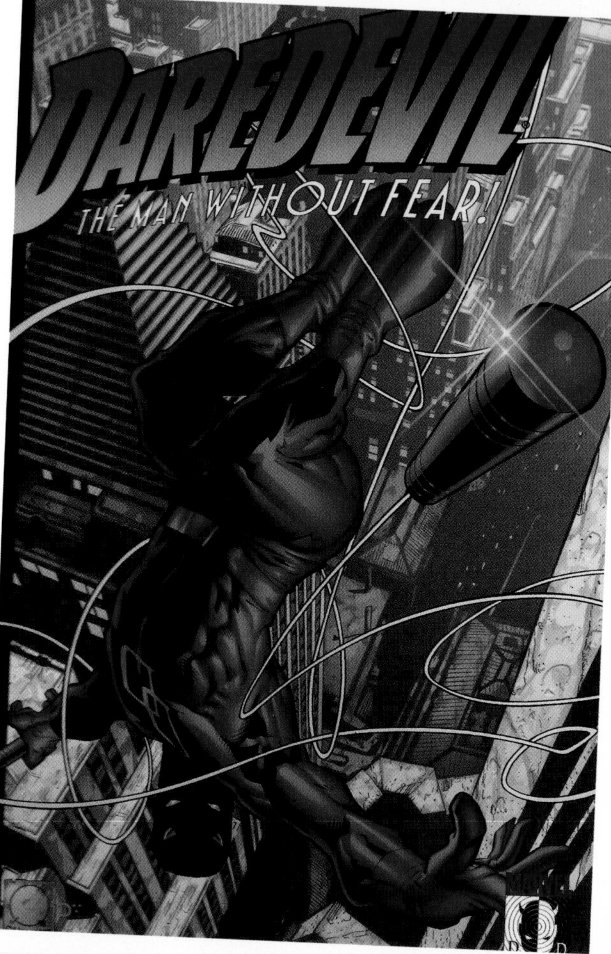

Affected Objects

A trick Joe Quesada used effectively while drawing *Daredevil* is the affected objects technique. He would use objects from the environment that were in some way or another affected by the action of the panel to create the illusion of movement. This was used most effectively with Daredevil's billy club. On this cover, Joe depicts Daredevil jumping around rooftops, and he uses the rope from the billy club in the same way that other artists use speed lines. The rope traces the path that Daredevil's arms and body have taken, creating the illusion that Daredevil has been flipping about. The result is a sense of motion and elegant-looking panels without using clunky speed lines.

***Daredevil* #1, cover: ©1998, 2008 Marvel Characters, Inc. Used with permission.**

THE 180-DEGREE RULE

In film, when a scene is established in a shot, an imaginary line is created that the camera should never cross. If the scene is of two people talking with one another, the 180-degree line is created by the characters' lines of sight—looking at each other. Once it's established that character A is facing to the right and character B is facing character A, looking off panel to the left, that's the line of sight. Assuming that neither character moves in the scene, they should always face the same way. The rule gets its name because the camera can shoot from any angle within 180 degrees on the camera side of the imaginary line.

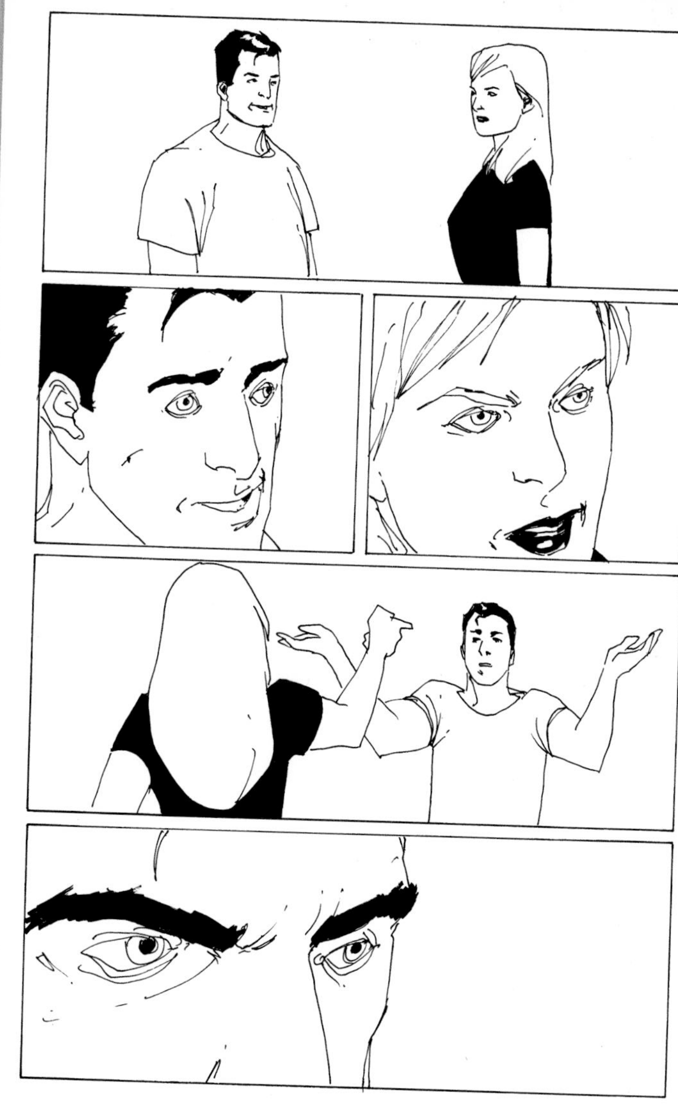

180-Degree Rule Goes Wrong
In this version, artist Khoi Pham crosses the 180-degree line in panel 3. It looks now like the woman and man are talking in the same direction, perhaps to a third person in the room. But all he really did was select the wrong place for his camera. In the last panel, Khoi breaks the line again. In panel 4, the man looks to the left of the page, but in panel 5, the close-up, he appears to be facing to the right. Is he addressing someone new? No; again, Khoi moved the camera to the wrong location and caused a confusing page.

CROSSING THE LINE

Crossing the line confuses the reader. If the man is viewed from one side of the room and the woman from the other, it creates an optical illusion. They will both appear on the same side of the panel looking in the same direction rather than sitting across from each other.

EXCEPTIONS

There are ways to do this that will not confuse the reader.

- Use a series of panels in which the camera stays focused on a person's face. In each panel the camera moves around the figure, changing the angle a little. It could go from a side view, to a three-quarters view, to a straight-on front shot, then move to the other side of his face in another three-quarters view. The camera is swinging around and crossing the line. This works because of the constant focus on

iNSidER PROFiLE

Klaus Janson

OCCUPATION: Penciller, inker, writer, colorist

DATE OF BIRTH: January 23, 1952

FIRST PUBLISHED WORK: Inked Rich Buckler's pencils when he started to draw Black Panther in a book called *Jungle Action* for Marvel back in the early 1970s.

INFLUENCES: From comics I read as a kid, the main guys were probably: Gil Kane, Wally Wood, Steve Ditko, Neal Adams, Dick Giordano, Tom Palmer, Jack Kirby, Joe Kubert, Jim Steranko, Will Eisner. From the current generation I like: Walt Simonson, Mike Mignola, Leinil Francis Yu, John Romita Jr., Bryan Hitch, Jim Lee, James Jean. But I also have been heavily influenced by film: John Ford, Alfred Hitchcock, Martin Scorsese, the film noir stuff from the 1950s, the black-and-white films of the 1940s. Music is a big influence: The Beatles, Talking Heads, Radiohead, David Bowie. Some of the painters of the last century: Milton Avery, Fairfield Porter, David Hockney, Francis Bacon, Edward Hopper. I think it's important to cast a wider net than comics when looking for influence or inspiration.

LONGEST RUN ON A BOOK: Probably *Daredevil* with Frank Miller.

BEST KNOWN FOR: I suspect that "inker of *Dark Knight Returns*" will be on the tombstone.

FAVORITE CHARACTER WORKED ON: The book that manages to combine some of my favorite elements–crime, superheroes and New York City: *Daredevil.*

DREAM PROJECT: Enough money to live on while I do some creator-owned material.

MOST PERSONAL WORK: The stuff that's in my notebooks.

ART TRAINING: No formal training, though I did backgrounds for Dick Giordano right after I got out of high school, and that was highly educational.

KLAUS JANSON is known by fans as an inker and a finisher, but the comics industry knows the truth: Klaus is one of the finest storytellers in the history of the medium. His approach to *Daredevil* and *Batman* revolutionized how dynamic stories are told. In addition to his body of work, Klaus is also a comics historian and teacher.

ALL-TIME FAVORITE ARTIST: I have a real passion for van Gogh. Great use of space, color and texture. I think the best time I ever had in my life was the time I spent in the van Gogh Museum in Amsterdam. But if we use the word "artist" in a broader sense, the artist that is never more than an arm's length away and that serves as a daily inspiration for me, it would be John Lennon and that group he was in.

BEST ADVICE RECEIVED WHEN STARTING OUT: It was Dick Giordano who told me to "meet your deadlines."

one character. But generally there is a more effective way to tell the story.

- The other way is using a neutral camera shot. Maybe a cut to an overhead shot looking straight down on the table and the man and woman. This is a neutral shot; it can go on either side of the 180-degree line from there. The next shot may establish that the camera is on the other side of the room now and the woman is on the left, looking across the table to the man on the right. This is more effective by virtue of using fewer panels. In both cases, you need a neutral shot to transition from.

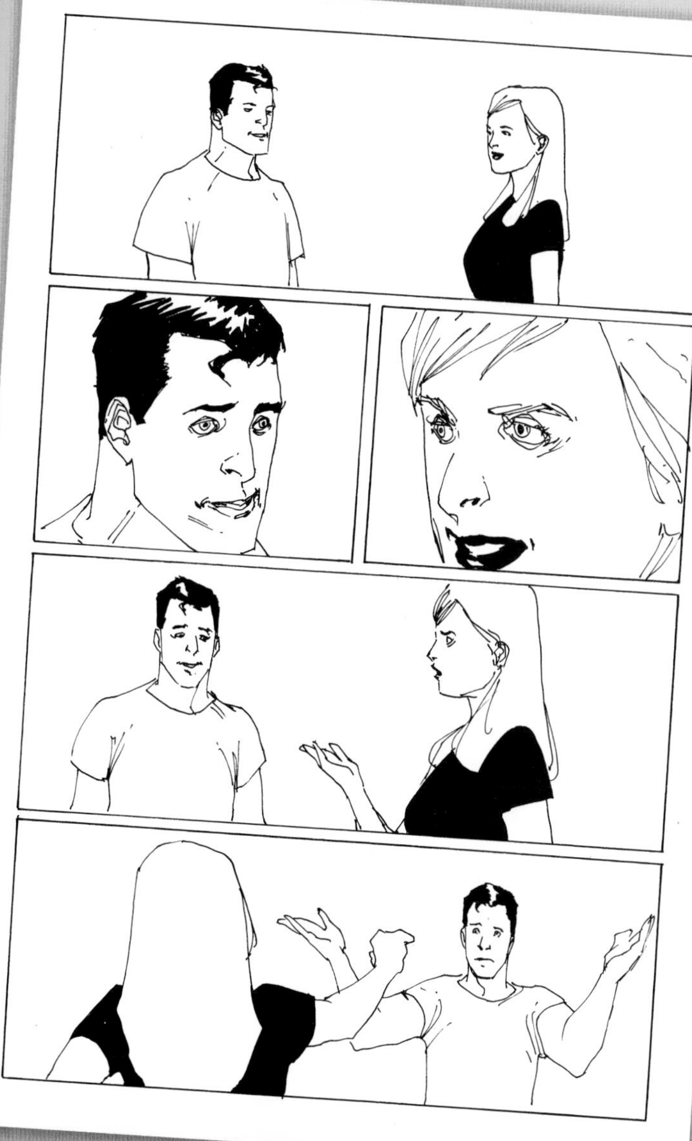

180-Degree Rule Done Right
In this version of the scene, Khoi illustrates the scene with an establishing shot depicting the man on the left and the woman on the right. The 180-degree line is now set on their line of sight. Khoi doesn't cross their line of sight until the last panel after he has disengaged to a neutral panel.

INSIDER VOICE

Klaus Janson on Goals

One of my favorite slogans that applies to comic book art and storytelling very well is: "If you're not doing something, you're doing nothing." Whenever anyone sits down to draw or ink or color, it's essential to be doing something. You have to have a goal, an agenda, an idea. Sitting down and drawing without thinking about what it is you are doing will result in certain failure. You can't just draw or ink or color a comic book page without saying something. And the ability to have an idea and execute it well requires education. So, no matter what your area of interest, immerse yourself in it, learn as much as you can about it, prepare yourself, get smart and get going.

4 CAMERA ANGLES

There's no camera in comics, but the analogy is useful when talking about framing compositions. The composition in a panel informs the reader where the "camera" is shooting from. So, if you're looking at a picture of a woman sitting in a park, and you can see her whole body and many trees all around her, you can intuit the approximate distance that the camera is from the woman. In comics, for simplicity's sake, we still refer to camera angles as though you were shooting a photograph rather than drawing a picture.

Throughout this chapter, we'll discuss various camera angles, define them, talk about when to use them, and what effects they have on the reader. Camera angles are used to effectively and intentionally manipulate audiences.

Look Up!

John Cassaday's cover to *Astonishing X-Men* looks straight up in the air as the characters come crashing down. This camera angle makes heroes look larger than life and villains look all the more sinister. Looking up exaggerates the illusion of power.

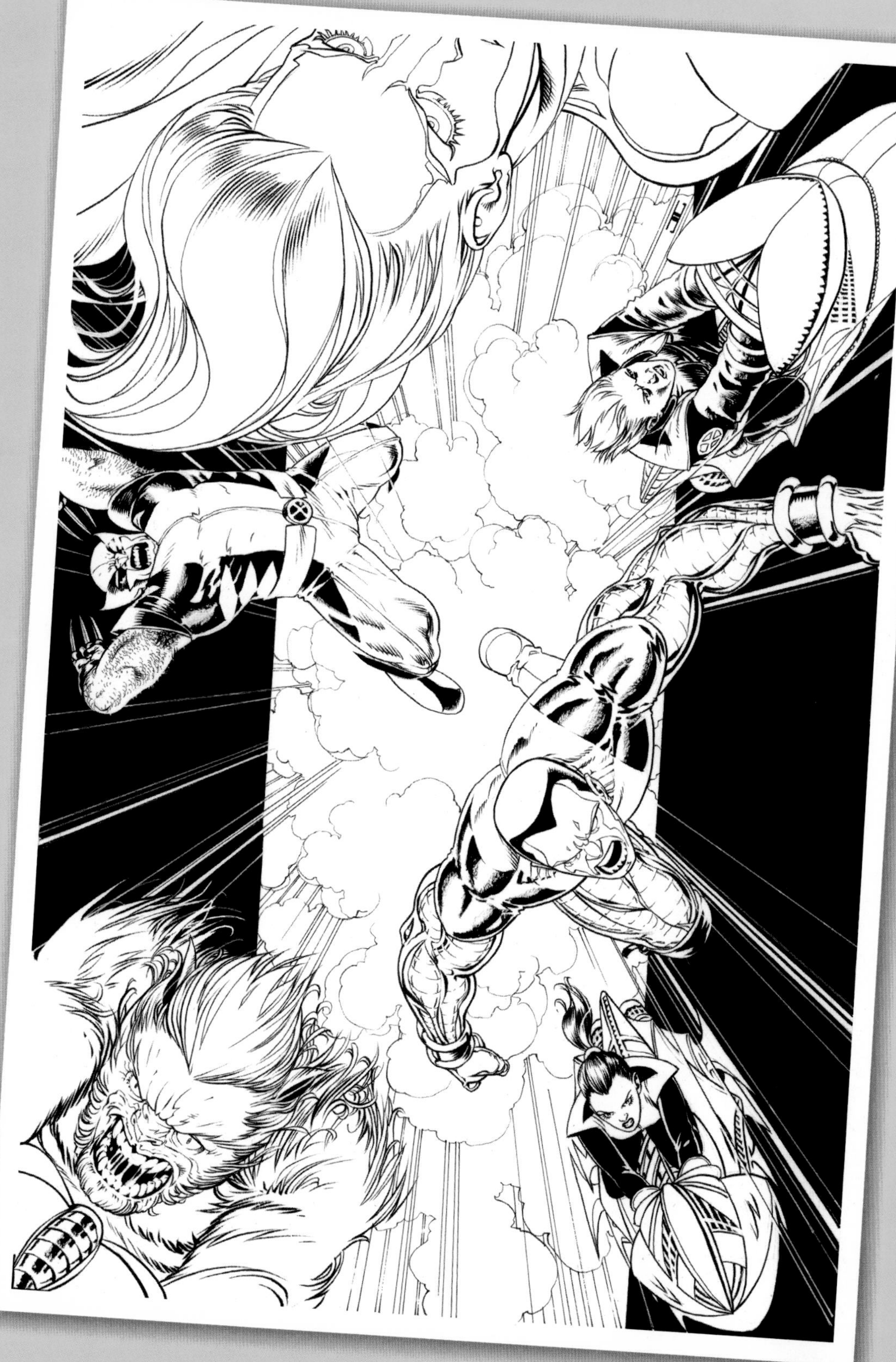

CHOOSING CAMERA ANGLES

The fun part of comics is entertaining. Camera angle has got to communicate effectively, but it can also shape the entertainment level of a comic. The camera angle carries information, just like everything else. If two people are framed talking off to the side of a panel and the camera's in an alley looking past a dumpster out at the people talking, the conversation automatically takes on a different tone than if the camera is right next to the two characters. Placing the camera with a slightly obstructed view creates the sense that the reader is looking in on a conversation that the characters themselves would rather the reader not be privy to. The selection of that particular camera angle is a part of the storytelling and a part of the entertainment—it's added tension, and tension is good.

There are a few quick definitions that will apply throughout this and subsequent chapters. The following all refer to the distance between the camera and the subject.

- **Extreme long shot** Everything in the scene is well within the panel borders. Figures are usually so small that they're in silhouette and all of the environment can be seen.
- **Long shot** Closer in, but characters are still seen as full figures. Details can often be made out.
- **Medium shot** The neutral shot. Usually most or all of the upper body can be seen on a figure from this distance. Details of the face can be seen.
- **Close-up** Tight enough in that we're only seeing the head and maybe shoulders of a figure. All facial expressions can easily be seen. Close-up shots engage the reader the most.
- **Extreme close-up** Closer in still. Only a face, or perhaps just the mouth or just the eyes can be seen. The face will encompass the entire panel.

Note on Subjects

The definitions here focus on a character and his face, but that doesn't mean that an extreme close-up must be on someone's face. The definitions are a guideline as to the distance of the camera from its subject. A close-up on a hand, or a gun, or anything else is perfectly fine and the terms are valid when used with any object.

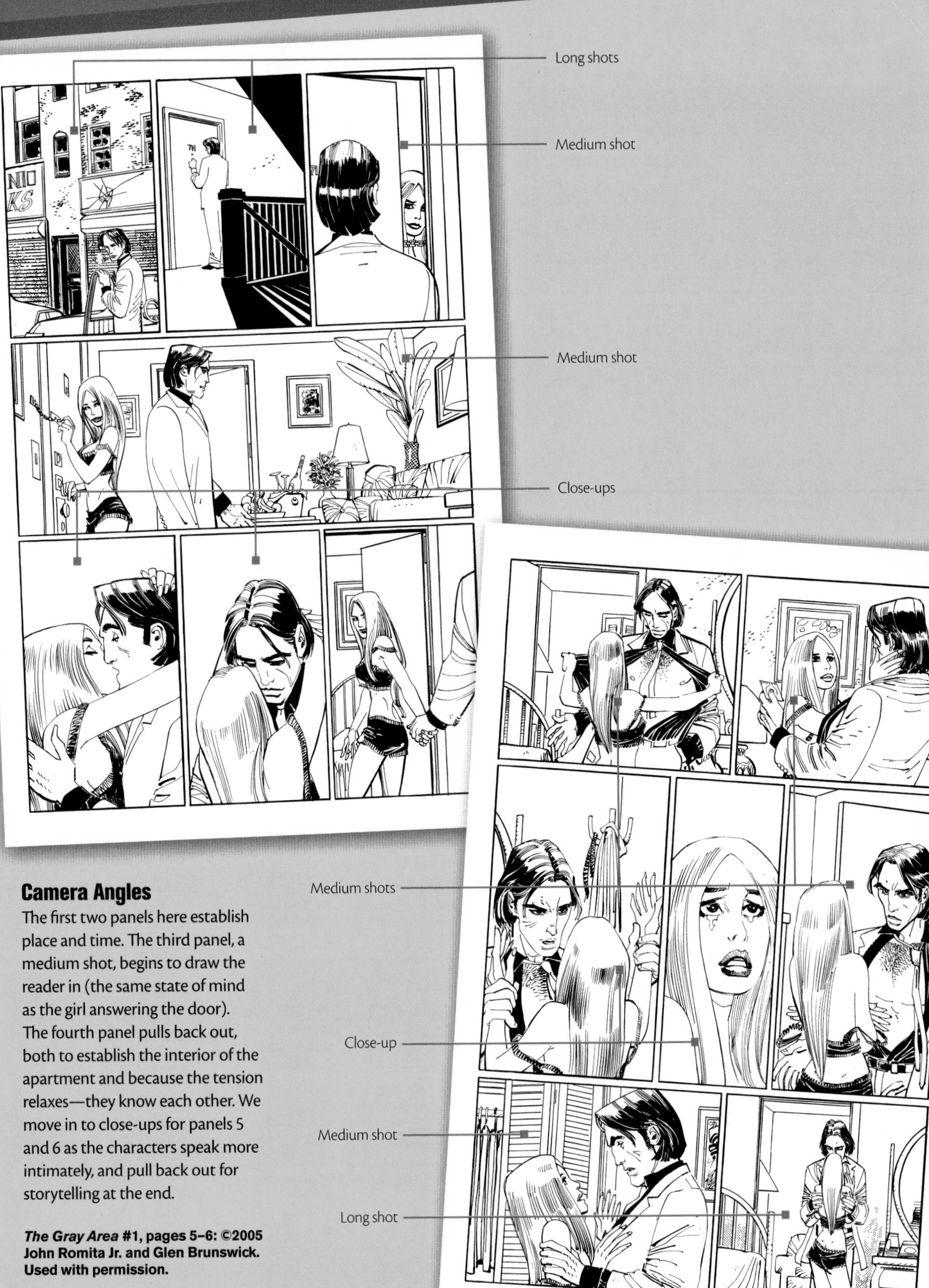

Camera Angles

The first two panels here establish place and time. The third panel, a medium shot, begins to draw the reader in (the same state of mind as the girl answering the door). The fourth panel pulls back out, both to establish the interior of the apartment and because the tension relaxes—they know each other. We move in to close-ups for panels 5 and 6 as the characters speak more intimately, and pull back out for storytelling at the end.

EYE-LEVEL SHOTS

The eye-level shot is the neutral camera position. It doesn't communicate anything extra to a reader. The camera is placed at a person's normal eye level, roughly five to six feet off the ground. And eye level only refers to the height at which the camera is placed—it can be combined with any of the shots listed on page 72. An extreme close-up at eye level all the way back to an extreme long shot at eye level is acceptable. An eye-level, medium shot is the most neutral shot. And it doesn't mean boring, only that it's not communicating anything beyond what is contained within the panel borders.

Eye-level shots are best used when the reader should be focused only on what is inside the panel. Sometimes, putting extra tricks into a panel sends an unintended message. The eye-level shot won't do that—it allows the reader to draw his own conclusions about the content within the panel.

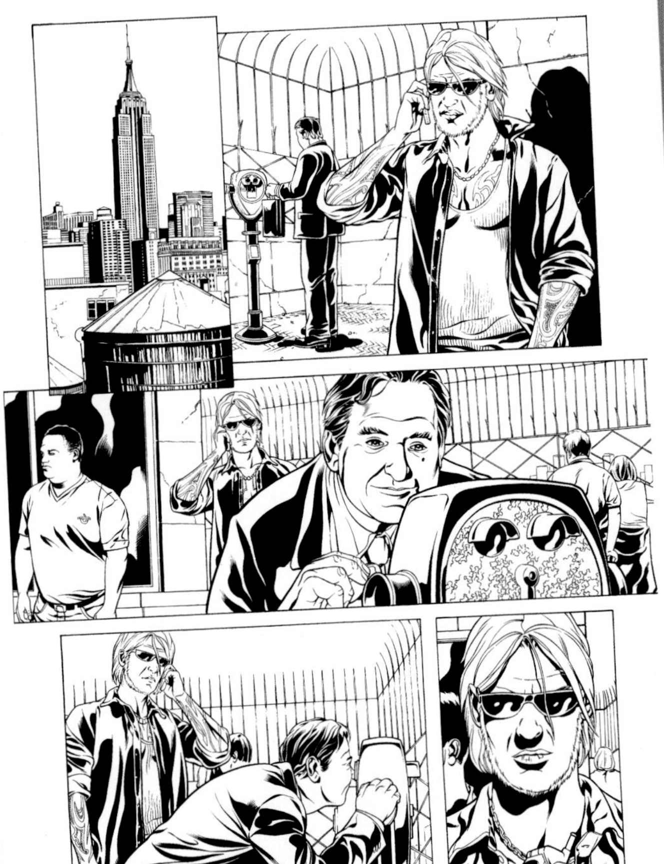

Eye Level All the Way

Pablo Raimondi's page here uses an extreme long shot, a long shot, two medium shots and one close-up. All of them are eye level and communicate only the actions within the panels.

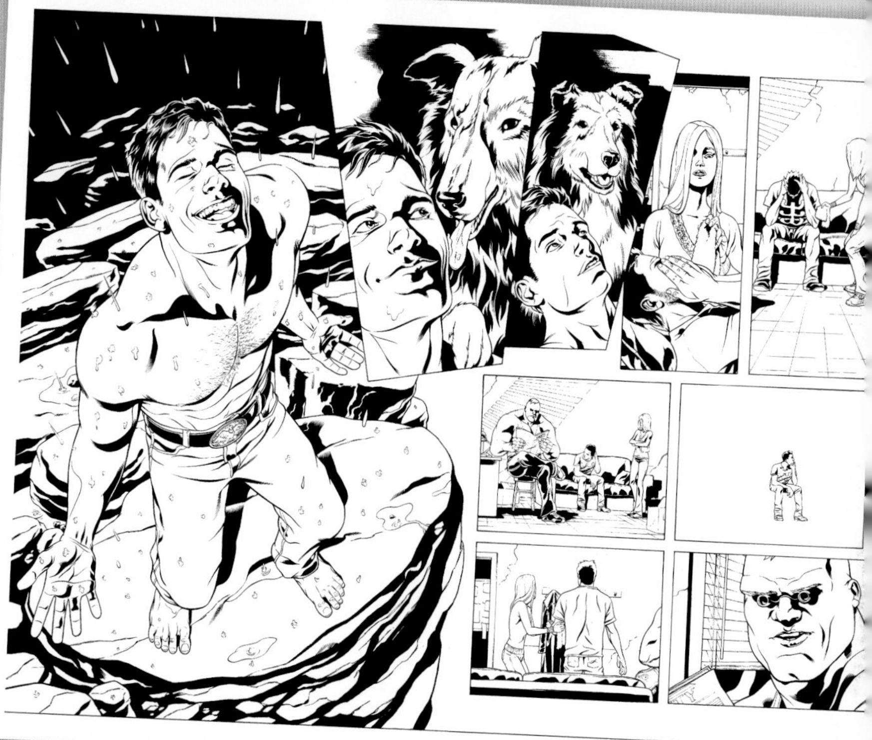

A *high-angle shot* is any camera angle from above the eye-level shot up to the overhead shot. This requires the camera to be tilted at an angle toward the ground so the reader gets a view looking down. In order to do this, the camera must be somewhere above him. A high-angle shot looking down on someone has a tendency to make the subject look smaller than an eye-level shot would. Artists use this angle when they are trying to manipulate the reader into thinking that the character in the shot is weak or afraid.

The *low-angle shot* is like the high-angle shot in that it is any angle from below the eye level all the way down to the floor. A low-angle shot means that the camera is looking up toward the subject. Like the high-angle shot, this also has an effect on the reader. When the reader is looking up at the man, even the same man seen in a high-angle shot, he will appear strong, confident and stable. This is a great way to make a character look heroic or trustworthy, or, if a villain, threatening.

Because both the high- and low-angle shots create specific effects, they're used generally only when artists want to affect an audience in such a way. I'm not saying that the camera angle should not move up or down, but it should not move so drastically as to give the reader an unintended message.

High-Angle Shot

Pablo Raimondi used the high angle here to create a sense of smallness while the character begins to realize that there is a higher power.

***Madrox* #1, page 20: ©2008 Marvel Characters, Inc. Used with permission.**

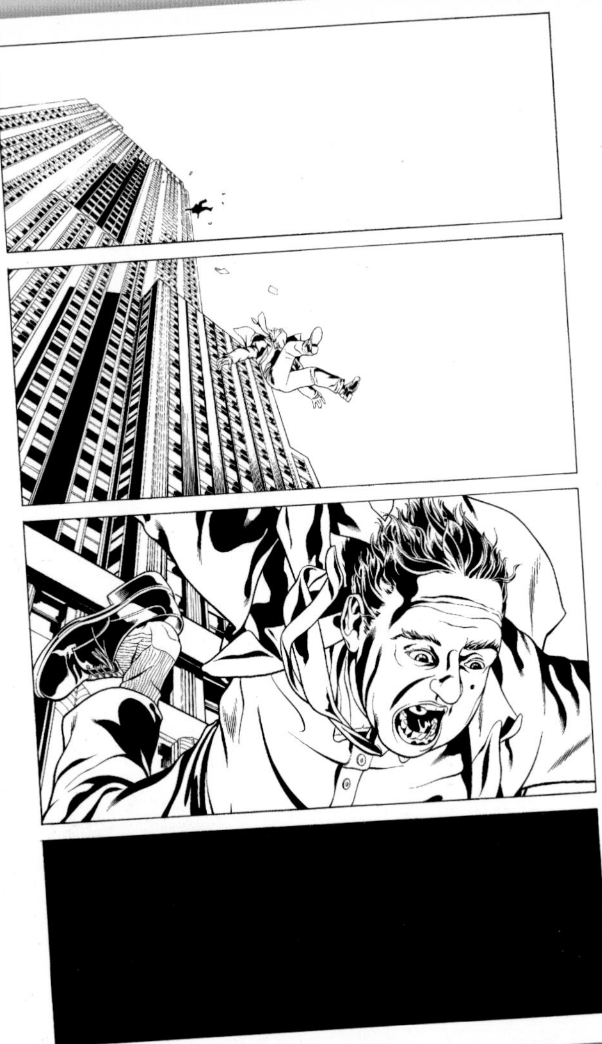

Low-Angle Shot

The low-angle shot that Pablo uses here accentuates how large and tall the building is, thus increasing the anticipation and effectiveness of the character's impending impact.

INSIDER VOICE

John Romita Jr. on What New Artists Should Work on First

Not the ability to draw, that will come. It's like being an athlete—you work out, you get strong, you get better and you become a better football player. But learning to play, in this case, learning how to tell a story, is more viable than the physical part of it. Now I'm testament to that: My artwork is OK, but because of my storytelling, my artwork looks better. So, as a young up-and-coming artist, learn to tell a story quicker than the actual artwork. Your artwork will improve.

And do not be afraid of background. Fill up the background.

CLOSE-UPS

Close-ups automatically intensify a scene. The tighter in the camera is on someone's face, the more intense the scene becomes. On the flip side, the wider out the camera goes, the less intense a scene becomes. For example, take a look at any fight scene. Chances are, you'll see that as the battle gets more and more heated over the course of five pages, the artist will have used the camera angle to manipulate the audience and intensify the scene just by slowly moving closer in on the action. The fight scene might start with a long shot of two characters, full figure, standing in front of one another in a heated argument. The camera might move in closer for the first punch. The camera movement alone can intensify the scene. As the battle continues and gets more heated, that camera might keep moving in to upper body shots only, then finally close-ups on faces and fists, and so on, until the fight ends, then returning to the long-shot position.

The key to using the close-up is to avoid going in too tight on the subjects until the scene is established either with an establishing long shot (see page 58) or with landmarks (see page 63) so that the reader understands where everyone is. If the reader is confused, he's not going to be nearly as entertained as he should be.

Also note how what's in the panel borders (and by extension, what's left out) carries an effect to the reader. An extreme close-up on smiling lips carries a different message than a close-up of the whole face.

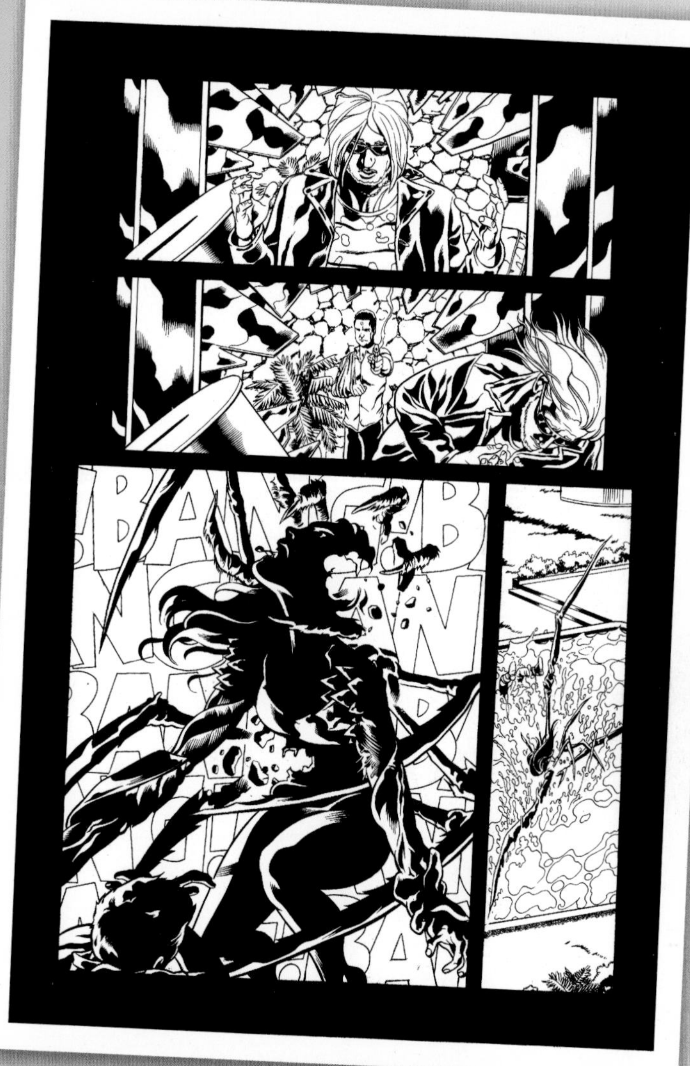

Moving In Close

Here, Pablo uses a larger panel and a tighter crop in panel 3 to intensify the climax of the action sequence.

TILTED HORIZON LINE

The *horizon line* is an imaginary line where earth and sky meet. Tilting the camera so the horizon line in the scene is slanted on the panel causes a scene to feel unbalanced or off-putting. Typically, when we talk about camera angles, the camera is assumed parallel to the ground; it may look up, down, to the left or to the right, but the horizon line is always a horizontal line parallel to the top and bottom lines of the panel. This is not the case with a tilted angle.

Humans are used to the horizon line remaining consistent and perpendicular to ourselves. Any time the horizon line is depicted on an extreme angle, the horizon no longer feels stable; there's a subtle uneasiness that occurs in the reader's mind.

Tilting the horizon line can be useful just to give a scene an uneasy feeling. Maybe a detective is exploring a crime scene and there's a hint that something unexpected may occur. Perhaps a character has been drugged and is off balance. Tilting the horizon line can help show these things.

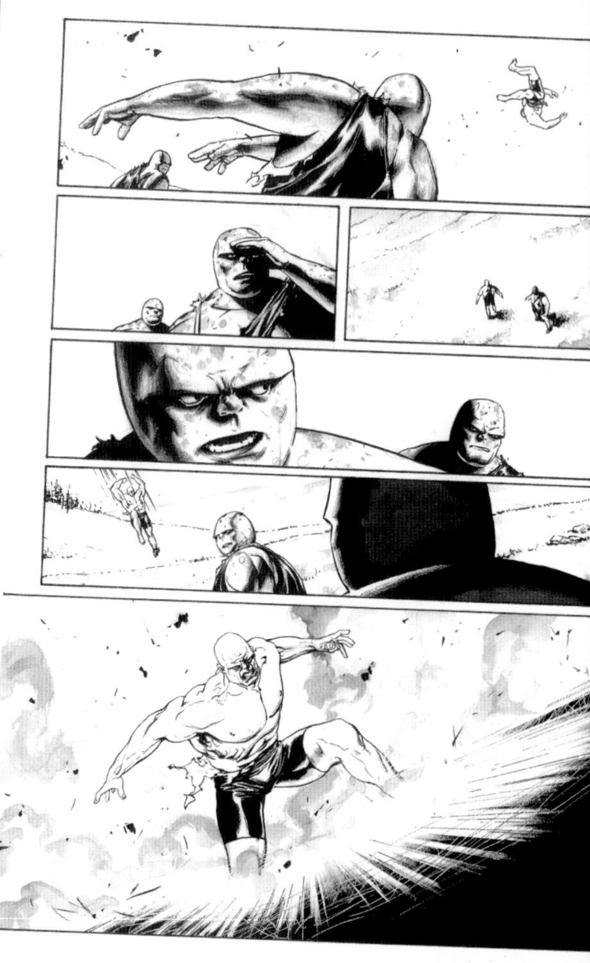

Tilted Horizon

On this page by Mitch Breitweiser, panels 1–5 do not tilt the horizon line, but the last panel does. It creates an effective and uneasy moment as Drax the Destroyer slams into the ground.

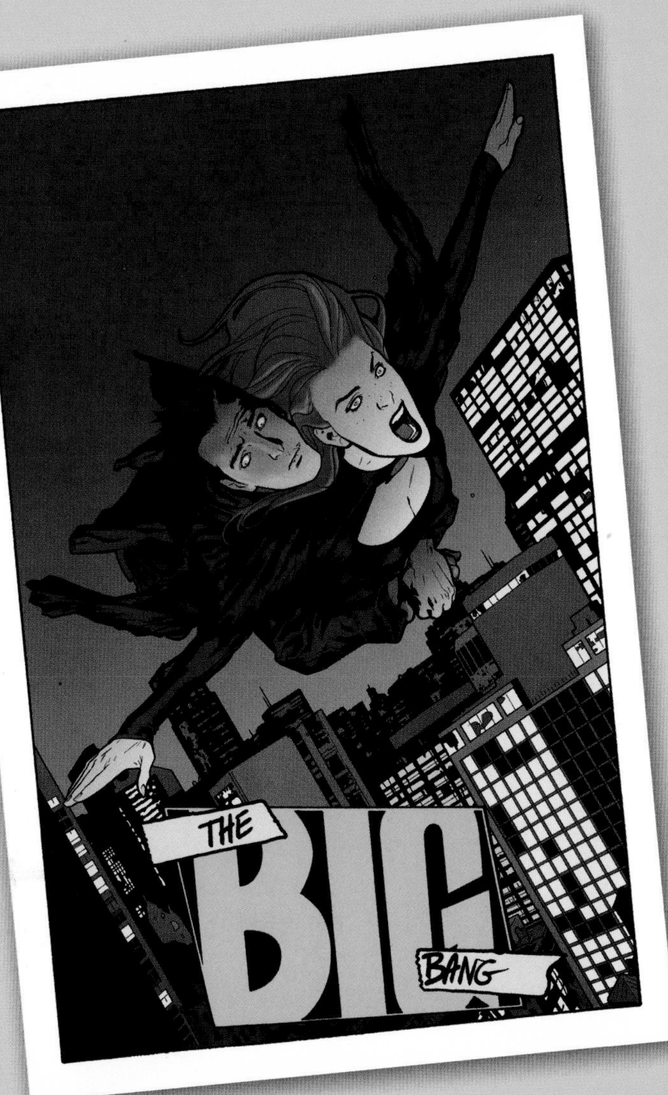

Off Balance
Artist Ryan Sook tilts the horizon line to approximate the panicked unease of Jamie Madrox, who is holding on for dear life.

X-Factor **#3, page 3: ©2008 Marvel Characters, Inc. Used with permission.**

INSIDER VOICE
Gene Ha on Voice

Bring something that's new to comics. The world doesn't need another artist imitating Frank Miller or Mike Mignola. If you want to be like them, bring in your passions from elsewhere in your life and teach the comics world something new. That's what they did.

When Frank Miller started in the industry, Japanese comics were almost impossible to find in the United States. The manga influences Miller introduced changed American comics. Nowadays every young artist has read *Naruto*. Look further afield. Show me stuff I've never seen before.

BIRD'S-EYE and WORM'S-EYE VIEWS

When I was a kid, I loved the video games I could play on the Atari game system my parents brought home. I remember a couple of them fondly to this day. They all had one thing in common: The camera shot on the action in the game was entirely from a bird's-eye view—a 100 percent overhead shot, looking directly down at the ground. Playing *Pac-Man*, I didn't ever have to worry about what was behind the next corner, because I could see the whole room at all times.

Recently, my wife and I took a trip to New Zealand (go there if you can!), and I learned exactly what a worm's-eye view was after bungee jumping off a bridge. Once at the bottom of a cavern, I slapped the river water with my hands, then I looked back up at the bridge with the water touching the back of my head for just a second. That bridge looked miles away and appeared to be the largest thing man had ever constructed.

Both the bird's-eye view and the worm's-eye view provide a look at the entire scene. Like the eye-level shot, the bird's-eye view is essentially neutral. The reader gets no extra information or feeling from the bird's-eye view—you're mostly relaying information.

The worm's-eye view, on the other hand, makes a situation seem bigger and more dramatic. The bottom border of the panel is the ground, so all the figures standing on the ground look like they're standing on the bottom panel border. The worm's-eye view tends to disengage the reader from the action. It pulls the camera out to get full figures in the panel and places the camera on the floor—a position most of us don't typically view the world from. So it pulls us away from the action and places us in a strange location.

Worm's-eye views can be great re-establishing shots. They can give the reader a sense that the events he's looking at are larger than life—it's great for superhero comics!

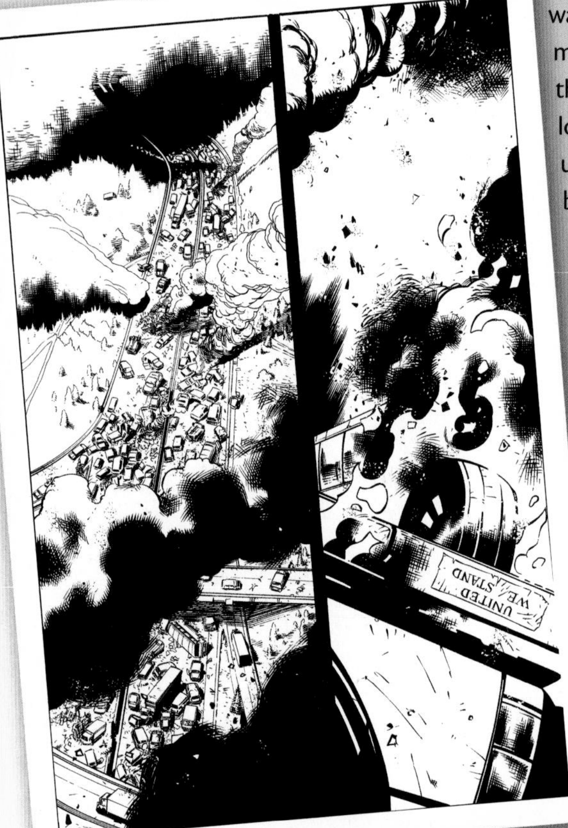

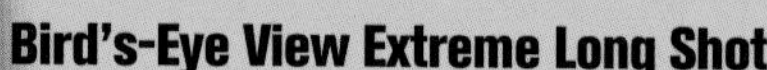

Bird's-Eye View Extreme Long Shot

Artist Olivier Coipel uses the bird's-eye view with an extreme long shot to show the reader the extent of a recent disaster.

***The Avengers* #69, page 6: ©2008 Marvel Characters, Inc. Used with permission.**

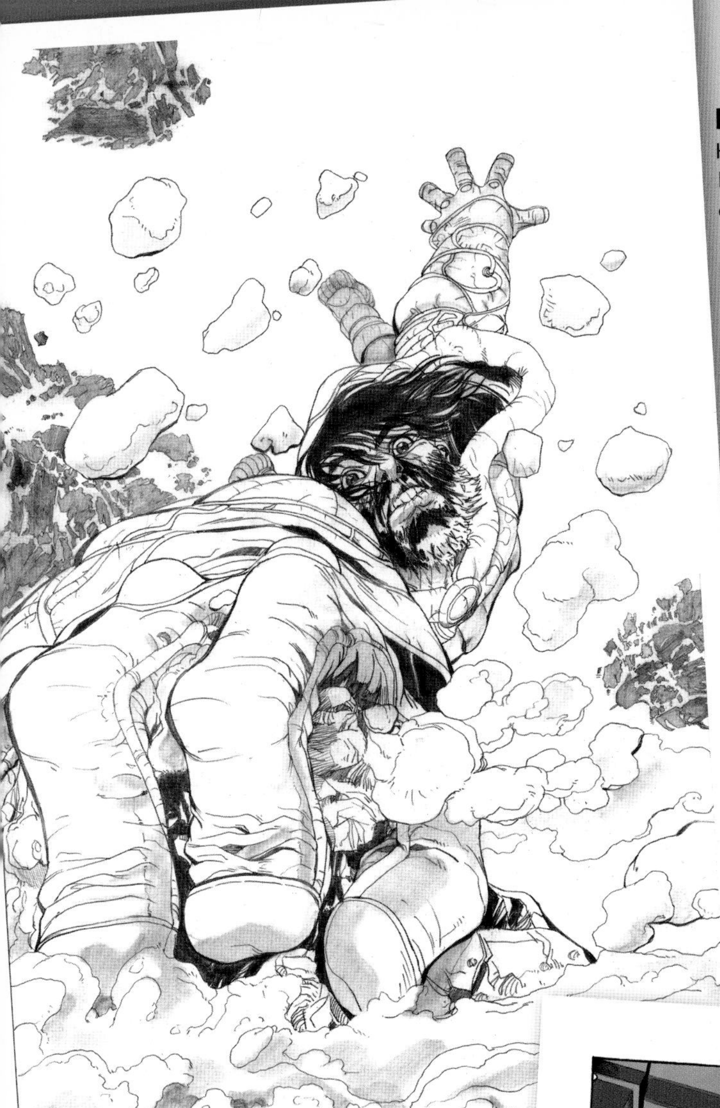

Bird's-Eye View Close-Up

Here, Chris Cross uses a close-up with the bird's-eye view to demonstrate the danger the character faces.

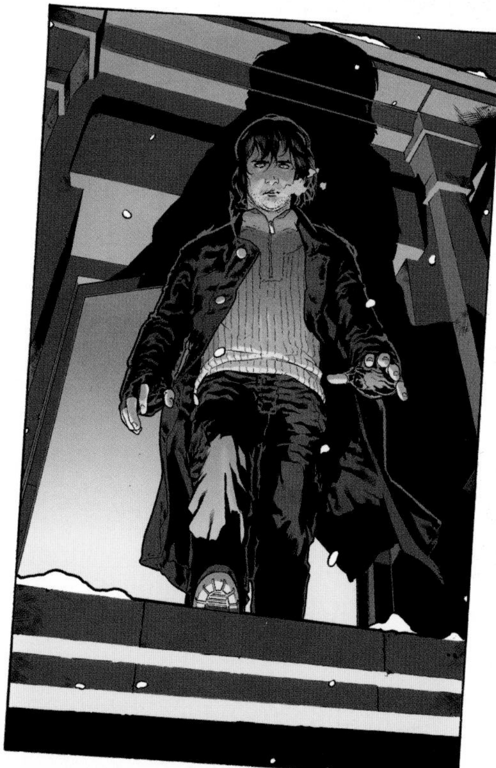

Worm's-Eye View

Ryan Sook chose the worm's-eye view here, emphasizing that the character is looking down, toward the reader, at the street below.

CAMERA IN MOTION

In comics, the camera can't constantly move. When artists want to create the illusion of a moving camera, they have to resort to some tricks.

There are three basic ways to trick the reader into thinking that the camera is moving. They are:

- Side-to-side camera movement
- Tracking shot
- Camera pan

SIDE-TO-SIDE

It takes a series of panels to create the illusion of camera movement. And the camera moves only about 30 degrees in each successive panel.

The movement occurs between shots, with the camera focused on the same object or objects throughout the sequence. The artist can't cut away to another shot, or he will break the illusion.

The objects can move, like two figures talking can gesticulate and perhaps walk around a little, but the camera angle can only move a little bit from shot to shot. If it moves too much, it will just look like the camera's moved to a different place. Jump too little, and it will look like the artist tried to repeat the previous panel but failed to do it well.

TRACKING SHOT

In film, moving the camera in a freeform style is called a *tracking shot*. The effect can be approximated in comics. A scene may open with a high-angle shot looking down on a shoe in the street. In the next panel, the shoe may be moved toward the bottom of the panel and at the top we see a woman's purse. In the third panel the purse may be at the bottom of the panel and at the top is the beginning of a trail of blood, and so on. This gives the illusion

Side-to-Side ↓
When used effectively, the side-to-side camera movement can add a little visual spice to what might otherwise be a less-than-thrilling talking-heads scene. Mark Bagley does it here as he moves the camera to the right, following J. Jonah Jameson.

***The Pulse* #1, pages 12–13: ©2008 Marvel Characters, Inc. Used with permission.**

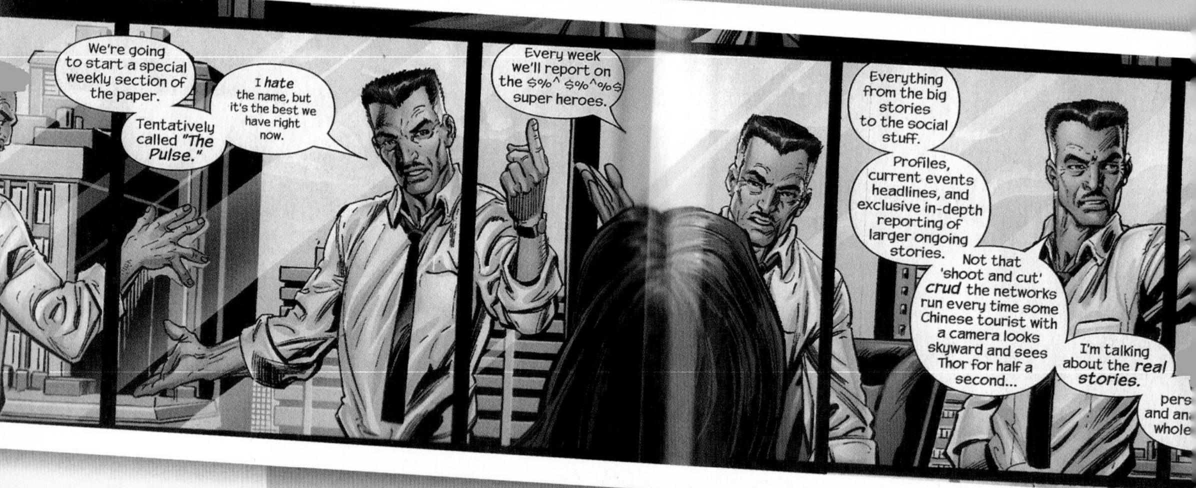

of the camera moving along the floor and slowly revealing a scene.

CAMERA PAN

The third camera movement is the camera pan. If a character is running toward the camera in panel 1, in panel 2 he'll get closer. The camera may "pivot" as the man begins to pass the camera, giving us almost a side view of the man in the third panel. In panel 4, the camera will continue to pivot or pan so it is a complete profile of the runner. In the fifth panel, we would begin to see the back of the man's head as he begins to shrink in the panel as he runs away from the camera.

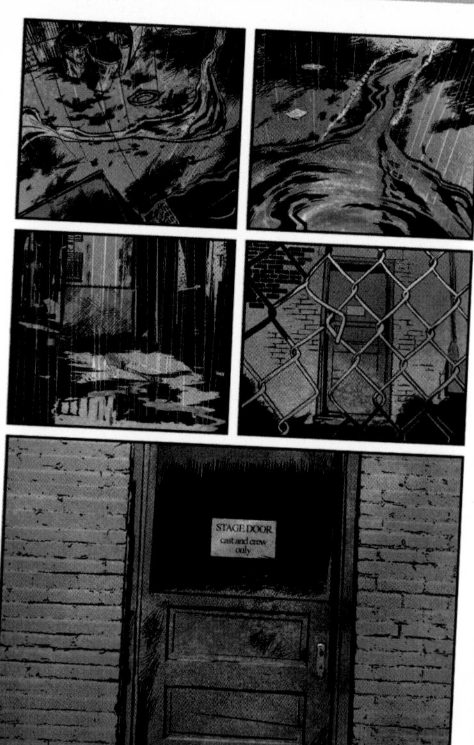

Tracking Shot

The tracking shot can use side-to-side or panning motions, but is not limited to them. In this page by Dennis Calero, the camera follows the water coming out of an alley, goes into the alley, pans up to see a fence, and moves beyond the fence to a door. This technique draws the reader in slowly and cautiously, causing an increase in tension.

***X-Factor* #5, page 3: ©2008 Marvel Characters, Inc. Used with permission.**

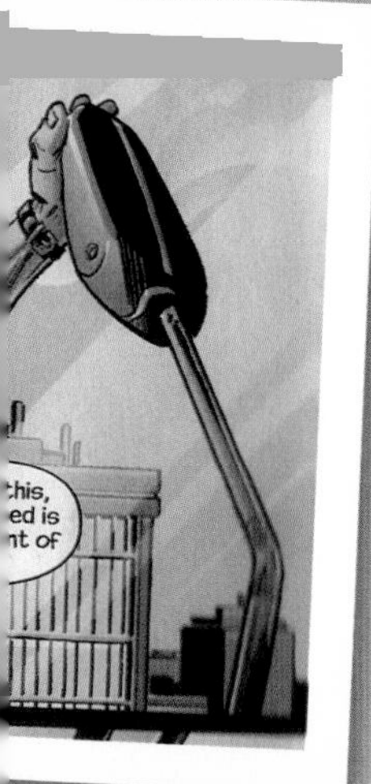

Camera Pan ➡

Here, artist Kevin Maguire leaves the camera in one place but simply pivots it to follow the character in motion. This forces the reader to feel like these four panels are all one very important moment. It emphasizes the action across the page.

***Defenders* #3, page 5: ©2008 Marvel Characters, Inc. Used with permission.**

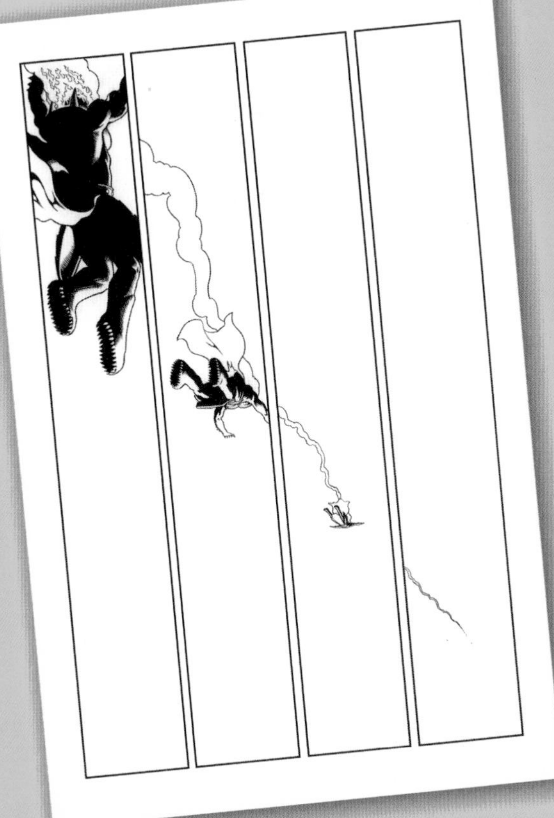

5 CHARACTER ACTING

Even the best layouts with the perfect camera angles and lighting will fail to stir up the reader's emotions if the characters within the panels can't act. Comics, in this regard, are similar to the movies. For me, the movie *Speed* was like this. It was a fun action movie—fast-paced, snappy dialogue, cool special effects, but the actors failed to convince me they were in danger. Both lead actors in that movie have given performances that I've liked in the past and since making *Speed*, but for whatever reason, they couldn't draw me in.

The same problem can occur in comics. If the body language and facial expressions don't communicate emotions to the reader, the comic will not be engaging. Let's be honest for a moment—this is the biggest shortcoming in superhero comics today. We put our superheroes in brightly colored costumes and dramatic situations so the body language is all that's needed to communicate. Those costumes are not a substitute for real emoting. This isn't to say that no superhero comics artists do great facial expressions—many, in fact most, of them can, but they're not required to do so while drawing Spider-Man. That said, Mary Jane Watson and J. Jonah Jameson, Spider-Man's supporting cast, have to be very expressive.

There are two basic forms of character acting:

1 Body language

2 Facial expression

Getting Angry

Artist Kevin Maguire is best known for his expressive facial expressions. Note how annoyed the Sub-Mariner becomes in panel 10, and then how defensive he is in panel 12.

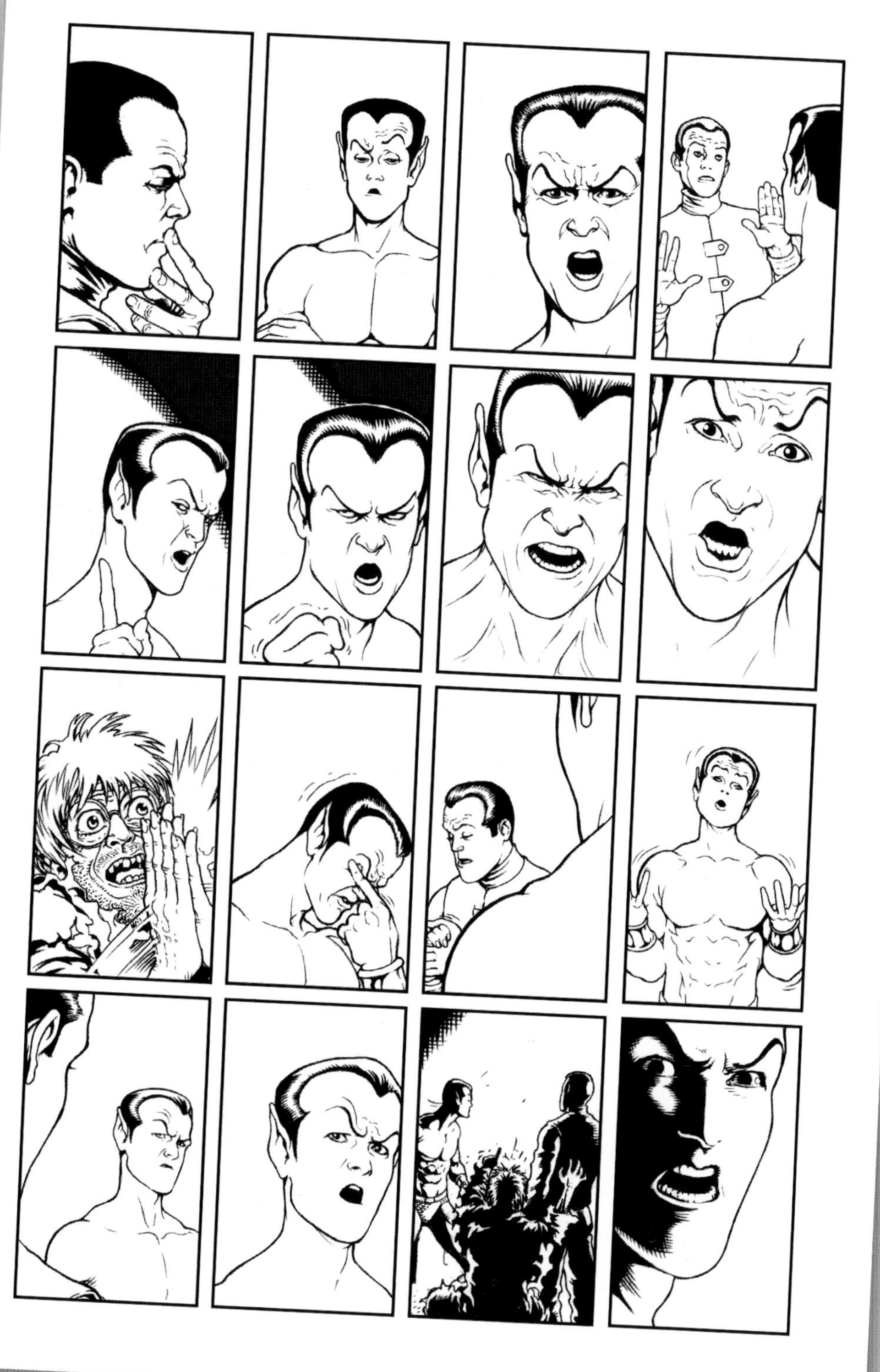

The importance of expression in characters boils down to one thing: It is through characters' expressions that readers will emotionally connect with them. Artists need to communicate the expression first, and then entertain. The good thing about body language and facial expressions is that they tend to be entertaining on their own. The characters' abilities to capture readers' imaginations propels readers to finish reading the story. If someone has read a third of a comic and doesn't relate on any level to the characters, that reader will probably put the comic down. On the flip side, if a reader's not a fan of the art style and finds the page layouts distracting but is interested in the characters, he will keep reading. It comes down to making a connection with your reader. And expressive characters are the means to form that connection.

Expression Through Facial and Body Language Drawing Tips

- Take a figure drawing class and a life study class. Artists must be able to imitate human anatomy as precisely as possible. Heck, get some medical books. Learn what muscles look like and how they connect to bones.
- Take an acting class. Classes for stage actors teach about body movement and expression with gestures and body position.
- Read books on the psychology of body language to learn what the different body positions mean. For example, someone with arms crossed and head cocked to the side probably isn't open to hearing what you have to say to him.
- Look in the mirror. Many artists just use a mirror and act out or role-play what their character is going through or saying.
- Read art books on figure drawing. Two great ones are Burne Hogarth's *Dynamic Figure Drawing* and Will Eisner's *Comics & Sequential Art*. Both of these taught me much of what I know about figures, anatomy and body language expression.
- Go to a park and watch from a distance how people interact with each other. What do you think they're saying to each other? What does their body language communicate to you?
- Practice. Always practice. Always be striving to improve. Almost everyone who comes up to me at a convention for a portfolio review could improve on their character anatomy and expression.

The biggest debate in character expression is which draws the reader in more: realistic representational art or more cartoony art like newspaper strips. That's not a debate I'm going to be able to settle here (or ever, probably), but I do have a few thoughts on the subject. The cartoon style has a wider appeal because the expressions are exaggerated and plain to see. Also, because the character doesn't look like a real person, it is easier for the reader to graft his own characteristics onto the character—the reader is more likely to see part of himself in the cartoon character. Representational art—more photorealistic—is better at creating a character that will be of some new interest to the reader. I may not recognize myself in the realistic art because the character may look like someone else I know or like characters from the movies, but if you're building a character that I'm not meant to identify with a lot, this is the approach to take. For example, if you're telling a story about a hit man, I'm not likely to connect a lot with the character. Of course, I want to connect enough to get involved in his story, but I'm not likely to have experienced a lot of the same events or react to situations in the same way that he will. But I can be drawn in—I can be interested in what this guy's life is like. If a hit man's story is told in a cartoon-like style, then I'm more likely to be grafting my own emotions and thoughts onto the character. My favorite comic of all time is *Calvin and Hobbes* by Bill Watterson. I saw myself in Calvin's character every morning. The cartoon style made that very easy. My favorite representational comic is *V for Vendetta*. I don't relate to the title character at all, but it's our differences that intrigue me. His ideas and motivations are so different from my own that I'm drawn in and I want to get to know him rather than see myself reflected back at me.

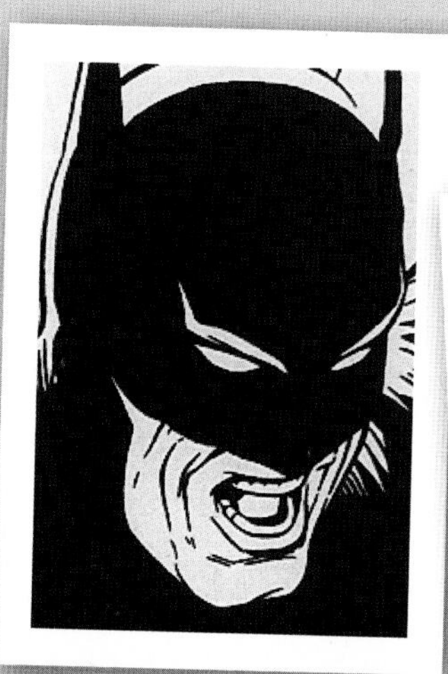

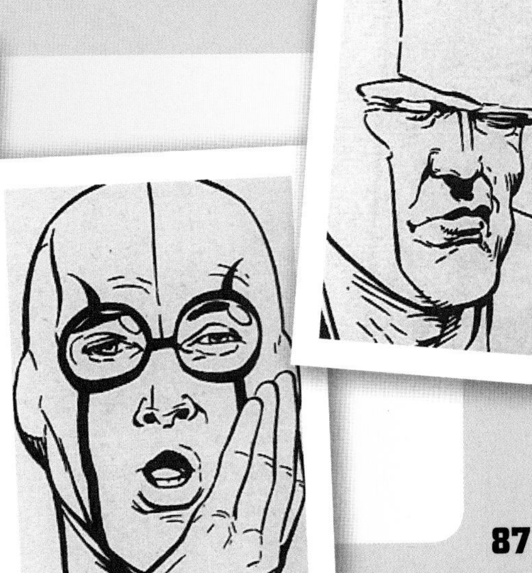

Honest Expressions
Kevin Maguire draws honest expressions.

TYPES OF EXPRESSIONS

Everything I know about body language and expression comes from life experience and Will Eisner. He was the best at communicating honest expression with his cartoon characters. His chapter in *Comics & Sequential Art* can't be beaten.

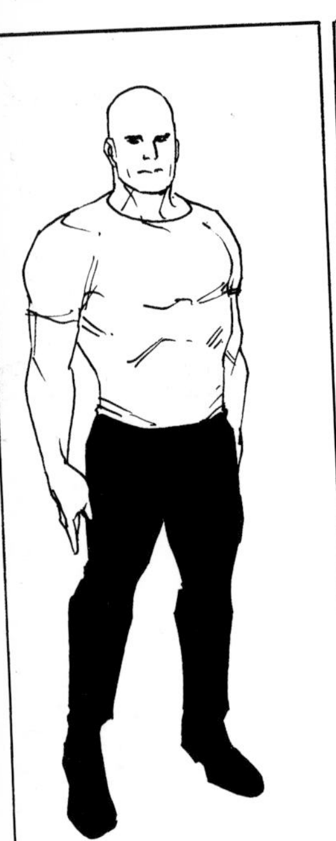
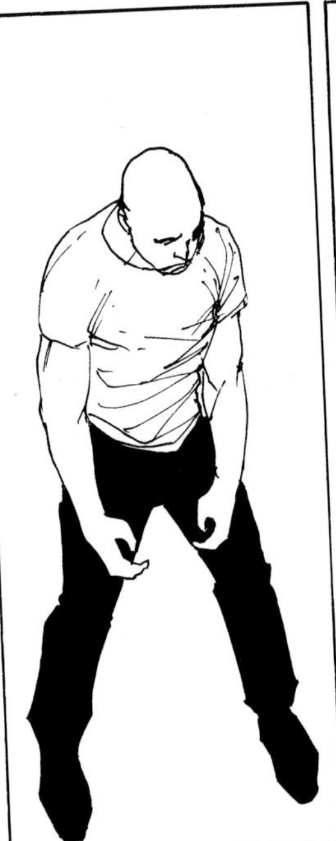
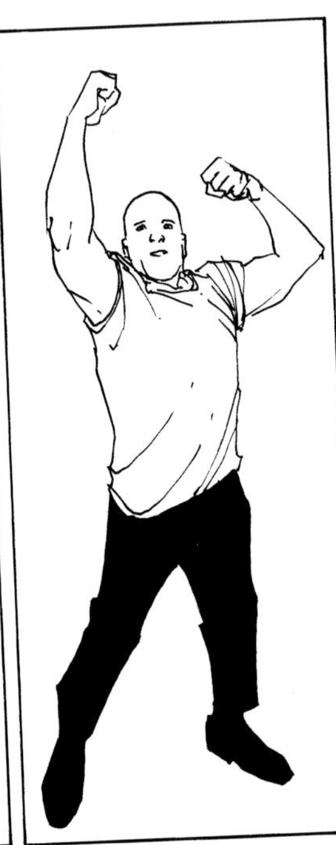

Body Language
Six figures. Same guy. Same clothes. Same camera angle. Six different messages. Across from top left: neutral, defeated, triumphant, pleading, angry, inviting.

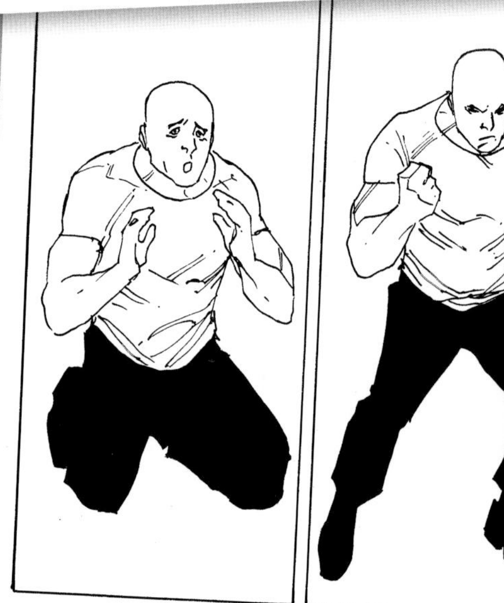
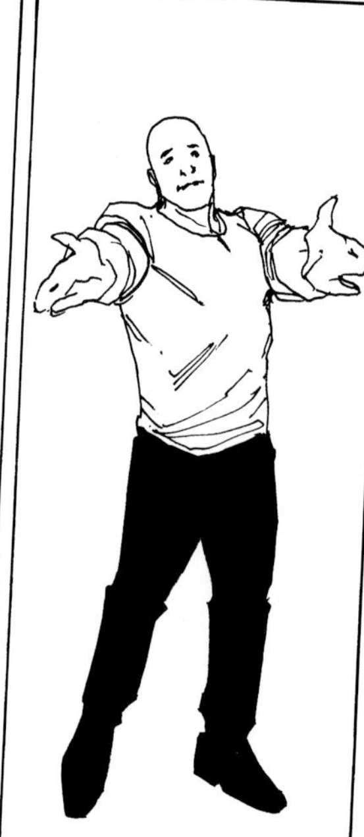

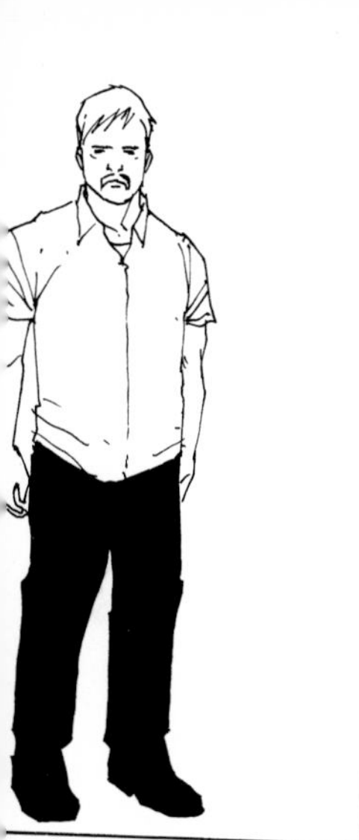

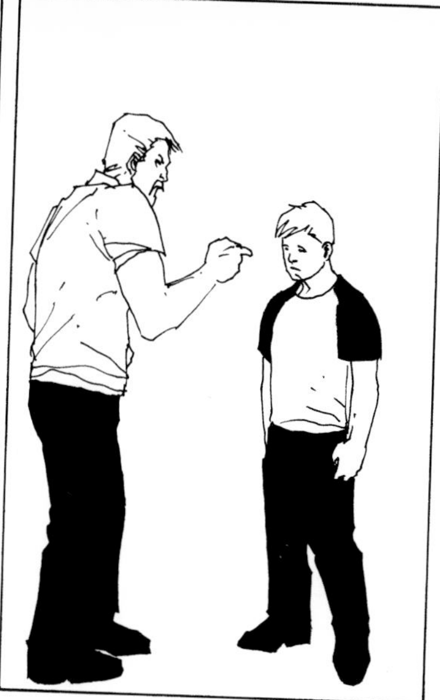

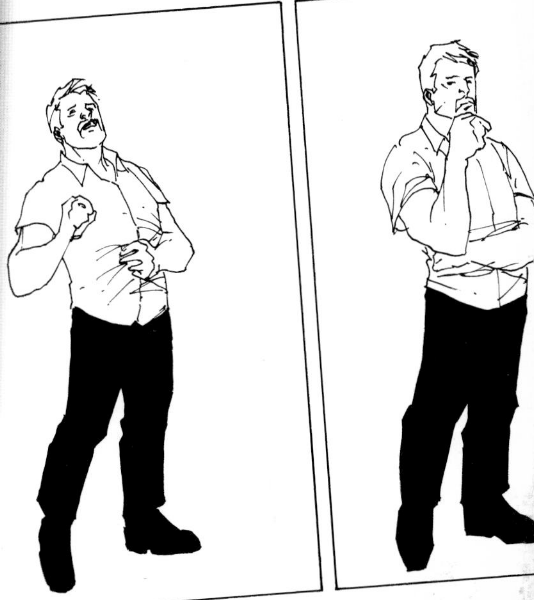

More Body Language

From top left: neutral, scolding and ashamed, happy, pensive.

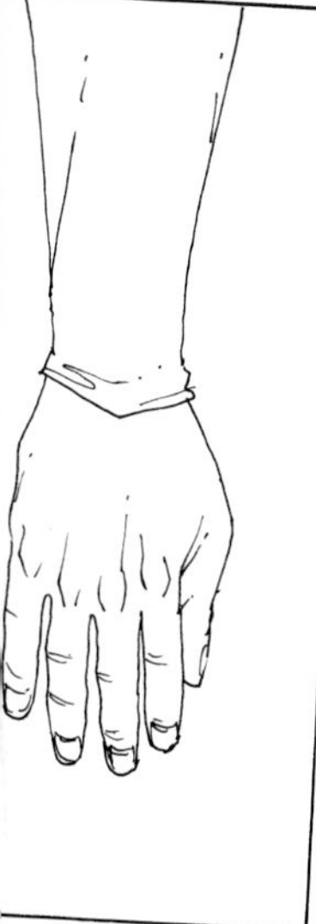

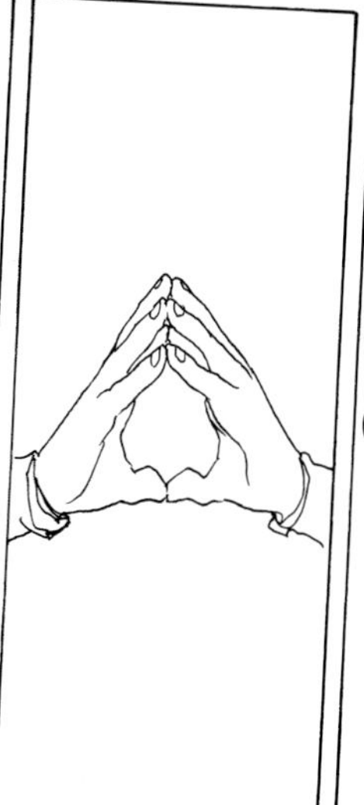

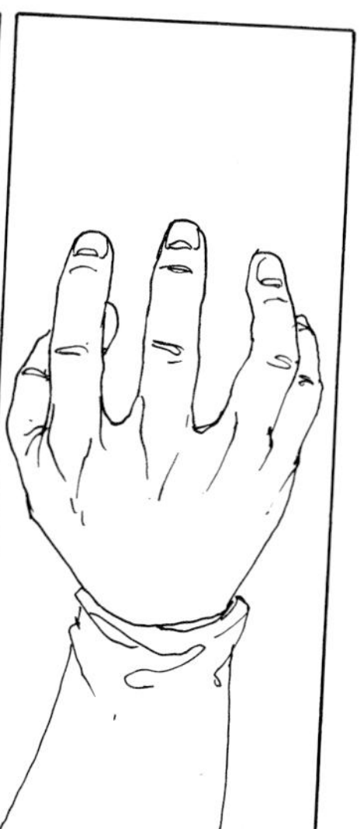

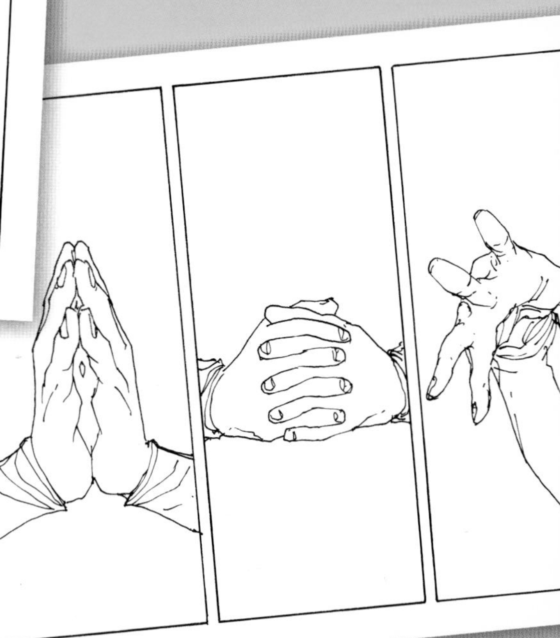

Expressive Hands

Across from top left: neutral, thoughtful, dominant or tense, thinking evil thoughts or praying, relaxed, shocked.

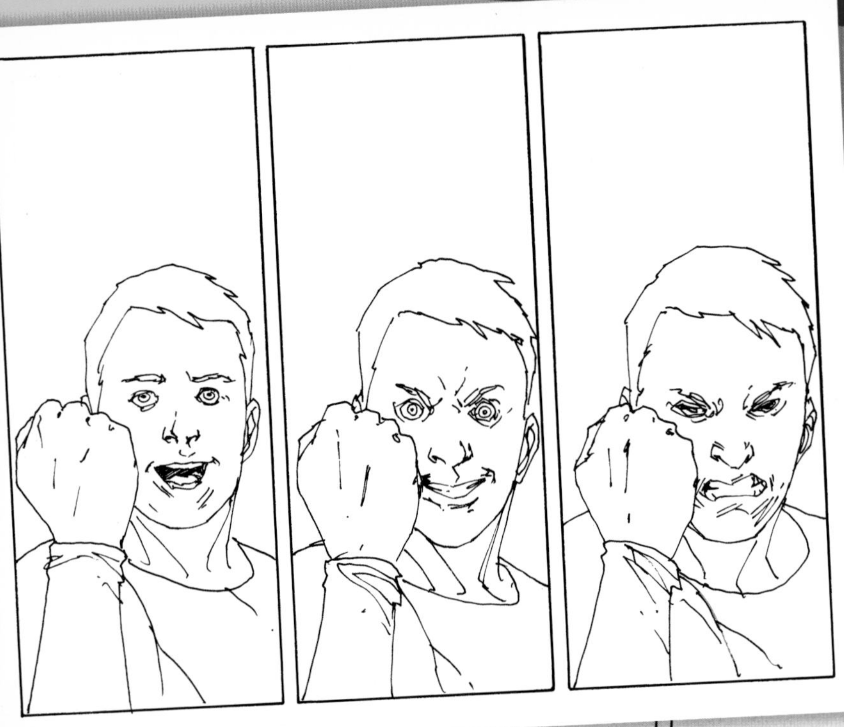

Faces and Hands

Here, Khoi used the same hands with three different facial expressions providing new meanings. Top row: excited, maniacal, angry. Bottom row: worried, defensive, celebrating.

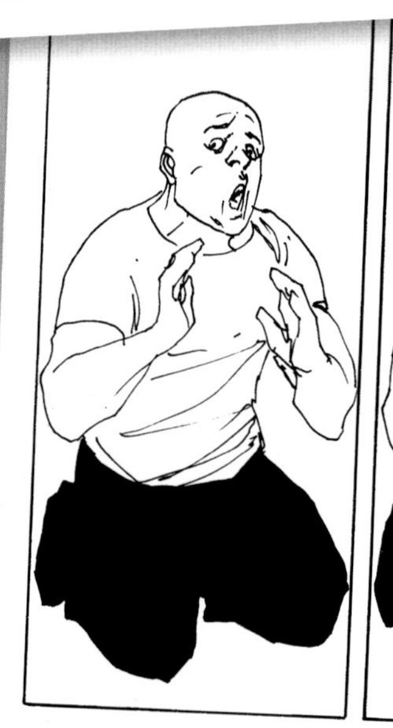

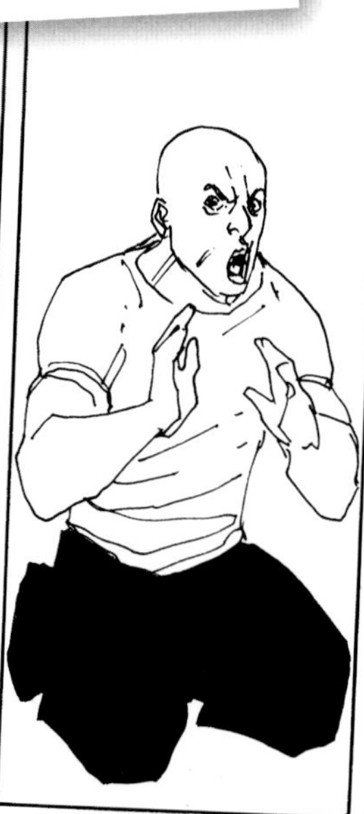

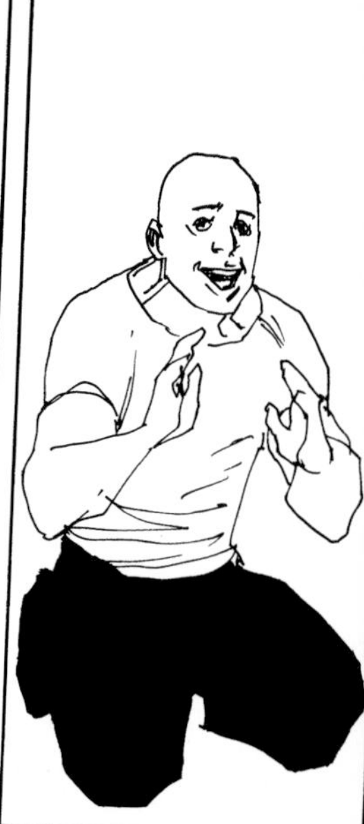

INSIDER VOICE

David Finch on Good Pencils

I want to see characters that look like they are just always on the very edge of wanting to kill someone, but are too stupid to know any better. I want to see lots of detail, heavy shadowing, inventive rendering, nice texturing and larger-than-life, over-the-top, powerful art.

Facial Expressions

From top left: neutral, happy, angry, scared, stern, mischievous, antagonistic, regretful.

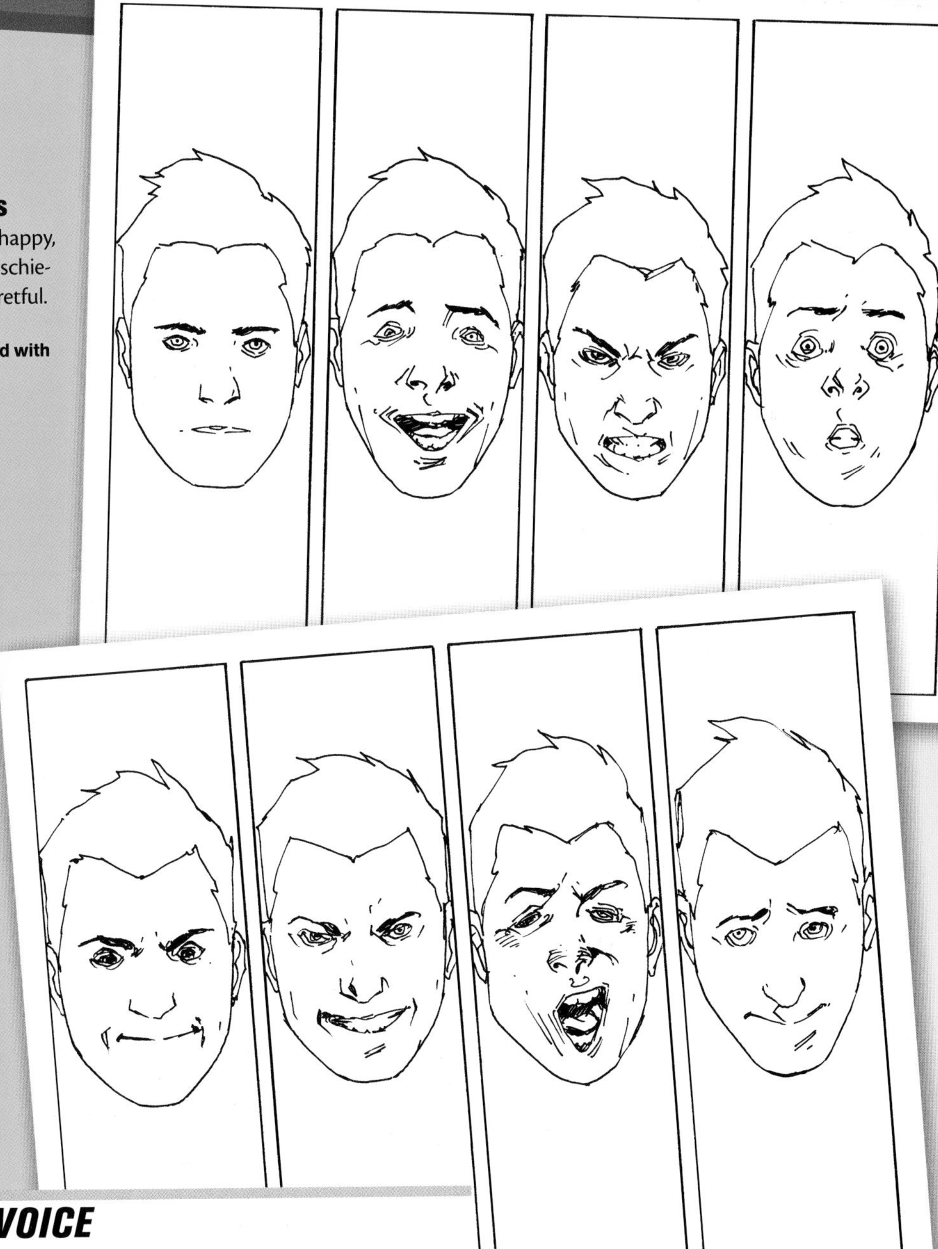

INSIDER VOICE

Gene Ha on Photo Reference

I do use photo reference. Every now and then I meet someone who'd make a great comic book face. I take extensive photos from all around and of various facial expressions. I try to do this with main characters. I don't use photos for minor characters or any character who's too distinctive to easily find a good model.

For my backgrounds I like using reference for details. My backgrounds are usually architectural fantasias. They're not based on any single building or city.

CHARACTERS and THEIR ENVIRONMENT

During portfolio reviews, I often find that, artists draw great figures and great environments, but can't draw the two of them together. Sometimes characters move from panel to panel in strange ways—they get taller or shorter, they move farther away or closer to other characters. Sometimes, they just look like they're floating somewhere in a room or outside. Figures and their environments should seamlessly blend together.

1 FIGURE POSITIONING

The first way to integrate figures into the environment is by selecting postures that show the effects of gravity. No matter what environment characters are in, they still have their own weight to deal with. Characters should be positioned so that they look like they are supporting weight on their legs, that their clothes are affected by gravity and that they're in some kind of motion. The classic "hero shot" of the man with his hands on his hips, chin up, and so on, doesn't feel like the character exists in a real space; it feels like he is posing for a camera.

2 UNIFORM LIGHTING

Light sources should be consistent. The reason for this is simple—light affects how people and things look. If a table is lit from the left next to a figure who is lit from the right, they won't look like they fit together properly. This is especially jarring when two characters in the same panel are lit differently from the environment. The best thing lighting can do to help integrate characters into the environment is to cast shadows of characters and objects onto the environment. Simply connecting the shadow to his feet and the floor instantly creates the illusion of the character standing on the floor. Without some form of shadow, the figure may look like he is floating above or in front of the ground.

3 CONTINUITY OF POSITIONING

Once character locations are established in a given scene, no matter where the camera goes the character positions stay the same (unless a character actually moves, of course). This doesn't just mean where the character is standing, or who is next to whom, though that's part of it. Another aspect of this is making sure character height is consistent. You may have noticed a scene in a comic where two characters can talk in long shot and one is significantly taller than the other, then the camera zooms in for a medium shot and suddenly they're the same height. Characters and their environment—the objects surrounding them and the lighting—need to remain consistent throughout every scene.

4 INTERACTION WITH ENVIRONMENT

In order for the reader to believe that the scene is real, the characters must look like they can interact with the objects surrounding them. There are two things that help to successfully create the illusion that characters and their environment exist in the same space.

First, the characters and environment are rendered in the same way. It's easier to tell when this is not done than it is to tell when it is done. If a figure is inked using hatchmarks for shading, then the environment is inked using an ink-wash technique, creating gray tones, the character and the environment will not feel like they exist in the same space.

The second is that characters must interact—at least to some degree—with the environment. This may mean that a character's shadow properly falls over an object, that a character's reflection appears in a mirror, perhaps a character sits in a chair, or it can mean that Professor Plum picks up the candlestick in the dining room and strikes the butler in the head with it.

5 INTERACTION WITH OTHER CHARACTERS

Similar to interaction with the environment, characters interacting properly with each other also helps complete the illusion. When two characters interact, make sure they're standing on the same plane. Characters' feet should be firmly planted on the same ground. If one stands higher than the other, it will appear as though one of the characters is floating inches above the ground. When one character touches another, there should be some indication on the character being touched that something is happening. In the case of a punch, it's relatively obvious that the character who is being punched should be reacting to the hit. If someone's arm is being grabbed, the sleeve on the man's shirt should wrinkle up around the hand grabbing it, or if it's a strong grab, perhaps the person jerks his shoulder up as he's being manhandled. Characters interacting should be looking at each other. Light sources should be consistent on both characters. For example, if two characters face each other and there are shadows on the left side on one face, the shadows should be cast to the right of the opposite man's face. It's like a film set. The light source doesn't move between camera angles, so shadows are going to be cast differently on one character's face than they will on another character's.

INSIDER VOICE

Neal Adams on Artist and Reader Responsibilities

It's not up to the audience to decide what the actors are supposed to do; it's not up to the viewer to analyze what the artist has done wrong. It's up to the artist to understand what it is about his art that is not appealing to people and to fix it. Figure it out.

FACIAL EXPRESSIONS

Humans have two basic emotions—fear and love. Everything else falls under one of those two emotions. Happy, depressed, wacky, maudlin, sultry—whatever mood you're in, it is based on either fear or desire. The way a person's physical face displays emotion is similar. Your face is either happy or not. The two most expressive parts of the face are the eyes first and the mouth second.

EYES

Typically, the wider the eyes are open, the more they are trying to communicate. When I'm really happy with a gift a friend has given me, my eyes go wide when thanking him. Or, if I'm deathly afraid of something, my eyes go wide to communicate this simple message to anyone whose eyes I can catch—"help!" The main difference between the two expressions (happiness and fear) is the eyebrows. With happiness, eyebrows shoot straight up equally across the brow. When expressing fear or concern, the eyebrows go up only on the nose end, staying low on the cheek end—creating two diagonal eyebrows moving up toward the center of the face. Your eyes can easily be set in a neutral position: open, but not wide, with relaxed eyebrows. Angry eyes are thinned out, squinted slightly with the eyebrows brought down right on top of the eyes. This creates an intensity of thought and focus. This positioning is used most often with characters like Batman or Wolverine. The stoic, angry types.

MOUTH

The mouth emotes in a similar fashion. When the corners are both up, that tells the reader that our character is happy or entertained. When the corners are down, that indicates sadness. When one corner is up and the other is in a neutral position, that's a smirk, meaning that the character is either saying something sarcastic or not really buying the line being said by the other guy on stage. It's also used when the speaker is saying something while being coy. Perhaps with, "I've got a plan." Thus saying, it's a clever plan and wouldn't you just love to know what it is! A wide-open mouth is usually a scream of some kind—either a scream of fear or of hearty laughter. The grin, an unusually large smile, is often used to show extreme happiness or evil, depending on the context.

All of the above works if you are depicting only the eyes or only the mouth. So the question is: What do the combination of eyes and mouth mean?

COMBINED EYES AND MOUTH

It is the combination of the eyes and mouth (with the rest of the face) that communicates more specific emotions. Try this exercise: Look in a mirror and adjust only one thing, either your eyes or your mouth, at any given time. See how many different expressions you can map. With raised eyebrows in the middle, you can adjust your mouth, jaw, tilt of the head, and direction your eyes are looking. Any of these changes can produce a different message. You should wind up with a very long list.

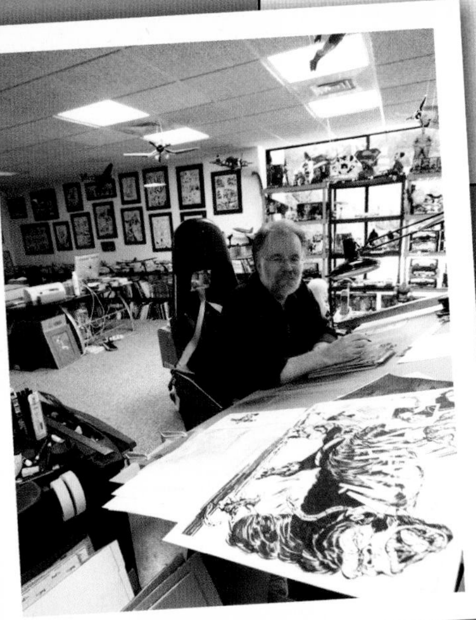

iNSidER PROFiLE

John Byrne

JOHN BYRNE is said to be comics' first superstar and it's not hard to understand why. His work on *The Uncanny X-Men* turned a loser of a property into an American comics dynamo. Without Byrne's work with co-plotter Chris Claremont, the X-Men would never have achieved the success they have. And Byrne didn't stop there. In the mid-1980s, when DC Comics decided to revamp and relaunch *Superman*, they turned to Byrne to re-create their mythological hero.

WEBSITE: http://byrnerobotics.com

OCCUPATION: Cartoonist

DATE OF BIRTH: July 6, 1950

FIRST PUBLISHED WORK: *The Monster Times*, "Do Not Disturb" (1973)

INFLUENCES: Everything I have ever seen.

LONGEST RUN ON A BOOK: *Fantastic Four*

BEST KNOWN FOR: *FF*, *X-Men*, *Superman*

FAVORITE CHARACTER WORKED ON: Batman

DREAM PROJECT: Finishing *X-Men: The Hidden Years*

MOST PERSONAL WORK: If I told you that, it wouldn't be personal anymore!

ART TRAINING: Alberta College of Art, two and a half years of a four year course; then, on-the-job training.

ALL-TIME FAVORITE ARTIST: Joe Kubert

BEST ADVICE RECEIVED WHEN STARTING OUT: "Aim high. That way, if you fail, at least it will be worth the effort." Don't remember the source.

INSIDER VOICE

John Byrne on the Critic

There was only one audience for whom I was really working, and that was my harshest critic: me!

6 TIME IN COMICS

Now we're getting into the heady stuff. Time. What is it? How do we as humans experience it? How do we express it in the comics medium? Time has essentially two categories.

1 Reference to a specific time or time period as it relates to another time period. Morning relates to night, the Dark Ages came before the twentieth century.

2 Reference to how long an action or sequence can take or appear to take on the page. Two different illusions that comics artists have to deal with.

Have you ever heard of Zeno's paradox? Zeno said that if it takes time (any amount of time, it didn't matter) for an archer's arrow to travel half the distance from the bow to the target, and it takes some measure of time to then travel half the distance from the midpoint to the target again, and then some time to travel half the remaining distance again, and so on and so on, and it always took some time to travel half the distance, there will always be half of a distance and always take more time to travel that half and therefore the archer's arrow can never actually reach the target. Did that make sense? No, in practical terms it does not make sense. We know the arrow will reach the target and reach it with some force.

Comics face a different version of Zeno's paradox. Any single event can be depicted in a single panel. Or, an event can be depicted in a series of panels. For Zeno's arrow, there could be a new panel for each "half-distance" that the arrow travels and therefore an infinite number of panels depicting the one action. But no one would do that. Why? First, someone could die doing it since the number of panels is infinite. Second, it'd be boring.

One panel depicting the arrow traveling the full distance and striking the target may not have the impact you require. It may work better in three panels: The archer takes careful aim, the archer looses the string, and the arrow strikes the target. By increasing the panel count, you've increased the tension in the scene and the amount of time the reader has spent paying attention to the action—it's equivalent to going into slow motion in a film. Eventually we'd all be filled with doubt about the archer's ability to hit the target, so the arrow's impact carries more weight with the reader. Knowing when to use multiple panels and how many is a skill that comes from practice. But there are a few guidelines that artists use to decide when is the right time to stretch the moment out.

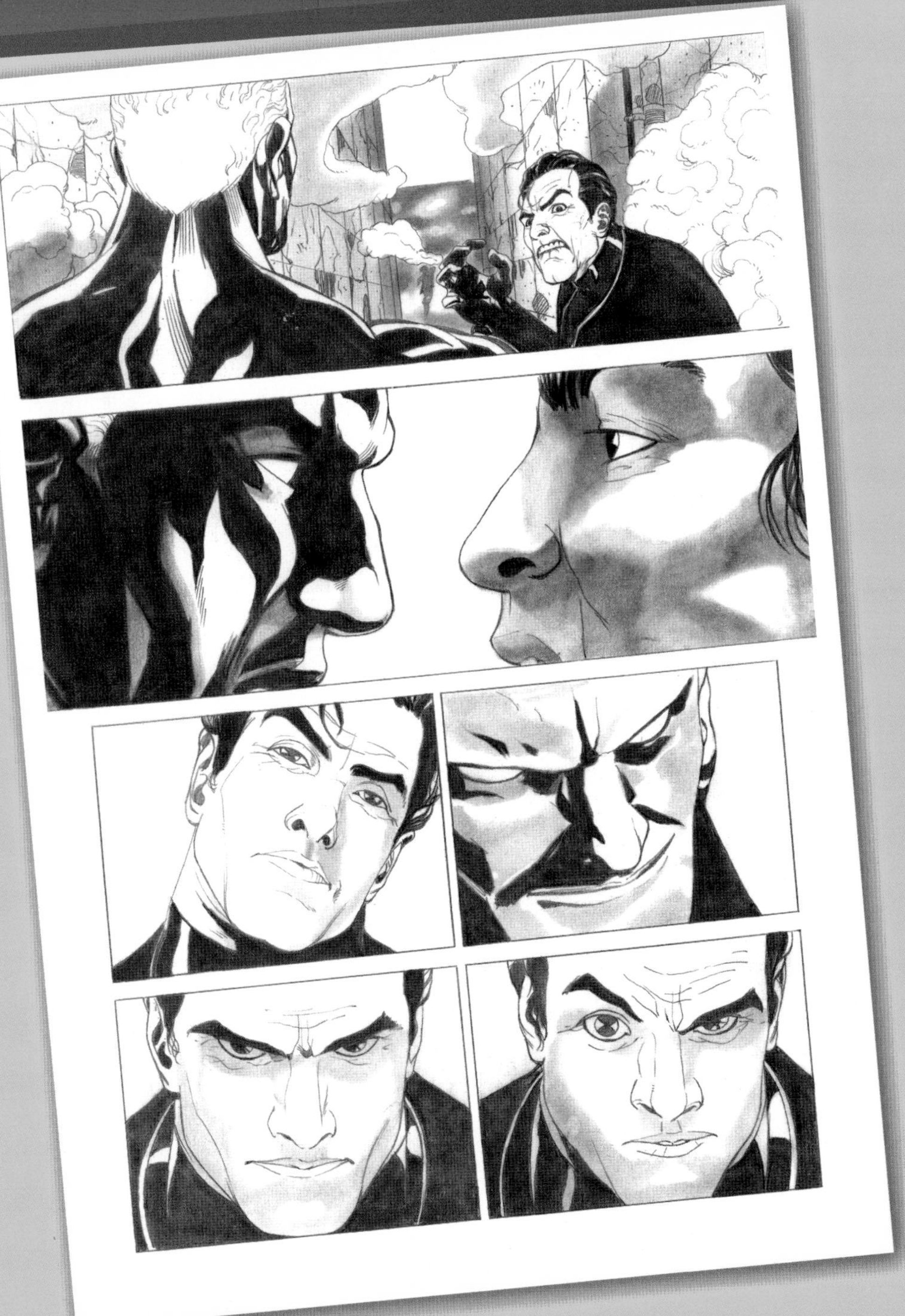

Conversation Beats

Look at this page by Chris Cross. It's one conversation broken into six panels. Why? How did he and writer Peter David choose the breaking points? Any conversation has beats. A *beat* is a moment in time when the conversation, story or character turns from flowing in one direction and begins moving in another. This is reflected in the art here. Notice the different facial expressions from panel to panel.

A flashback is typically a scene that takes place before a scene you're currently in or scenes that have come already. The cliché flashback occurs at the end of a story when the hero is trapped and the villain is about to do the hero in—but instead decides that this is the time to reveal his motivations and origin and we're taken back in time to see the villain's origin as it unfolds.

When I started as an editor at Marvel Comics, they had just instituted a rule: no flashbacks allowed. The rule is no longer in existence, but the reason for it still has merit. Flashbacks are extremely difficult to communicate to a novice reader. I mean, how does anyone know that we've jumped back in time? It's the same artist drawing the pictures, it's the same characters—how do we know?

An older technique used to delineate flashback sequences is to round the corners of the panels. This was common in the 1980s and early 1990s. It hasn't endured in recent years and I think that's because it was created for comics specifically. Most of the color techniques used to express something about time come from more communal experiences.

The artist or the writer must tell the reader he is reading a flashback, or a flashforward for that matter. No amount of frilly designs in the panel gutters will communicate a flashback clearly. Comics don't have that uniformity of experience or the early introduction from many of its readers to draw from.

TIME CHANGE: FORWARD OR BACK

Artists and writers clue in readers by providing reference points—or establishing shots, if you will—that indicate specific points in time. So, if there's a close-up of a man's face, the next panel might zoom in on the eyes. The next panel might repeat the close-up of the eyes, but now they look old. And the next panel might pull out to reveal the same man's face, but it has aged thirty-five years and the background has become futuristic. That's probably enough to indicate to the reader that they're in a different time period (the future). The man seems to have aged roughly thirty-five years, so we're probably in the future about the same amount of time. Readers aren't stupid, so they can do some of the work, but they need a reference point, just like a spatial reference point.

A panel might show an old motorcycle, rusted and missing parts, cobwebs spread all over it, and the next might cut to the same motorcycle in the prime of life—all put together, on the open road, polished to a mirror-like shine, bright headlamp shining down the road ahead. The juxtaposition of the two images is probably enough to indicate that we've jumped from the present (in which the motorcycle has died) to the past (in which it was someone's prized possession). The main thing that creators must avoid is switching between time periods without a reference point or a proper segue (like the two transitional beats described above). The reader will not instinctively make the connection.

Other simple ways to denote a change in time include:

- Adding a caption that says something like: THREE DAYS AGO, or 1944, JAPAN, or even just THE FUTURE. For what it lacks in finesse it makes up in clarity.
- Using a character's narration to tell the reader that his story takes place in the past. Writers can decide to do this. Artists can add this element by finding some clever background element to help incorporate a time period in the story. Perhaps it's the style of cars if the story suddenly shifted to the 1950s, or perhaps it's a newspaper headline with a date on it. Maybe it's a landmark of some kind—the 1928 world's fair, Mount Rushmore with the faces not fully carved yet. If readers have context and a reference point, they'll stay tuned.

From the Editor: In Defense of the Time Stamp

I once edited a twenty-five comic project that was told over the course of six different series with different titles. It was a complex science-fiction war story told on many different planets with about a hundred characters. To make things easier on my different creative teams and the readers (okay, really just easier on me!), I decided to use a time stamp caption. In the very first issue of the series, we established a day-one marker—a particular event that I would then use as a reference point for the rest of the series. It was a war story, so it worked pretty well with the genre. Instead of reading D-DAY, PLUS 1 it read ANNIHILATION DAY, PLUS 1. I think we wound up going all the way to day 222 before the story was over.

INSIDER VOICE

Klaus Janson on the Most Important Job in Comics

You can debate whether a penciller is more important than a writer or whether a colorist is more important than an inker, but the reality is that if any one of those contributing parts doesn't do the job well, the whole comic falls apart no matter how important you may think the individual part is. So, to me, the argument over what is more important is irrelevant. Get me people who know what they are doing and I'll show you what's important: The sum is greater than the parts.

CONTROLLING TIME with PANELS

In comics, time is a nebulous and indefinable thing. One reader may think an action takes minutes, another reader might think days have passed—it's all in the eye of the beholder. That said, there are tricks artists use to manipulate the perceived passage of time. The size and shape of panels is one thing that makes an impact on how time is perceived in a scene.

NEUTRAL TIME

In the typical grid structure of three tiers with two square panels on each tier, time is set in neutral. This means that the scene is perceived as moving at a normal pace, like a conversation scene in a movie—not too fast, not too slow. When this layout is altered, time begins to shift.

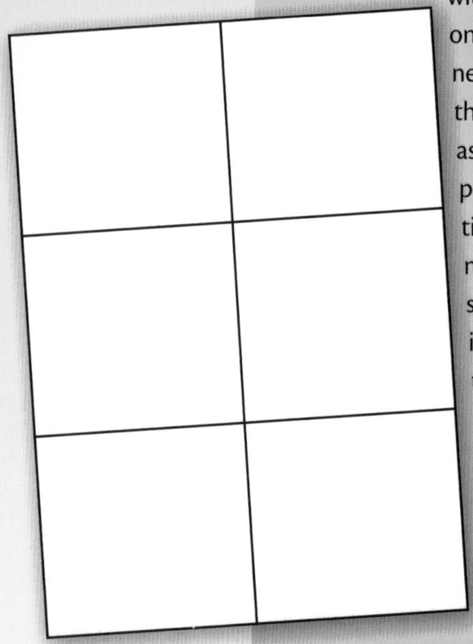

Typical Grid Structure = Neutral Time

This layout communicates nothing in particular, just the normal flow of time.

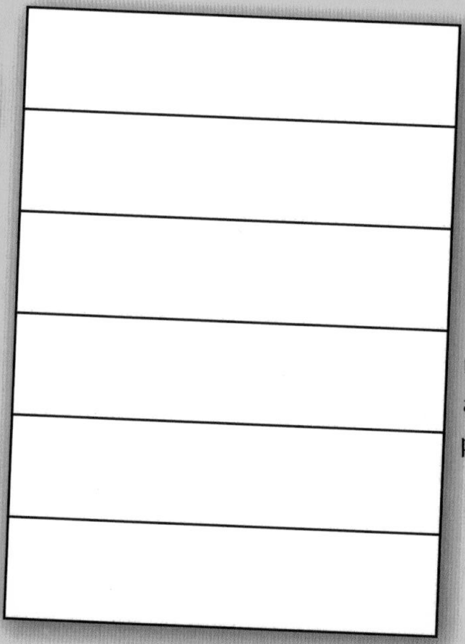

Widescreen Panels = Longer Period

Widescreen panels focus the reader's attention on only one panel at a time and create the illusion of more distinct moments in time.

SLOWER TIME

Six horizontal panels that stretch the width of the page and are all stacked on top of one another appear to take more time than the six panels in the neutral position. The reason for this is that while the panel count has stayed the same, the number of tiers to the page has doubled. The panels feel like wholly separate beats and feel less connected to one another. Of course, these panels may not take place over a longer period of time than the neutral position page, it's just the perception.

SLOWER PERCEIVED TIME

Chopping a tier of panels into tall thin panels—say, six or more on one tier—often slows the reader down and thus slows down the perceived passage of time. The smaller panels don't need to be overloaded with dialogue to slow the reader down. Simply digesting a new image every inch or so is enough for the reader's brain to process and feel like the action is slowing. This approach tends to be particularly effective toward the climax of a scene or during a Mexican standoff. If there are three gunmen about to fire on each other, a series of quick close-up shots of the gunmen's faces, their guns, their trembling hands and so on, can really expand time and increase the suspense in the scene.

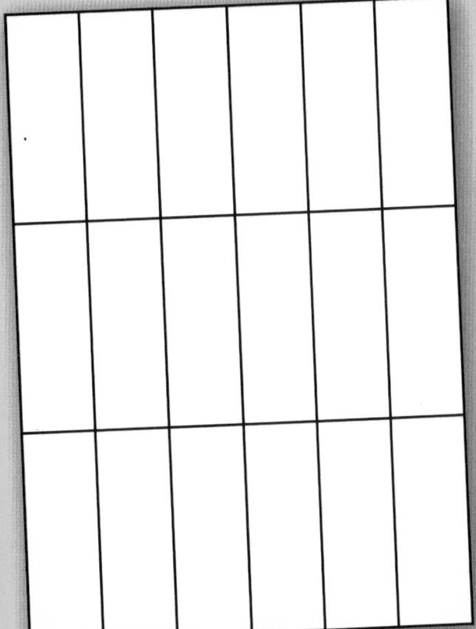

Vertical Panels = Slow Time
Vertical panels help to slow down time.

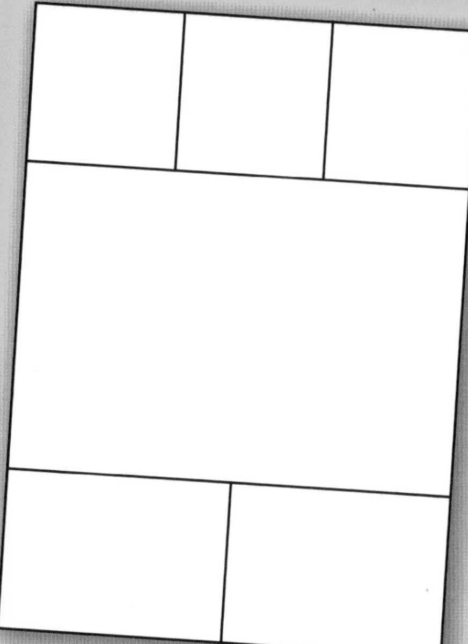

Large Panels = Illusion of More Time
One central large panel communicates importance or magnitude and often an event that takes more time.

ANOTHER WAY FOR SLOWER PERCEIVED TIME

Large panels that take up two-thirds or more of a page can pack a lot of information in them with many background elements, or they can show one big splash image with little background detail. Either way, very large panels create the illusion that they take more time in a scene. It usually is not true, though. For example, you may turn the page at the end of a comic to reveal the big bad villain on a splash page cliffhanger, but the villain may only have three words of dialogue. That wouldn't take much time at all, but it feels like it does because (if the reader is engaged in the story) the implication is that the reveal is shocking to the heroes as well and the reader intuits a shocked response following the few words of dialogue.

A Word of Caution for Artists

Just because a writer has created a ten-panel page does not mean that he intends to slow the action down. If there is no reason for so many panels, it's worth seeing if you can get another page. You don't want to unintentionally slow a reader down or speed him up. It can be very disorienting.

OVERLAPPING DIALOGUE

Overlapping dialogue refers to one of two things. The first is word balloons that literally overlap one another and may even cover the words inside the bottom balloon. The second is dialogue that overlaps panel borders and continues into another panel.

BALLOONS OVERLAPPING EACH OTHER

Dialogue balloons that overlap one another give a sense of characters all talking at the same time and at the same volume.

In Establishing Shots

This is used a lot in establishing shots of parties or crowded areas when creators want to give the idea that there's hustle and bustle. We used them a lot in *The Pulse*. We'd cut to the interior of the newspaper main room and there would be people running around and shouting all kinds of stuff with overlapping balloons. The reader would get snippets of different conversations. It works well to establish a mood, but not to relay important information. So creators cannot include important information in any of the dialogue because the likelihood of it getting covered up or ignored by the reader is high.

Between Two or Three characters

Overlapping dialogue between two or three defined or important characters carries a different meaning. If these are three important characters, the reader needs to know to pay attention to what they're saying and the overlapping nature of the dialogue balloons can increase the speed that the reader reads the scene. Having characters cut each other off or correct one another in fast succession creates the illusion that the characters are speaking quickly.

BALLOONS OVERLAPPING PANELS

Dialogue that overlaps panels doesn't speed up a scene or slow it down significantly. Instead, it gives a scene fluidity. If it's all one conversation and the balloons and tails stream across panel to panel, it helps the reader fill in actions between panels. Brian Michael Bendis is a master at this technique. Flowing from panel to panel doesn't mean the speaker needs to be in every panel. It's helpful if the speaker is in the first panel and the last (or at least in one of these two). Placing the speaker in the first panel is the most clear because there is no mistaking who is talking.

Overlapping dialogue can stretch over three or four panels at a time without the reader losing track of who is speaking (and it can be more than one speaker as long as all the balloons are connected to the proper speaker by linking tails). The images in the panels don't have to depict the speaker, but should depict something relevant to the dialogue flowing over them. Because the dialogue will be inside or on top of the image, the reader will naturally draw a connection between the dialogue and the images inside the panels. The most common example of this is when one character starts to tell a story about something that has already happened and the dialogue spills over into the next panel, which depicts the events within the speaker's story.

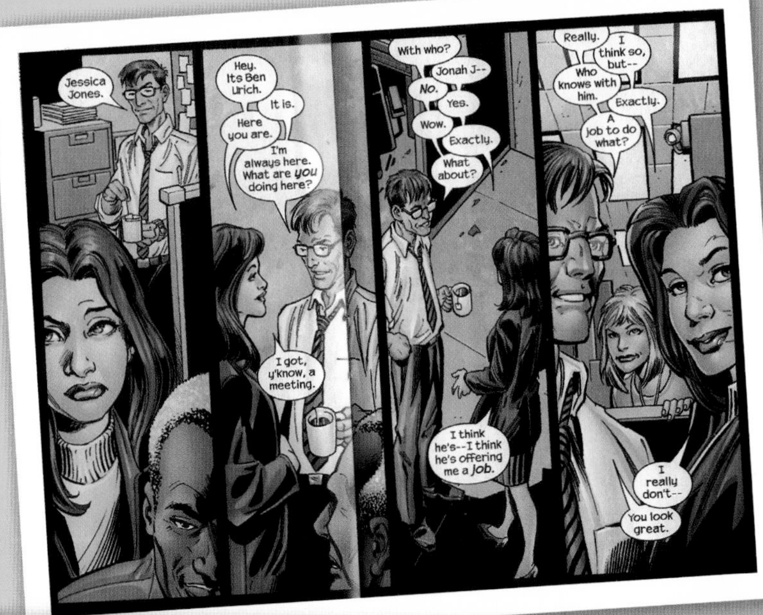

Overlapping Balloons Can Convey Natural Conversation

In this page by Brian Michael Bendis and Mark Bagley, Jessica and Ben's dialogue overlaps often, giving the reader the sense that this is a fast-paced and natural conversation.

***The Pulse* #1, pages 8–9: ©2008 Marvel Characters, Inc. Used with permission.**

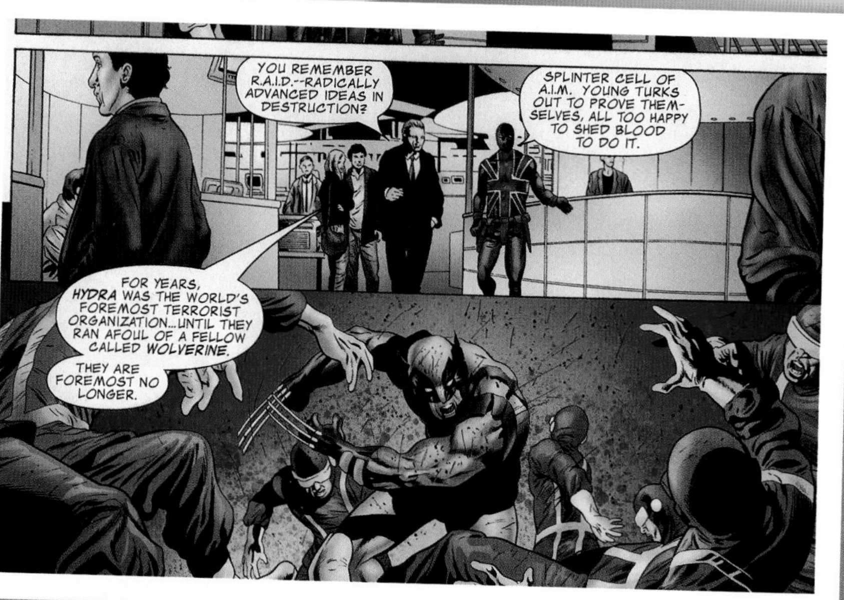

Balloons Overlapping Panels Can Signal Time Changes or Flashbacks

Christos Gage and Mike Perkins used a balloon overlapping from the top panel into the bottom panel to give the seemingly random image of Wolverine context. The dialogue lets the reader know that the image is a flashback.

***Union Jack* #1, page 5: ©2008 Marvel Characters, Inc. Used with permission.**

Color is not the basis of clear storytelling, but it can enhance storytelling significantly, especially when dealing with issues of time.

MOTION BLUR

A motion blur approximates a photographic effect. On a camera, the shutter allowing light to hit the film is open for a fraction of a second. Whatever light hits the film imprints itself there. If an object or person is moving while the shutter opens, the image on the film will blur whatever is moving for whatever distance it moved during that fraction of a second. The resulting blur, called a *motion blur*, is caused by objects in fast motion. In an action sequence, the color effect called a motion blur can, when applied properly and sparingly, communicate to the reader the great speed at which actions are taking place. A talented colorist can smudge the color and line work in Adobe Photoshop, stretching them backwards from an object in motion, thus creating the illusion that the smudged object is traveling quickly.

The motion blur is the least effective time-manipulating power that good coloring offers, as it only manipulates time slightly and in one specific application.

DIFFERING COLOR SCHEMES

If a story has multiple scenes that take place in different time periods—this could be anything from centuries apart to only a day apart—then a different color scheme for each time period is effective. In cases where the two scenes are significantly far apart, like years or more, knocking out all pages of the earlier scene of the story in sepia tone communicates that it takes place in the distant past. Sepia tone is a tan and yellowish washing out of all of the color on the page. It makes the page

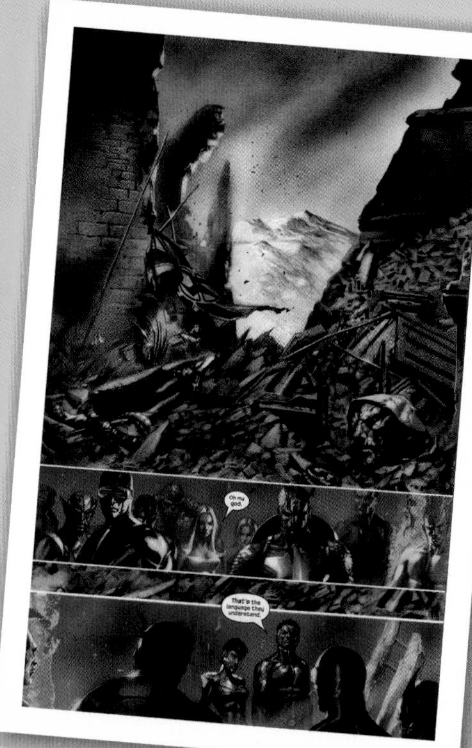

Different Color Schemes on the Same Page

Painter Gabriele Dell'Otto uses a natural color scheme for the panels set in the present, and a different one for the large flashback in panel 1.

***Secret War* #5, page 24: ©2008 Marvel Characters, Inc. Used with permission.**

look like an old, faded photograph. It's the faded photograph look that most people identify with that creates the illusion.

COLOR CODING

If the scenes run closer together in time, it may be enough to color code the gutters of the page so that present-day pages have white gutters and scenes taking place in the past have some other gutter color—though brightly colored gutters tend to detract from the art inside the panels. As an alternative, artists also give the images inside the panels different color tones or themes to set them apart. I've found that when dealing with scenes that take place in the past, it's often helpful to make those scenes monochromatic—meaning all but one color is washed out from them.

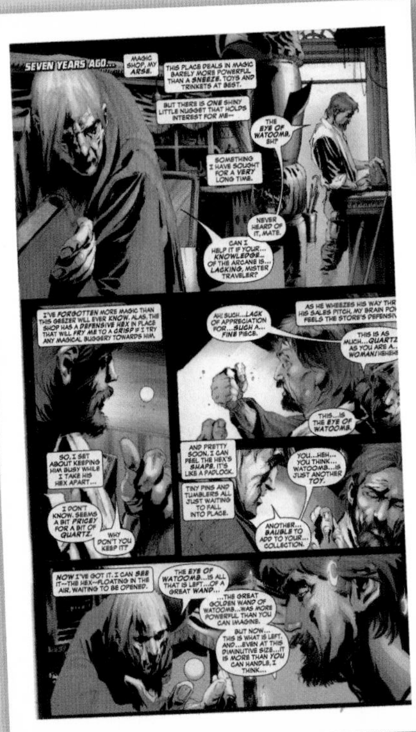

Monochromatic Color Scheme

Colorist Chris Sotomayor washes out this entire page to indicate that it takes place in the past.

***Ms. Marvel* #4, page 1: ©2008 Marvel Characters, Inc. Used with permission.**

COLOR TEMPERATURE

Color can also be subtle. We tend to think of high-energy activities as being hot, intense, brutal, etc. We also associate lighter or warmer colors with these activities. If a colorist uses warmer and warmer colors in the scene as the action rises, the action will speed up on the page just a touch and in an almost imperceptible way. By the time the big climactic panel arrives, the colorist might knock the whole background out in red or orange to bolster the speed and energy of the panel. Cooler tones, soothing blues and dark greens will slow things down a bit and give the reader a chance to breathe.

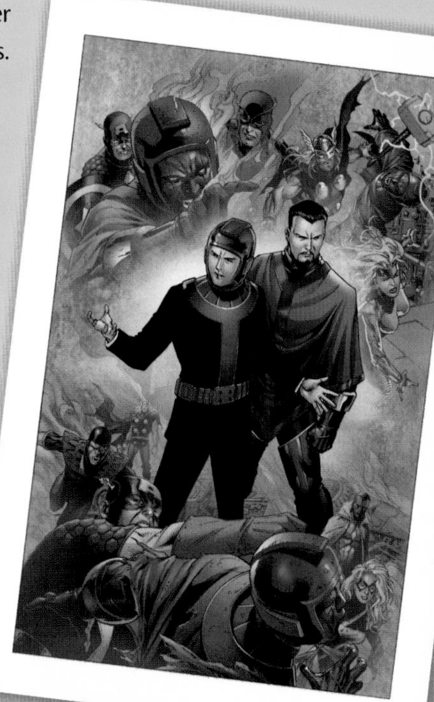

Temperature Contrast

Justin Ponsor uses warmer colors to separate the two characters from the present from the cooler background and events that have already happened.

***Young Avengers* #2, page 8: ©2008 Marvel Characters, Inc. Used with permission.**

7 DYNAMICS

If you go back to the beginning of this book, you may remember that I (thank you, Klaus Janson) mentioned that comics artists have two functions. The first is communication. But the second, and no less important, is to entertain the reader.

Entertainment comes in many different forms. Artists will always debate what is entertaining (readers won't always be able to tell you, either). But when we talk about entertainment as a different thing from communication, what we're really talking about is dynamics.

The granddaddy of dynamics in comics is Jack "King" Kirby. He, with Stan Lee, formed the foundation that would become Marvel Comics. Stan plotted the stories that led to the *Fantastic Four*, *The X-Men*, *Iron Man*, *Thor* and *The Incredible Hulk*. Jack Kirby is the one who gave these characters life on the page. It was his dynamic artwork that propelled those characters off the page and into the eyes (and hands) of young readers of the 1960s. Kirby tended to stick to simple grid layouts, but within those square panels, he delivered characters who were always "doing." Kirby never had a talking-heads scene—not because one wasn't written but because he found things for his characters to do to expand on any conversation that might be taking place. His characters didn't talk—they argued, pranked, loved, flirted, fought, kidded, joked, jabbed, boasted, declared, interrogated, taught and punched their way through scenes.

In the late 1970s, Neal Adams came along and changed the way comics artists would draw layouts and choose "camera angles" forever. Adams's intense layout design would send the reader's eye darting in different directions for massive impact and his camera angles were designed for highest possible contrast. The reader never got a chance to relax while reading a Neal Adams comic.

These two artists invented American comics style. No two other creators have changed the face of comics in America the way Kirby and Adams did. They brought dynamics to the drawing table and delivered it to the page.

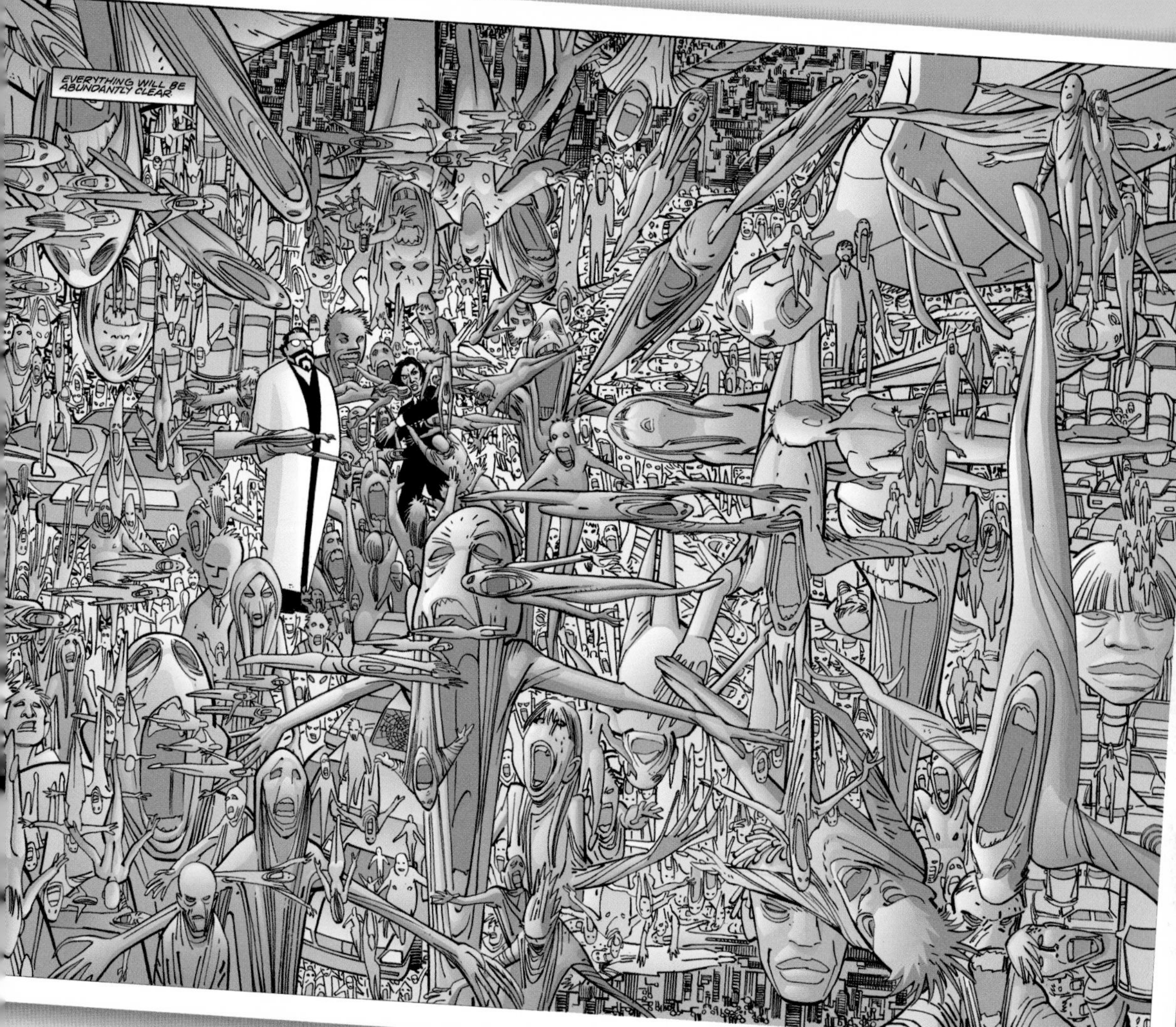

Punching It Up

At its core, dynamics is about pushing the artist's imagination. Not just illustrating what a script asks for, but imagining what that panel, scene, even story can *really* be—and then illustrating that.

***The Gray Area* #1, pages 30–31: ©2005 John Romita Jr. and Glen Brunswick. Used with permission.**

SPLASH IMAGES

The most impactful image is a splash image. Typically, a splash is the only image on a single page. It often bleeds off all four edges of the page, filling every centimeter of space with exciting color. Also a relatively new option is the double-page splash. It's two full-bleed splash pages next to each other that connect in the middle. Not so long ago, doing one image that stretched across a comic's stitches wasn't possible. But as presses became more accurate and the stapling of pages became more precise, these double-page spreads became viable options.

We know that the most important panel on the page should be the largest (if using a freeform layout). The splash page is an extension of that. So important and monumental is the action taking place in this panel that it's not just the biggest panel on the page, it's the only panel on the page.

The thing about splash pages is that many people don't understand how to use them properly. Here are some guidelines:

- The splash implies story-driven importance. If the climax doesn't happen on page 7, but page 7 is a splash, there's a problem. Is this event on page 7 more important than the climax? Probably not. Revision may be better so that page 7 is a six-panel page so the climax on page 20 can get a full splash.
- Splash pages are used to their utmost effect when surrounded by smaller panels—the impact comes from the contrast to the surrounding panels. So if there are a series of smaller panels—say, twelve—on the page before, turning to a full splash will be twice as shocking than if the previous page had only six panels.
- Again, the splash implies story importance. If there's a splash page of the main character getting shot (let's say that happens on page 7), the implication is that the rest of the story will deal with (in some regard) the shooting. Either the story will follow the hero's recovery or it will be about his funeral or finding his killer. If page 8 depicts the hero getting up and brushing off the wound Teddy Roosevelt style, the splash page doesn't belong there.

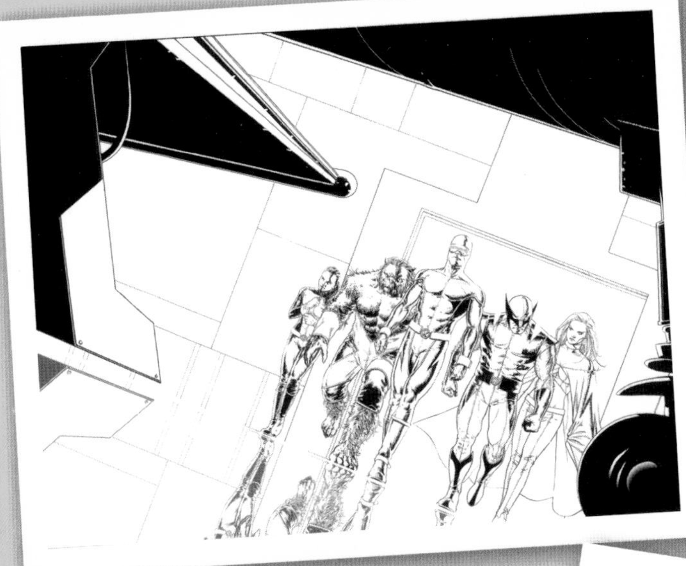

Ending With a Splash

This double-page splash by John Cassaday ended the first issue of *Astonishing X-Men*. They are walking to a jet. It's not all that important from a story perspective, but this splash made a big statement. It was the first time the X-Men had been seen in costume for about three years and it basically said: This comic is about superheroes. Any X-Men fan who saw these pages had to come back for the next issue.

Astonishing X-Men **#1, pages 22–23: ©2008 Marvel Characters, Inc. Used with permission.**

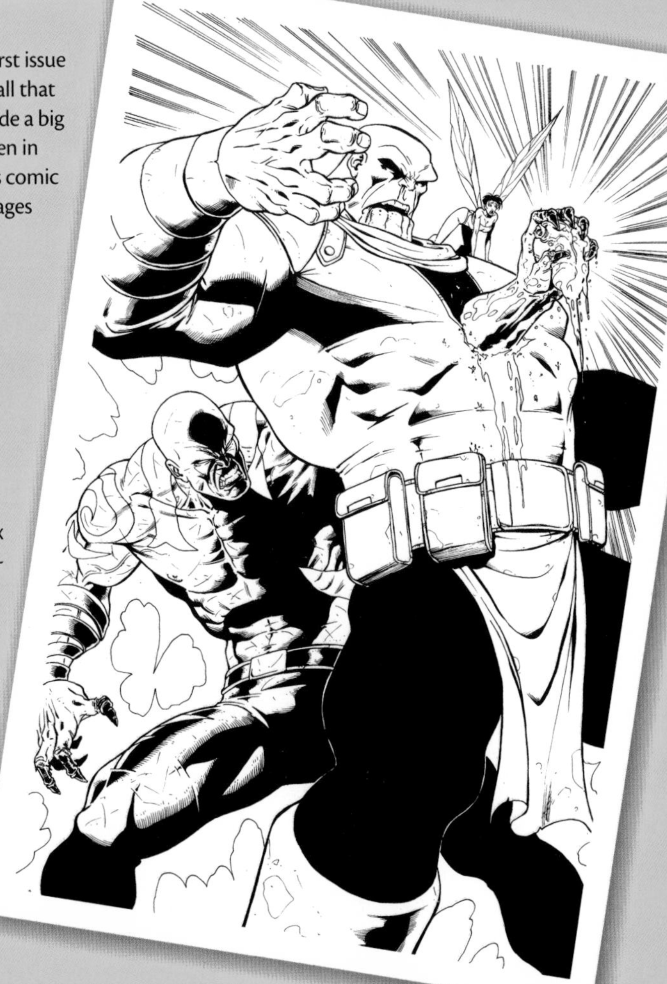

Climax!

For the better part of a year, this subplot between Drax and Thanos and their eventual conflict had been brewing. When the battle finally came, its climax needed a splash page, drawn here by Andrea Di Vito.

Annihilation **#4, page 24: ©2008 Marvel Characters, Inc. Used with permission.**

ZOOMING IN

A lot of younger artists, especially ones who are rightfully conscious of their storytelling, have a tendency to use too many medium shots. *Medium shots* get all the information into the story. *Long shots* establish where everyone and everything is in relation to everything else. But the *close-up* and the *extreme close-up* shots are often ignored almost completely. A tight close-up on just a villain's sinister smile can be more effective than a detailed medium shot. (See page 72 for more on camera angles.)

The close-up and extreme close-up shots focus the reader's attention on one small thing. In most cases it's a face or even just a part of a face. An extreme close-up on a character's eyes can tell the reader instantly and viscerally everything he needs to know about the character in that moment. A medium shot showing the head and shoulders of that character is more likely to need a dialogue balloon or caption to tell the reader what is going through the character's mind.

Close-ups also allow the artist to break up the monotony of a boring scene or introduce a scene in an intriguing way. By giving the reader only close-ups at the start of a scene, the reader is coaxed into guessing where we are and who is there. It helps make the reader a more active participant.

A good close-up during a conversation can also be an effective storytelling tool. In a scene between a man and a woman talking, close-ups on things like the woman curling a lock of her hair, the man's knee bouncing nervously or the woman's hand reaching over to the man's provide visual cues that tell us there is an attraction between them even though they're not saying it out loud.

Like the splash page, close-ups are great when used in contrast to the surrounding panels. But unlike splash pages, it is often better to shift less dramatically from extreme long shots to extreme close-ups. A number of panels in between the two extremes provide a kind of zooming effect.

INSIDER VOICE

John Romita Jr. on Pacing a Story

I don't start drawing until the whole script has been plotted out, played out, thumbnailed out, and I know that it fits into the number of pages required, every scene has the right size, the right delivery. There should be a couple large panels, and a double-page spread here. Certain sequences should have nine panels on a page if there's a rapid-fire conversation and the writer wants close-ups for expression's sake, you know, boom-boom-boom.

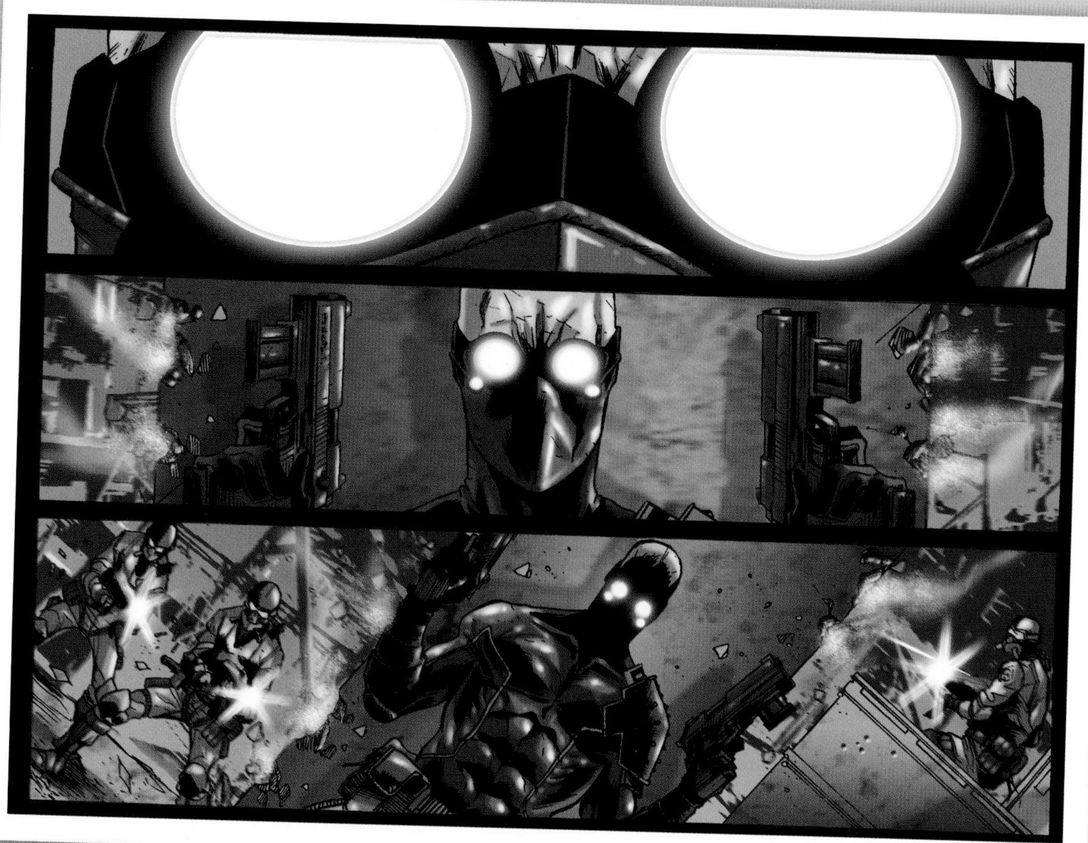

Zooming Can Establish Scenes While Inviting the Reader to Question

In panel 1, Marco Chechetto uses an extreme close-up—of what, the reader isn't sure. In panel 2, we pull out and see it's a person's head and that he has two guns. But what is he doing? In panel 3, we can see that he's pinned against a column with three people shooting at him.

The whole scene is established, but in a way that invites the reader to ask questions and become active.

***The Courier* #1, page 1: ©2008 Andy Schmidt and Marco Chechetto.**

The CASE AGAINST BREAKING OUT of the PANEL

It looks cool when characters break out of panels, but it's also disruptive and calls attention to itself. It's one of those things that makes a page look dynamic at a glance but often interferes with the storytelling. In general, I advise artists against panel breakouts. Here are the common issues that explain why.

DISTRACTION

Breaking the panel is distracting. The reader's eye goes immediately to it and skips anything preceding it. If characters do break out of the panel, it should be because they are doing something so exciting that it just can't be contained within the normal panel. All the reader's attention is drawn to the panel breakout. So the panel being broken had darn well better be the most important panel on the page (if not the whole issue!).

READING FLOW DISRUPTION

When something is breaking out of the frame, it better lead the reader to (and only to) the next panel in the reading order. Far too often, I see characters break out of a panel and not just into the gutter area between panels, but overlap into a neighboring panel—and usually it is not the next panel in the reading order. What seems to happen most often is that a character or object breaks out of the panel in a downward movement and leads not into the next panel, but the panel after that. The reader's eye will follow whatever breaks out of the panel border and go directly into whatever panel is overlapped. This is true even if the panel the reader is led into is a panel he has already read. It causes the reader to stop, break out of the world the artist has created, and figure out where he's supposed to go to next. And that's bad.

LOSS OF IMPACT

It all comes down to contrast. As you'll see in the next two chapters on inking and coloring, contrast is a huge part of storytelling in a visual medium. This is true of breaking through panel borders. The more often it's done, the less impact it will have. If it's done more than once in a twenty-two-page story, that's probably too often. It should be reserved for only when it can be done in such a way that serves the story. Breaking out of the frame is a tool like a knife. And every time you use it, it dulls.

INSIDER VOICE

John Byrne on How to Stay Productive

People ask me this often, and I think they want me to say something like, "I put my left foot in a bucket of warm water and face east." When I tell them the real story, their eyes glaze over. Because, unfortunately, there is only one way to do it. Something Kirby understood, Ditko understood, both Buscemas, Romita, any of the guys who came in with a professional attitude understand. It's simply nose-to-the-grindstone. Work. Discipline. The hard part!

BREAKING OUT OF FRAME EFFECTIVELY

Here's when it works.

- It's done with only a panel of great importance and action. Note that I said great importance *and* action. It should have both.
- The page is designed so that whatever breaks out of the panel does so in the direction toward the panel immediately following it in the reading order.
- It doesn't overlap another panel unless absolutely necessary.
- If something breaks out of one panel (let's say it's a spear being thrown) and overlaps into the next panel, that same spear isn't depicted in the following panel. If the following panel is a shot of, say, someone being hit by the spear, then the one spear exists in the second panel in two places. It's not something anyone has ever said to me, but it always bounces wrong for me to have the same object appear twice in the same panel, even if one of those times it is clearly a part of the preceding panel. It's weird and it always—always—takes me out of the story.

DYNAMIC LIGHTING

The lighting in a scene involves the light itself and its effect on shadows, reflections and highlights, as well as color. The penciller indicates to the inker and colorist where the light source is in a scene. Dynamic lighting casts shadows or eliminates them for dramatic effect.

CAST SHADOWS

By indicating shadows on characters and objects, the penciller communicates to the inker and colorist that the light source is in the opposite direction from the shadow. One dynamic shadow effect that works in comics was often used in the television show *The X-Files*; any time something out of the ordinary happens, they use one very strong light source, usually below the action so it casts long shadows upwards.

MULTIPLE LIGHT SOURCES

Artists can also use multiple light sources in a single panel, sometimes to both cast shadows and eliminate them. In his creator-owned series *Hellshock*, Jae Lee often uses one light source off to the side, casting much of his figures in black. He then uses a kicker light behind the person or object that creates a slight outline or impression of where the darkened side of the person or object ends. This technique is also used in film. It creates stark contrasts and a dynamic brooding effect.

CENTER SHADOWS

Some pencillers use a technique that puts light sources on either side of a character so a dark shadow falls directly down the

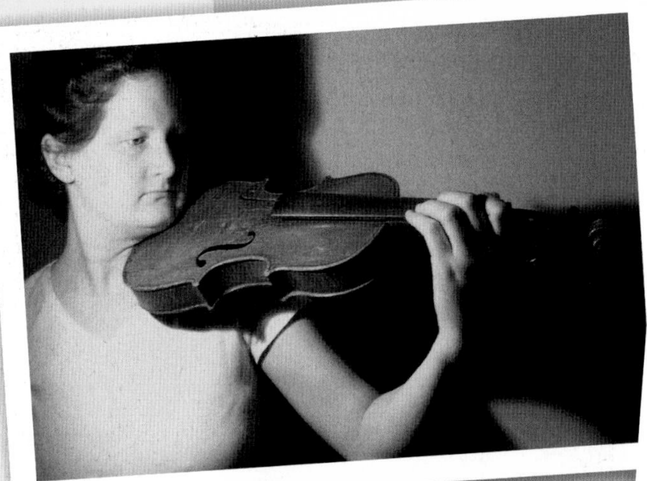

Shadows Tell Where the Light Is
It's clear, here, that the light source is on the left, casting shadows on the right.

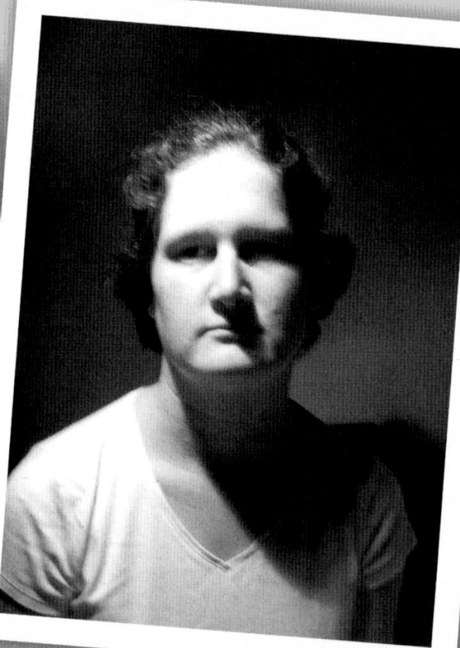

Neutral Lighting
Even neutral lighting with a single light source has strong cast shadows in comics.

center of that person's face. It creates a kind of symmetrical Rorschach inkblot effect. It's great for depicting anger.

FEW SHADOWS

On the flip side, washing something out with loss of light and very few shadows can also be extremely effective. It is much like when a camera opens its shutter wide to let a lot of light in. This effect is used to indicate great heat or great power, but also great tranquility—as though someone may be dying and seeing "the light."

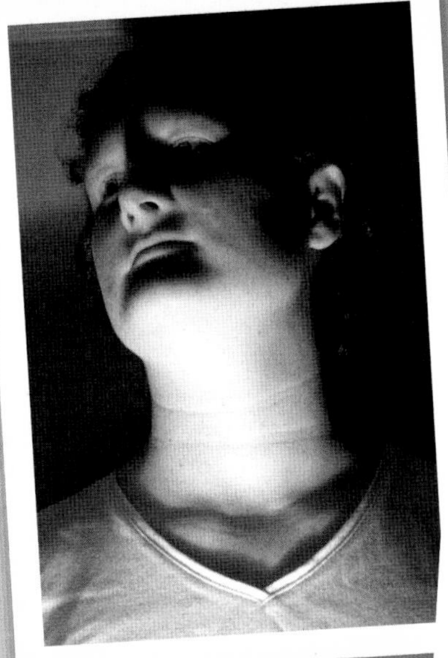

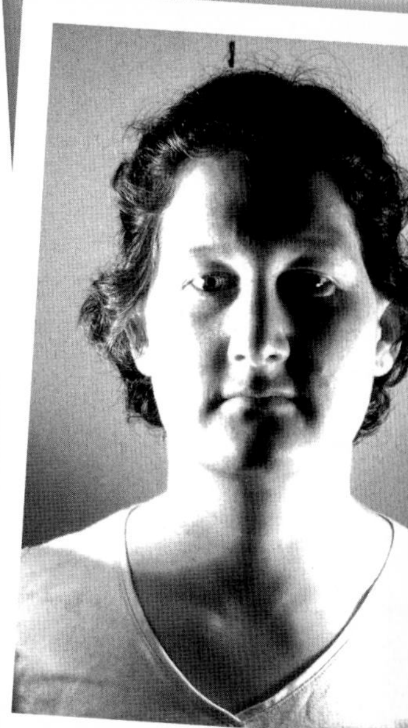

Light Source Location Is Telling

Strong light from below almost always indicates something creepy going on. Light sources from either side, with a shadow down the middle, generally means anger. (Notice how this character doesn't have an angry expression.)

INSIDER VOICE

Neal Adams on the Contract With the Reader

With comic books there's a contract with readers. And it works like this: I'm going to tell you a story. If you will be good enough to read my story, I will not trick you, I will not slow you down, I will not give you something that you don't understand. Unless, we agree at this time, it's time not to understand something but I'll explain it to you later on. But I won't keep you in the dark for so long that you get bored. So if you take my hand and read my story, at the end it will have a good ending and you will be happy, and you will come back next time and read another story.

I think that's the contract that you make: You're a storyteller, and you don't disappoint the reader, and you don't confuse the reader, and don't make the reader crazy.

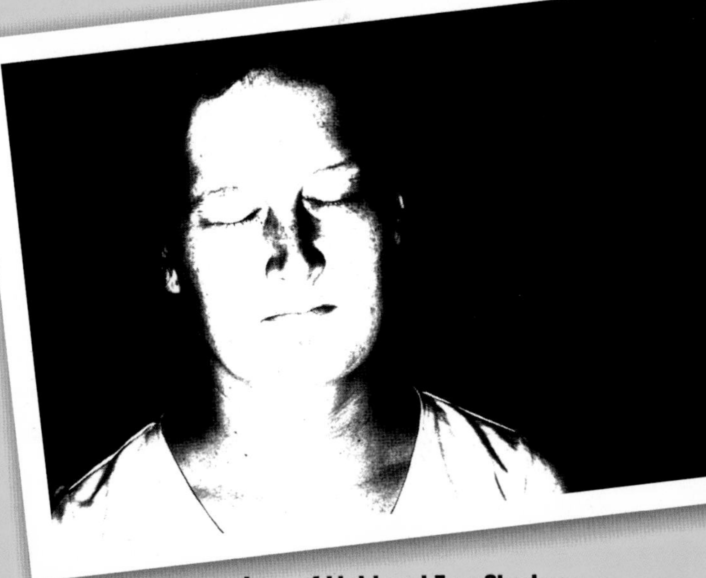

Loss of Light and Few Shadows

This often indicates heat, power or tranquility, or all three. The divine.

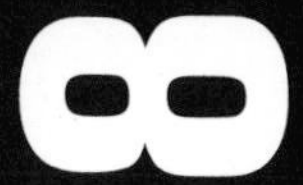

INKING

Inking is a funny discipline. Its role has changed over the years. Originally, the inker was supposed to trace the line work the penciller had laid down on the page. The way the printing press operated at the time, it needed thick black lines to reproduce, so the inker's job was to make sure the penciller's work made it onto the final product.

Over time, printing presses got better and the need for inkers started to dwindle (it never disappeared, but it became less necessary). As a result, inkers began to experiment with their craft, making it something more than tracing.

Today, the inker must bring something unique to the drawing board. The right inker on a project can make it really sing and the wrong inker can destroy good pencilled pages. Inkers now expand on the work of the penciller. It often depends on what the penciller wants the inker to do. Some pencillers like an inker who can do something different to his work; others want the inker to strictly follow their line strokes. A good inker is able to look at the page in front of him and figure out how he can bring out the best in the line work. The inker deals with light and dark contrasts. He deals with light sources, with foreshortening, with separating planes in the three-dimensional field, and with a hundred other factors. His work is not easy and it is often overlooked by the public.

For this chapter, I went to three of the finest inkers working in comics and asked them to tell us what they do in their own words.

- Klaus Janson, famed inker of *Batman: The Dark Knight Returns* and *Daredevil*, among other things.
- Mike Perkins, inker on *Captain America*, among others.
- Karl Kesel, who has worked on hundreds of fine comic books, most notably *Fantastic Four*.

All three of these gentlemen are fantastic pencillers in their own right and so make ideal candidates to talk about the separation of inking from pencilling. Trust me, the line can get blurry.

Inker's Tools

The inker uses many of the same tools as the penciller, including a drafting table and light boxes. In addition to these tools, the inker uses:

Ink

Brushes

Eraser

White correction fluid

Photocopies of pencils

Scanner

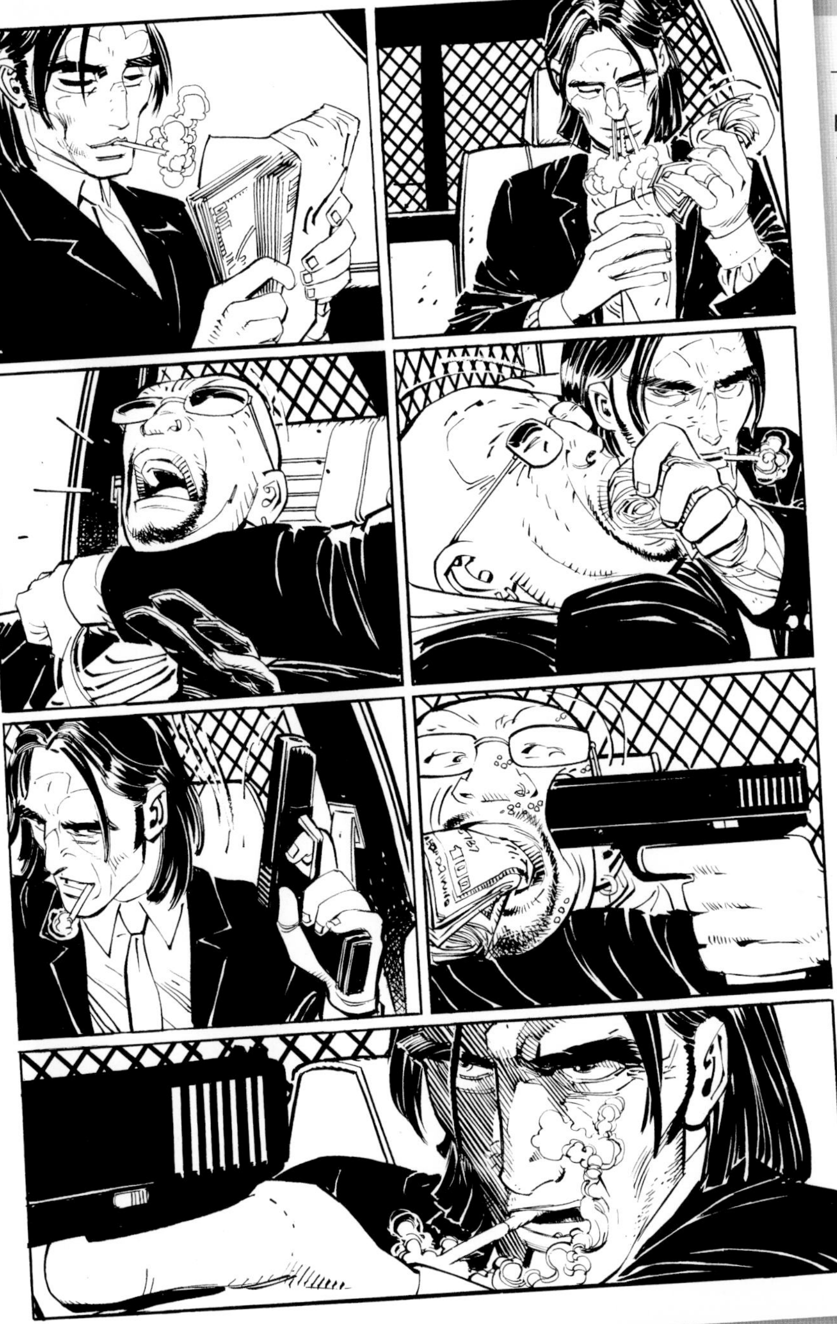

The Inker's Job

Inkers must make sure that all the information on the page is portrayed clearly. Adding shadow to certain planes and people will emphasize the prominence of a particular element. A good knowledge of anatomy and an understanding of the structure of real-world surroundings is not only the responsibility of the penciller.

Klaus Janson's Inks Over John Romita Jr.'s Pencils

John lays down very deliberate lines and Klaus extrapolates from what John indicates. Note the thick shading on the face in the last panel. That shading was reserved for only the final panel to give it a more ominous tone.

iNSidER PROFiLE

Mike Perkins

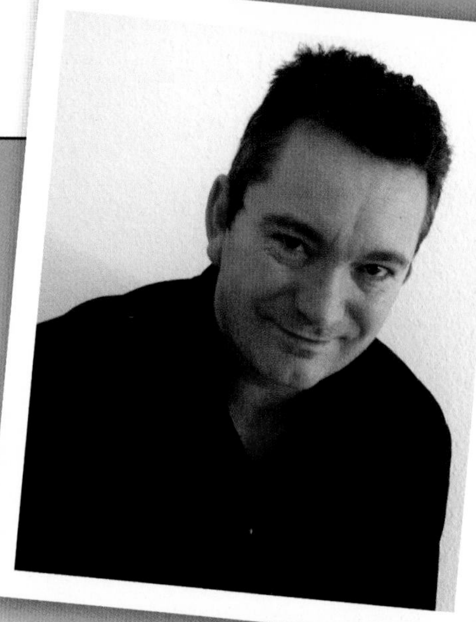

OCCUPATION: Illustrator, comic book artist, storyteller

DATE OF BIRTH: November 20, 1969

FIRST PUBLISHED WORK: *Tharg's Future Shocks, 2000 A.D.*

INFLUENCES: Steve Dillon, Brian Bolland, etc.

LONGEST RUN ON A BOOK: *Captain America* #8 to present (#39), give or take a few issues.

BEST KNOWN FOR: *Union Jack, Captain America, Ruse, Spellbinders*

FAVORITE CHARACTER WORKED ON: All of the above plus Judge Dredd.

DREAM PROJECT: A nice long run on something, pencilling and inking, and that Macbeth idea I have with Mike Carey.

MOST PERSONAL WORK: Probably *Captain America* #23, everything just flowed on that issue.

ART TRAINING: Bournville College of Art, then one year of intensive business training, then on the job.

BEST ADVICE RECEIVED WHEN STARTING OUT: Steve Dillon said, "Get a thicker pen!"

MIKE PERKINS hails from merry ole' England, where he started his comics pencilling and inking career. But it was a small company called CrossGen that brought him to the United States. His phenomenal work on comics such as *Kiss Kiss Bang Bang* and his inking over greats like George Pérez and Steve Epting garnered the attention of Marvel editor Tom Brevoort, who hired both Steve and Mike to relaunch the wildly successful *Captain America* title in 2006. Since then, Mike has accepted an exclusive contract with Marvel and has pencilled many projects on his own in addition to *Captain America*. He is currently illustrating the adaptation of Stephen King's *The Stand*.

On the comic book page the creator is fundamentally attempting to create a three-dimensional world working in a two-dimensional environment.

The penciller will most likely turn in pages that lack line weight and depth. It's the inker's job to bring a certain amount of depth perception to the pages provided. This can be accomplished using various approaches, depending on the subject matter and the desires of the penciller. Some techniques include:

- Going from a thick line in the foreground to a thin line in the background (one of the most widely employed techniques).
- Darkening the figure or fixture in the foreground, leading to a shadowless background.
- Varying tones using combinations of gray washes, lighter pencils, "flecking" and solid blacks.

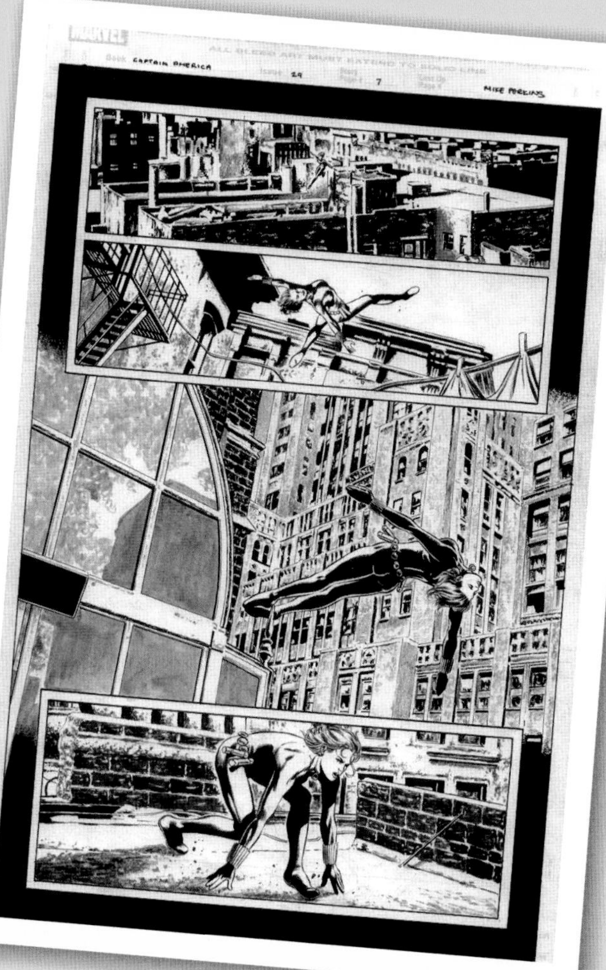

Keeping Figure and Setting Separate

The script required a page of Black Widow bounding, leaping and jumping through a cityscape. By necessity this would be a highly detailed page, and if the inker is not careful, the figure and surroundings could easily melt into one mass.

***Captain America* #29: page 7, ©2008 Marvel Characters, Inc. Used with permission.**

Textural Techniques

From Mike Perkins

A lot of the comic books on the stands today are concerned with real-world occurrences where the actions of their characters are just a bit more harsh. Sometimes those situations and environments get downright mean and dirty. Often the inks need to reflect that. This requires inkers to create environments they would not want to be a part of.

Here are some of the tools I use, why I use them and what I do with them. All these textural techniques won't be necessary on every page—just one or two will usually suffice—but when adding that "grit," the best advice is to practice and get increasingly more confident in wallowing in the dirt.

INSIDER VOICE

Klaus Janson on Inker Responsibilities

The first obligation is to do whatever works best for the story. The second obligation is to make the penciller look good. And that depends on what the pencils are lacking. Sometimes the anatomy needs an assist, sometimes the inker can separate the shapes a bit and make the composition more clear, sometimes a special effect is appropriate, sometimes texture can help the panel, sometimes a well-positioned black can pop an image, etc. It helps to be able to think quickly and have the options and knowledge that experience brings at your disposal.

1 X-Acto blade

Once the page is finished, it may still need some extra roughing up. This is where the blade comes in. All those nice smooth lines laid down with a brush can easily be obliterated with one swoosh of its sharp surface. Here I used it to emphasize the graininess of the roof structure by pulling the blade along the lines there already and breaking up the solid edges. The blade is also one of the best tools for throwing a rainstorm down on the page—just flick the blade upwards away from the raindrop to create an atmospheric streak. Confidence is needed in the use of this tool. You can easily obliterate the parts you didn't particularly want to get rid of.

2 Prismacolor pencil

A black colored pencil can provide some amazingly rough textures. The Prismacolor is one of the roughest. Look at the walls of the bar where it's used to show the effects of fifty years' worth of cigarettes and alcohol. By pressing down on the pencil you can bring forward and backward the depth and density of the mark.

3 No. 1 round brush

Not only useful for getting those delicate lines in there but also good for a dry-brush technique. This is a process that can be invaluable when portraying a little more grittiness than usual or just to soften a line. The excess ink needs to be dried off the brush using a piece of paper or a paper towel before sweeping the line along the page. This creates a ragged edge—it takes a lot of practice to get it to a point where you can be relatively happy with it. Here, I used it prominently on the pool table so the ridges on the sides are not so sharp and more rounded (as they are on an actual pool table). The drybrush is also appropriated on the baseball bat the barman is brandishing—it gives it that "used to beat heads in" look that's needed in this scene.

4 Col-Erase pencil

This is the smoother of the two pencils I use on my pages. It gives a much softer line and a more consistent tone. It's great for softening jaw lines, indicating eye shadow and portraying the texture of leather catsuits (a staple in any comic book).

5 Gray wash

This one's a little repetitive but artists get used to feeling like caged animals stuck in their little freelancing studios. I always have a small cup of water close at hand—usually for cleaning brushes. (Note: Always look when you're taking a sip from your coffee cup. We inkers may have ink in our blood but it doesn't taste so great when it mistakenly slides down to your stomach. Also, attempt to clean your brushes in the water provided for such use…not in your coffee.) To get the best wash effect, I keep adding a brushload of ink to the water each time I take a pass at placing the grays on the page. This provides a great sense of depth and texture.

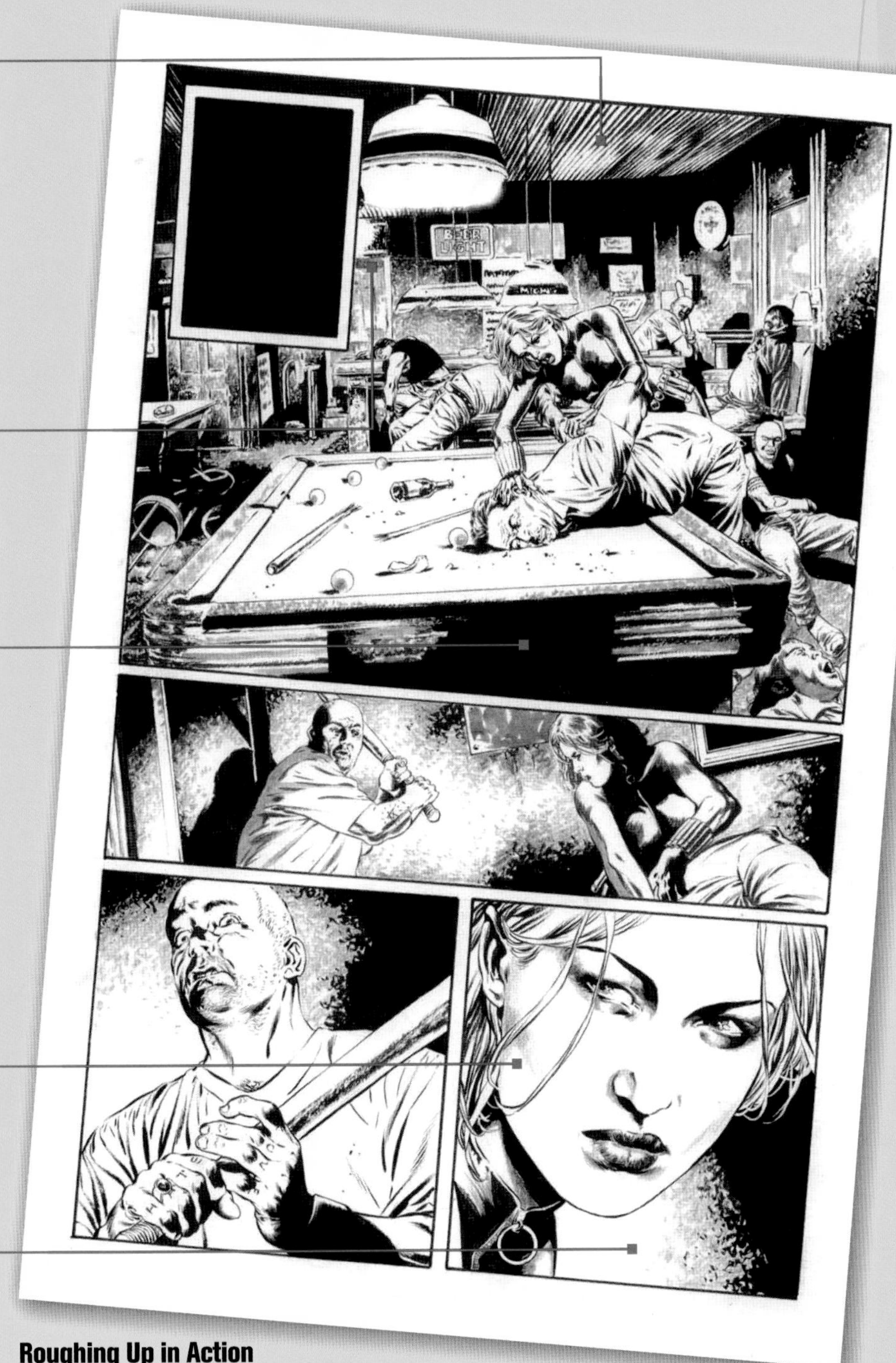

Roughing Up in Action

On this page I wanted to portray the grungy atmosphere of this hole-in-the-wall bar. Roughing it up was, by far, the best way to go.

Choosing an Inker

One of the most difficult things to figure out as an editor or as a new penciller is how to choose an inker. I spent the first couple of years as an editor really trying to figure this out and it's not easy. I mean, I understand exactly what a writer and a penciller bring to a project. I even understand what a good colorist and letterer can do. But inking I found elusive.

It's not easy to choose an inker, so I suggest this process:

1 Visualize what you want the final printed page to look like.

2 Look at a lot of inkers and their work. What aspects do they have that remind you of your vision?

3 Talk with your inker about what you want and ask him if he can deliver the goods.

4 Keep in constant contact with your inker. Give constructive feedback on his work.

Not all inkers ink the same way. They use different kinds of ink, they use different tools to apply the ink, and they certainly use different styles. At first, I just wanted to make sure the inkers I was working with were inking everything on the page. There are more than a few inkers who won't always ink everything laid down by the penciller. Once I figured out who was legit and who was cutting corners, I started looking at who could separate the background from the foreground well. Slowly, I started to realize which inkers were best for certain kinds of things.

Often, pencillers have their own ideas of what kind of inker they want over them. More than once, I've gone with an inker requested by a penciller. Nothing wrong with that; keeps the penciller happy and the pages coming in on time—I liked that. The penciller and I would then discuss what we wanted the final published comic to look like and what other projects had aspects of what we wanted. I'd then look at what those inkers (and colorists, too) did that I thought would be helpful for the project in question. Usually, I would picture in my mind what I wanted the final printed page to look like, and I would look for those aspects in an inker's work.

Also, a lot of people don't do this, but just talking with an inker about what you want is extremely helpful. A lot of editors and artists assume that each inker has only one style, but that's not always the case. Giving someone a target to hit is always better than just asking someone to ink a page. At least the inker will know what's expected.

Every now and again I'm approached by an editor to not only ink a project but to finish it. He's not asking me to hurry up as I fast approach my deadline. He's not even asking me to color, letter, edit and print the comic. What this means is that, for whatever reason—whether it is because of time constraints or the strengths of a particular penciller—I'm being asked to, essentially, strengthen up the pencils in my inks. Sometimes, I'm being asked to have a hand in the actual finished style of the job in hand.

Being invited to do this means that I obviously have enough confidence in my abilities that my editor has noticed that I'd be able to handle it, no matter how complete the pencils are—and sometimes there's very little to work from.

When finishing a job in the inks, I follow the penciller's intent. It's similar to the relationship of a director and a director of photography or cinematographer—all of the storytelling is there, it just needs drama and depth.

To illustrate this welcome predicament, let's take a look at one of the pages from *Captain America* #10, which I finished over Lee Weeks's always strong pencils.

INSIDER VOICE

John Byrne on Pencillers Inking

It took me a while to get my inks to a point that I was remotely happy with, and literally years and years after that to get to something I could say I really liked, no qualifications. But in the end, it gave me more control over what the finished product looked like, which is probably why many pencillers prefer to ink their own work.

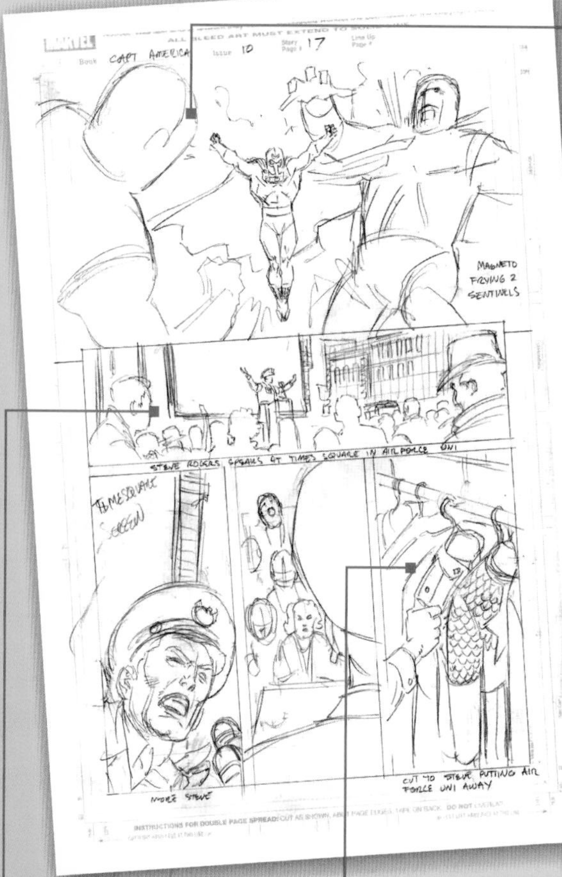

The first panel is shapes with a little more detail on the Magneto figure. If it were inked line for line, you wouldn't be able to figure out what the giant figures are and the power of Magneto's attack would be nonexistent. This is where research comes in handy. It's my job to find out what a Sentinel looks like—I can't just rely on my memory.

The next three panels consist primarily of a crowd scene in a New York street. In the pencil version, shapes are indicated in order to establish figures and faces. The buildings are represented as basic boxes with rudimentary windows. Do NOT draw this! Finish it! See in panel 4 how the crowd is indicated but not fully realized. This is an indicator that the page needs to be finished. A fully pencilled page would have very deliberate lines. Look at life. Look at photos. Study the fall and texture of clothing. Put the most prominent shadows in the foreground and drop those buildings back. Add more figures if needed to give the crowd some substance. Think about where you're adding the blacks—your page has to flow, it has to be composed. Those solid blacks need to balance the page and lead the eye.

The final panel, though simply a hand reaching into a wardrobe, must be approached with the same kind of commitment and drama as the others. Otherwise, the whole page could fall apart. Add depth with shadow and give the clothes a few more wrinkles, especially where the hand is grabbing the jacket. The wrinkles on the shirt sleeves of the arm and sleeve of the jacket lead the eye to the action.

Figure out where the lighting will originate from. In the first panel, I've used the figure of Magneto as the power source, using a central shadow to show the magnitude of the force emanating from within him. I've also accentuated the flow and ripples of his cape to lead the eye toward the focal point. This lighting is followed outward to the now metallic figures of the Sentinels with the foreground figure capitalizing on the placement. Magneto is the darkest element on the page, creating the illusion that he is standing far in front of the background elements—your brain is fooled into thinking this is a three-dimensional image.

Radiating lines show further power—once again pointing to the focal point of Magneto—being cut into by the electrical effect achieved using a white correction pen or white ink.

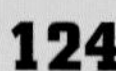

Build on the Basics

As you can see from the pencilled page, all the basic information is there; it just needs a little more depth and refinement. It's up to the inker to determine how much refinement is needed. There are some projects that are given to particular inkers so their own style can shine through. The inks of Kevin Nowlan are a perfect example. Unless I'm asked to take a specific approach, I usually try to go in a different direction when I'm offered such an undertaking. I'll take a look at the penciller's previous work—something the penciller was pleased with or something he inked himself. This exercise can put you on the fine road to less friction with the penciller (and to more work in the future).

INSIDER VOICE

Klaus Janson on the *Chasing Amy* Question

If we can imagine the inking community lined up on a continuum where "tracers" are on one end and "nontracers" on the other end, you would see that most of the inkers would fall into the middle range somewhere.There are inkers who "trace" to a greater degree than others, and I don't have a problem with that. It's a choice that the inker and penciller make and they should be allowed to make that choice. But that doesn't mean that all inkers are tracers or that inking is tracing. You just have to look at the inkers who have inked Jack Kirby. If inking were "tracing," Jack's pencils would look exactly the same no matter who inked them. The reality is quite different. Everyone who knows Jack's work knows that the look of it varied quite a bit depending on if Frank Giacoia, Vinnie Colletta, John Romita Sr. or Joe Sinnott inked him. Honestly the inker couldn't even help influencing the pencils if he wanted to. It's a question of degree.

INSIDER PROFILE

Karl Kesel

OCCUPATION: Cartoonist (writer/penciller/inker)

DATE OF BIRTH: January 7, 1959

FIRST PUBLISHED WORK: *Indiana Jones* inking sample page in *Marvel Age*, 1983. Even got paid fifty dollars for it!

INFLUENCES: Milton Caniff, Jack Kirby

LONGEST RUN ON A BOOK: As a writer it was *Adventures of Superman*; as an inker, probably *Fantastic Four*.

BEST KNOWN FOR: Co-creating (with Tom Grummett) the Conner Kent Superboy. Also well known for my love of Jack Kirby's work in general, and his *Fantastic Four* and *Challengers of the Unknown* runs in specific. Plus, irrational fondness for the late 1950s, early 1960s Marvel monsters like Sporr, Taboo and Groot! Love those guys!

FAVORITE CHARACTER WORKED ON: Hard to say. I've always been most attracted to and had the most fun with oddball fringe characters, and for that reason I'd have to choose the 24-Hour Bug, a character from Tom Grummett and my creator-owned book *Section Zero*. The Bug was a teenager who had a cursed tattoo, and every time he scratched it he became a weird bug-boy for twenty-four hours! I really got a kick out of that character, his situation and his name. Now THAT'S comics!

DREAM PROJECT: Other than one of a million creator-owned projects that I wish I could afford to actually do? *Fantastic Four* and/or *Challengers of the Unknown.*

MOST PERSONAL WORK: Probably *Spider-Boy*. Not that I bared my soul in it, but it captured a certain excitement and tone that I think comics do better than any other medium. It boiled down what I consider the essence of comics better than anything else I've written.

ART TRAINING: One year at the Joe Kubert School; three and a half years at Hartford Art School; many, many years scribbling away in class after class instead of taking notes.

KARL KESEL has been working in the comics industry for over twenty years and has not only attempted, but mastered nearly every creative job there is. Practically born a die-hard Jack Kirby fan, Karl's creative voice stands out as a champion of exciting, dramatic and clear storytelling as a writer, a penciller and an inker. His previous credits include some work on nearly every major title from both Marvel and DC Comics. His run on the *Fantastic Four* with writer Mark Waid and penciller Mike Wieringo holds an especially warm place in his heart.

BEST ADVICE RECEIVED WHEN STARTING OUT: Karen Berger was my first editor and did one thing that changed me forever and made me the cartoonist I am today. I handed in an inked issue of *Legion of Super-Heroes* and Karen was clearly not very happy with it. She called in editor-in-chief Dick Giordano to critique the work. Besides learning a lot from Dick's (very kind and insightful) talk, it made me realize that "good enough" was not good enough. From that day on I have never given any job less than 110 percent. And I've always tried to make my next job better than my last. It means I'm not the fastest inker (or writer or penciller) in the business, but it also means that any editor who hires me knows he or she is going to get high-quality work every single time. Thanks, Karen!

The Slick Line

From Karl Kesel

I'm a Brush Man. That means when it comes to inking comics, my weapon of choice is a brush. Not a nib, not a technical pen and (God, no!) not a marker—a brush. A Winsor & Newton Series 7 No. 3, to be precise. Why? Glad you asked...

First of all, a brush is what many of the greatest artists in this industry have used, from Milton Caniff (of *Terry and the Pirates* and *Steve Canyon* comic-strip fame) to Joe Sinnott (who inked Jack Kirby's groundbreaking work on the 1960s *Fantastic Four*, which really established the traditional look of the modern-day superhero story). If it was good enough for them, who am I to argue?

But more than that—more important than anything else, really—is the simple fact that I love the kind of line a brush puts down on paper. A good brush is like a great sportscar—an extension of yourself, instantly responsive, almost knowing what you are going to do before you do, a thrill to take for a ride. And, like a sportscar, if you don't know how to handle it, you're gonna crash and burn.

This is the basic difference between a brush and any other inking implement: A nib, pen or marker creates a line very easily, but using it to fill in areas of black is much more difficult. A brush creates areas of black very easily, but controlling it enough to produce a thin line is much more difficult. Gaining that amount of control with a brush takes patience and practice, but if you ask me, the end result is well worth it. Because once you master the brush, it can give you almost any kind of line or look you want.

By its very nature, a brush produces a line that goes from thin to thick to thin. It is a much more "lively" line than you can get with any marker or technical pen, and most nibs. It's extremely organic, and that's a good thing since we happen to be organic beings living in an organic world. A brush can produce a soft, supple, sensuous line that perfectly captures the feel of

Kesel's Rules for Professional Inks

- I always separate a panel's three planes–foreground, middle ground and background–using heavier line weights around objects that are closer to the reader, and lighter line weights on objects farther from the reader. This gives a sense of depth to the art, and makes it easier to tell if, say, a Ford Mustang is a real car somewhere in the distance or a toy car up close.
- Another helpful trick is to place black areas (called "spotting blacks") so they will help direct the reader's eye to what's important in the panel. For instance, placing a normally rendered figure in front of a heavily shadowed area will "pop" that figure forward and draw attention to it.
- A third thing I do is make sure different objects have distinct and identifiable textures. A tree shouldn't look like a rock; metal shouldn't look like water.

flesh. It can lay down wet, bold marks that evoke a rushing river or peaceful lake. It can give you the hard outline of a mountain as well as the deep shadows thrown by its craggy peaks. Even mechanical objects like cars and planes benefit from brushwork, gaining a warmth that makes them a part of the world, not apart from it.

Most of the projects I ink end up having what is usually considered a "professional" look: clean, smooth and slick. It isn't "professional" just because I use a brush, of course—although my brush style produces line work that is almost frighteningly clean, smooth, and slick—but also because I follow a few simple rules that add to that feeling.

What all this does is result in a finished style that might be best summed up with two words: reader friendly. Even at first glance it produces a look that is inviting and appealing to readers, creating a world they want to enter into. Then the style helps the storytelling be as clear and understandable as possible, and keeps the reader in that world. After all, it doesn't matter if you're telling the greatest story in the world if no one wants to stick around to read it.

This doesn't mean other inking implements are worthless. I use nibs for some of my fine detail work (a very flexible nib that produces brushlike line work), and many excellent comic artists use nibs and pens and sometimes even (>shudder!<) markers with wonderful results. But like I said, I'm a Brush Man.

And as far as I'm concerned, there's only one meaning to that old adage: a brush with greatness.

INSIDER VOICE

Klaus Janson on the Inker as an Endangered Species

I think that technology will improve and more pencillers might have their pencils colored, but there are other reasons besides the technology that might inhibit putting inkers on the endangered species list. Some pencillers who tried coloring their pencils complained that it took too long to tighten up their pencils enough to have them properly scanned. It actually slowed the pencilling process down. So they can turn out more pages and create more revenue if they use inkers. And the line is different. You can darken the pencil line enough to color over it but you'll never be able to replicate a brush line. It's an entirely different look when ink is colored compared to the look achieved when coloring just the pencils. There will always be some pencillers and readers that prefer the look of ink under the color.

INSIDER VOICE

Klaus Janson on the Most Important Inker Trait

Know how to draw. An inker is not going to be able to convincingly communicate light, or anatomy, or folds, depth, etc., unless he understands the mechanics of it. The best inkers have always been the artists who can draw: Tom Palmer, Wally Wood, Dick Giordano, Kevin Nowlan, Murphy Anderson, Joe Sinnott, Sal Buscema, etc.

9 COLORING

I love colored comics. There's something about those vibrant colors that really brings the pages to life for me as a reader. But here's the thing: Coloring is becoming a more and more technical craft in the comics business. Originally, coloring was done by hand coloring the page and indicating to the printer what combination of colored ink you wanted that color to be. It was almost mathematical and it wasn't precise by any means.

As technology of the printing press and the computer developed, that method of coloring died. Gone are the days of completely hand coloring anything. Gone are the days of physical color guides. Now, the colorist gets a digital file of the inked page and he uses primarily Adobe Photoshop to do the coloring work. However, you don't need to be a computer whiz to understand what makes good coloring.

The first thing to realize is that colorists are artists—not computer operators. The most important thing a colorist needs to do is understand color theory.

The second thing a colorist needs to know is how comics storytelling works.

The last thing a colorist needs to know is how to work in Adobe Photoshop or whatever program he uses. Be an artist first, figure out the computer stuff later.

Like with the inking chapter, I'm turning this chapter over to a colorist I've worked with consistently for the last six years. His name is Chris Sotomayor and he has colored *Captain Marvel, The Avengers, The Vision, Ms. Marvel, Annihilation: Super-Skrull* and *X-Men,* and that's just for me! He's a top-notch colorist and one of the best in the industry. So, without further ado, here's Chris!

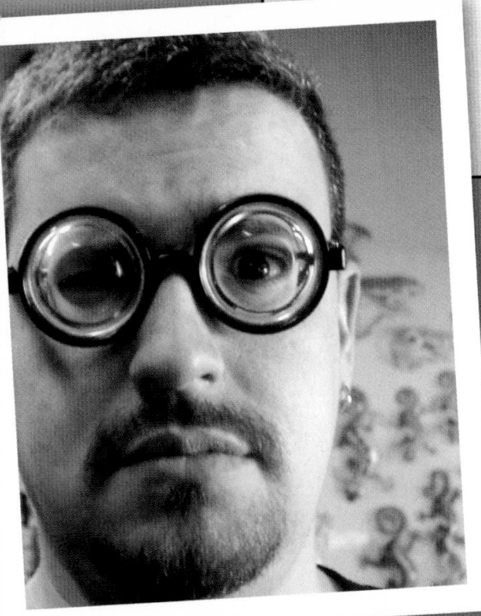

iNSidER PROFiLE
Chris Sotomayor

CHRIS SOTOMAYOR took the comics industry off guard with his revolutionary coloring over Chris Cross's pencils (no inks) on Marvel's *Captain Marvel* series in 2003. Until this point, no penciller/colorist team had managed to make production of a comic book look better without an inker than with one. Chris's success on *Captain Marvel* led to his other popular work on such titles as *Supreme Power, The Avengers* and *X-Men*. Beyond just being great at his job, Chris is also a teacher and, as such, has helped several young colorists hone their craft and jump-start their careers.

OCCUPATION: Freelance illustrator/digital color artist

DATE OF BIRTH: January 27, 1973

FIRST PUBLISHED WORK: *Triumphant Unleashed* #0 (a special "mail-away" book for an indie company named Triumphant)

INFLUENCES: My parents, my wife, Arleen, Maxfield Parrish, Lynn Varley, Richmond Lewis, and pretty much anyone working in comics right now.

LONGEST RUN ON A BOOK: *Captain Marvel* (thirty-plus issues across two volumes)

BEST KNOWN FOR: Probably *Captain Marvel.*

FAVORITE CHARACTER WORKED ON: That's a three-way tie between Captain America, Captain Marvel and Hulk.

DREAM PROJECT: A long run on a *Silver Surfer*, *Spider-Man* or *Daredevil* book.

MOST PERSONAL WORK: Again, that's gotta be *Captain Marvel.* I feel like I was firing on all cylinders and had a lot of creative freedom to experiment thanks to everyone involved. *Supreme Power/Squadron Supreme* comes a close second, though.

ART TRAINING: Aside from attending the School of Visual Arts in Manhattan, I interned at an illustrator's studio. That's probably where I learned the most. That experience especially helped me with the business side of comics, which is often overlooked.

BEST ADVICE RECEIVED WHEN STARTING OUT: An illustrator named Michael Davis probably gave me the best life lessons/experiences for my career. But the best single piece of advice was probably when Denys Cowan told me, "If you screw something up on a page, you have twenty-one other pages to make up for it. Don't sweat the small stuff."

Color Theory

From Chris Sotomayor

You wouldn't think that two small words would create such a heavy concept, but they do. Many people have a hard time wrapping their heads around color theory, probably because it's theory, not fact. It's easy to point to a physical object and name it. But to understand and use an abstract theoretical concept to provide clarity to the masses—that's quite a feat. The goal of color theory is to provide color combinations that will elicit a certain emotion and work well together aesthetically.

COLOR BREAKDOWN

Here's a simple breakdown:

Complementary Color

As suggested by Isaac Newton's color wheel, opposite colors cancel out each other's hue. If you look at the basic color wheel (a very important tool for a color artist), you'll see that certain colors fall on the opposite side of others. These are called *complementary colors*.

Basic thinking is that using these complementary color combinations will produce some kind of tension with the reader and also look pleasant together (which we may or may not want, depending on the emotion we're trying to evoke). Complementary color combos always work. This includes the shades and tints of colors as well (e.g., a darker or lighter version of a particular color, such as pink is a lighter tint of red—the complement of which is a mint green). That's why you can always find some kind of blue/orange color combo in comics. But of course, those aren't the only combos that work.

Other Color Combinations

Colors next to each other on the color wheel are called *analogous colors*. These combos are handy when driving home

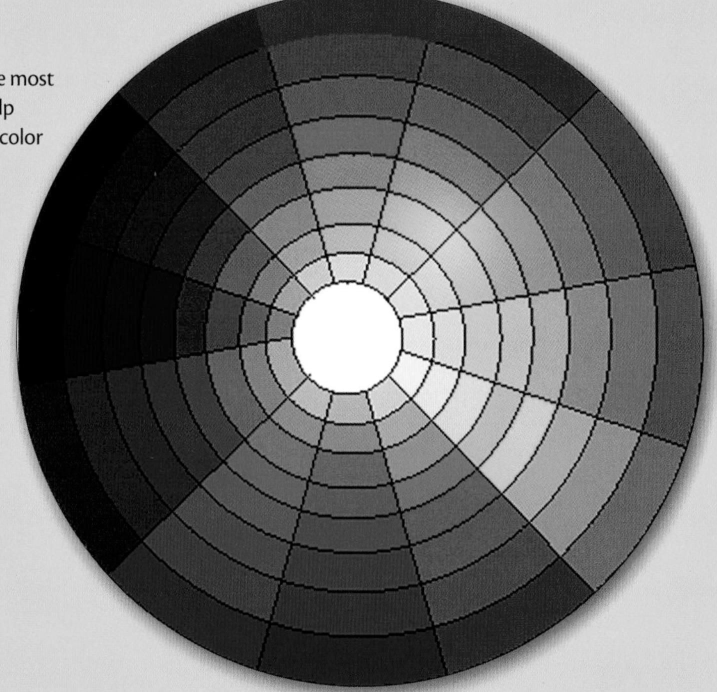

The Color Wheel
The color wheel is the most important tool to help understand pleasing color combinations.

a particular point—a singular idea, in color—like a sad image that's painted in blues and purples. Then there's a split complementary color scheme, which is a color presented with the two colors on either side of its direct complement: for example, blue accompanied by red and yellow. Now, this doesn't mean color combinations should be limited to these rules. These are just some simple rules to apply in order to keep color choices aesthetically pleasing.

Color Temperature

The task of any true creator is not just to know when to use the rules, but also when to break them. All this depends on the emotional reaction you're looking for from the reader. Using *color temperature* is also important in this respect. Color temperature is pretty easy to understand, and a good way to invoke reaction from the reader.

Generally, using warm colors (yellows, oranges and reds) will cause excitement, like if there's some kind of dramatic conflict or tension. Conversely, cool colors (blues, purples and greens) will slow down a scene or bring the mood down. These kinds of colors turn up in sad or quiet moments. These principles are the foundation for designing and conveying information through the use of color.

Quick Color Definitions

PRIMARY COLORS Red, blue and yellow; all colors come from these three.

SECONDARY COLORS Green, orange and purple; these come from mixing primary colors: blue + yellow = green, yellow + red = orange, red + blue = purple.

COMPLEMENTARY COLORS Any two colors opposite one another on the color wheel.

ANALOGOUS COLORS Colors next to each other on the color wheel.

SATURATED COLORS More intense, purer hues.

DESATURATED COLORS Colors that tend to be more dull, achieved by adding the hue's complement.

Storytelling

From Chris Sotomayor

When Spider-Man rushes into a burning building to save a baby, there's a reason why everything's doused with red. That's because the red color will really drive home the urgency of the moment. Sure, the flames cast a lot of red light, but that's just a convenience that nature gave us to make storytelling easier.

Let's back up a little bit. This is my favorite part of coloring. Remember in the previous section, when I mentioned that certain colors (and color temperature) can elicit certain responses from the reader? It's important to know when to use certain colors, and in what combinations. It's just as important to know when *not* to use certain colors.

If two characters are having a quiet moment, it's best to stay away from using reds, oranges or yellows. Any of the warmer colors will conflict with the solemnity of the scene. Something else to keep in mind is the strength of the colors you use. Saturated colors really pop off the page, so those choices should be saved for the more important elements—anything we want to move the reader's eye toward. Desaturated colors will recede and are usually a great choice for background or secondary information.

There are other ways to move the reader's eye from varying focal points. Again, this comes into play using combinations from the color wheel. Warm and cool contrasting colors can be used to this effect (think of that popular orange and blue combo again). So can using tints of colors, such as lighter colors in the background and more saturated colors in the foreground, which is most likely the main focus of the page.

When the topic of storytelling comes up, we should be thinking of mood, clarity and pacing. Clarity is pretty obvious. When telling a story, the information needs to be served to the reader as quickly and concisely as possible. Readers should not have to spend more time on a given panel or page than was intended. And there should be no confusion as to what the reader's being shown. All relevant information should be easily seen and consumed, with all the secondary information to serve as window dressing. The reader's eye should be trained on the important elements.

The absolute first thing to take into account when sitting down to color a page is mood. Mood dictates the palette and plays a big part in pacing the story.

Like I mentioned before, cool colors will slow the pacing while warm colors will speed it up and provide a lot of energy. Being able to shift the mood is also very important. Starting a scene off slowly and adding a dramatic impact can increase the tension.

What artists need to keep in mind is contrast. Whether it's light vs. dark or warm vs. cool, contrast is key in telling a clear story.

CHECKING CLARITY

There are a couple of tricks to see if a colored page is clear. The first is to flip the page upside down and see if the important elements are still where your eye is drawn to. That may not work well for computer coloring, but it'll still work for traditional painting. Another trick is to simply squint at the page and see if the focal points are still there. If the eye while squinting is still drawn to the proper places, the focal points are clear.

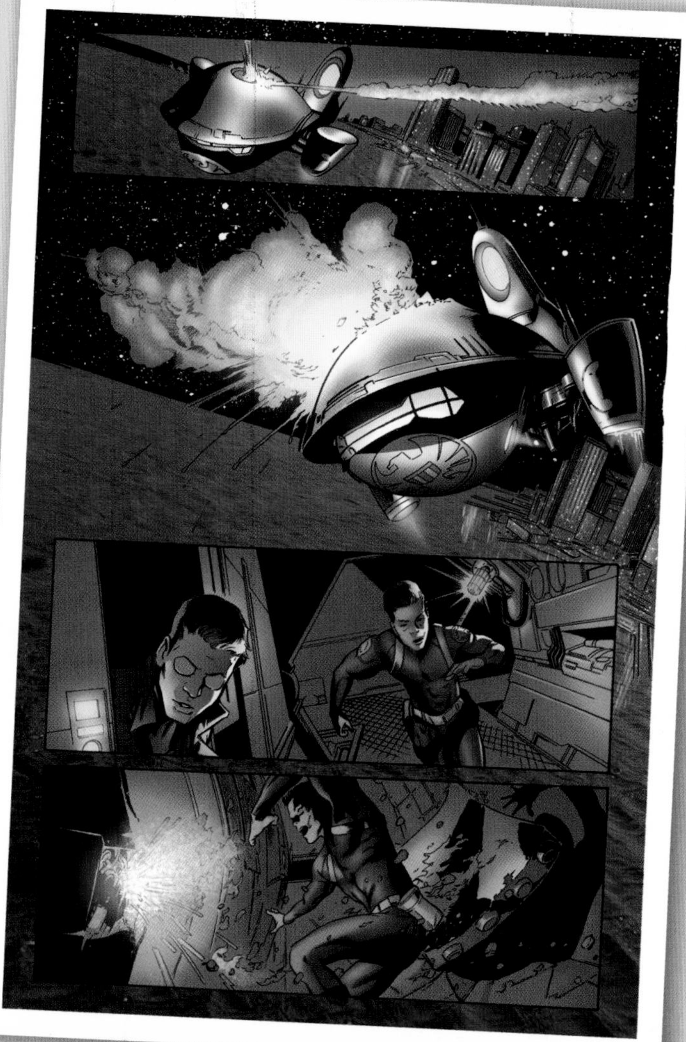

Mood and Well-Placed Highlights

Use the mood of the story to plan out the palette that will best tell the story and keep the reader interested.

This page starts off with a lot of blue to convey the idea of a quiet night with something disturbing it. When the calm is suddenly disrupted, everything goes red. The reader gets an instant feeling of danger.

You may think that's an easy call. Red and blue are always eye-catching colors, so you can't really go wrong. But what if the story calls for an evil plague-infested city that's full of dirt and disease? Browns, oranges and greens might work to drive that effect—a sickening combination, I think.

Well-placed highlights will keep moving the reader's eye to different points of contrast. I added bright rim lights on the sides of the characters' faces to help the reader find the more important element of the page, which can be difficult in a sea of monochromatic color.

INSIDER VOICE

Neal Adams on the Healthy Artist

One of the people I look up to very, very much is Joe Kubert. I look up to Joe Kubert because he represents things that one might not easily understand outside of the fact that he's a terrific artist. He does wonderful work. He's easy to read and he has a standard for himself that's very good. He also has a tremendous work ethic, which he had to learn, just like the rest of us. He has a family, he has children, he raised his children well. He puts his focus on his family. He's healthy and strong. That's very important to me. I believe personally that it doesn't matter how good an artist you are–it's about how you balance your life. And how you balance your life is between three things: Your health, your family and your work. All three must be equal.

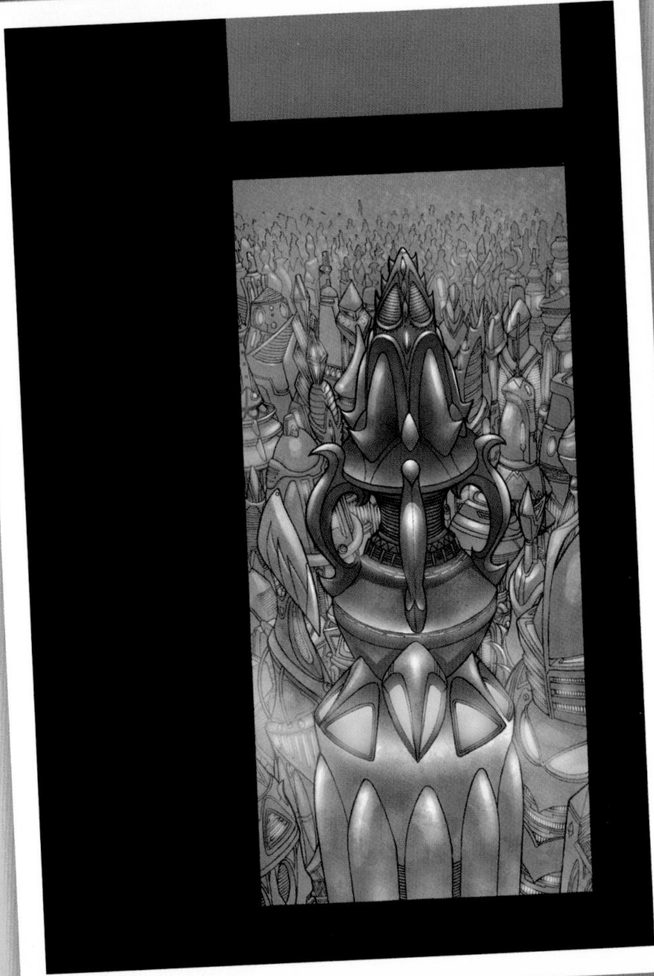

Isolating the Focal Point

Isolating the focal point of an image keeps the reader's eye trained and allows a colorist to control the pacing.

It can also be lit in such a way as to bring in the reader's eye, such as a harsh rim light on the edge of something, or dropping a highlight behind or on top of the main focus.

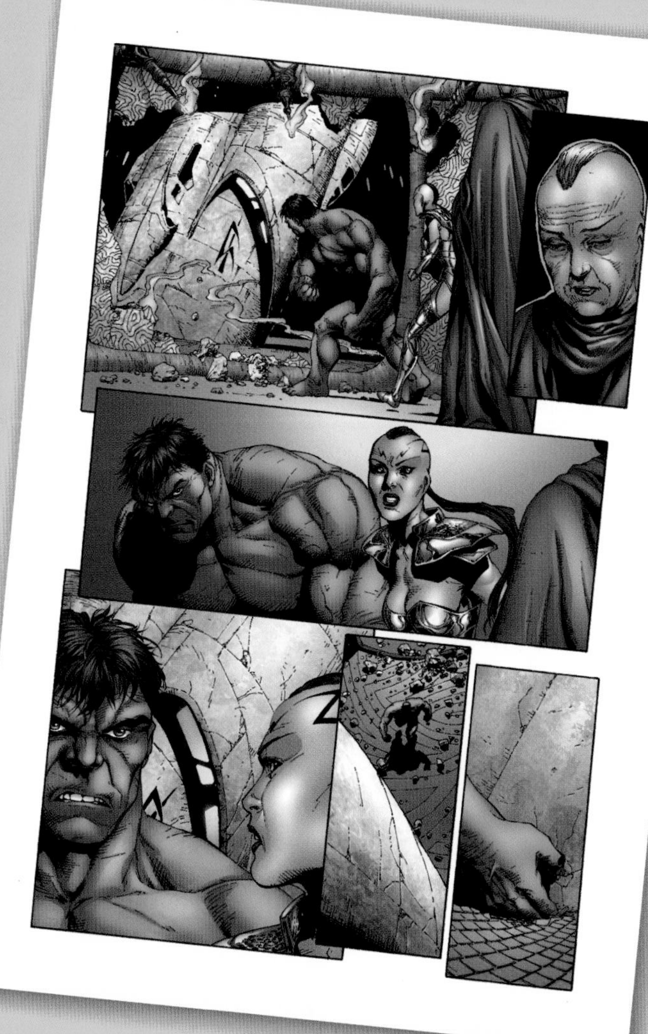

INSIDER VOICE
David Finch on Quality

The only thing that you can really control is the quality of your own work. No big break or high-profile job can ever compensate for the quality of the work, and if the work is good enough it will make something big out of a small project.

Colors Will Elicit Reaction and Make the Reader More Vested

Experiment with different color combinations, keeping in mind which moods or reactions certain colors will elicit.

Once a palette is set, the colorist concentrates on keeping the reader's eye focused on the important things—like the main character or a specific action. A standout color will bring that element out (as you can see, the Hulk stands out pretty well on this page and is colored accordingly).

***The Incredible Hulk* #101, page 7: ©2008 Marvel Characters, Inc. Used with permission.**

Coloring for Accuracy
From Chris Sotomayor

A big part of storytelling is knowing when to color for accuracy and when to take liberties with accuracy. It's all relative. What's it relative to? Value.

Value is the lightness or darkness of any given color. Using value, we can create forms and spatial relationships. Value contrast separates objects in space, while value gradation suggests mass and contour of a surface. Hue also has value. When contrasting hues are made similar in value, the spatial effects are flattened out.

Now, we all know that the grass is green (actually, my lawn is quite brown), and the sky is blue. And that's all well and good. If I were to color those things like that in a comic book, I'd be correct and within reason to do so. I would most likely go with this approach under normal lighting conditions, or the introduction of a character.

However, this doesn't always make for an interesting page. And if the page isn't interesting, we're going to lose the reader's attention. So in order to hold the reader's interest, we have to know when to play a little fast and loose with reality.

One of the most effective ways to do this is finding a light source and pushing it into a color. Some light sources have a color, a volcano for example. So if a character is hanging upside down over a volcano, the lava will be lighting the scene, making everything red. Thus the red is pushed into the coloring of the scene.

Multiplane Images and Montages Present Different Kinds of Problems ➡
Here the colorist must choose a focal point and build out from that. There are lots of characters for the reader to look at, and it's a little difficult to determine where the reader's eye should go.

So I isolate the planes that the characters fall on. The two characters in the back are washed in blue, so they look a little separated from the foreground elements, while those foreground figures are colored in their normal colors.

In the back, the girl has blue skin, which works well because her skin is actually blue. But you'll notice the orange circle on her temple, her hair and her eyes are actually a brown color. It's just perceived as orange because the reader's eye (that's you) is already making the adjustment to the blue colors over the background figures. The same thing applies to the background male figure on the other side (with his arms stretched). His shirt is reading as the appropriate red, white and blue, even though his sleeves are light blue. His chest is blue, and his chest emblem is purple. But it all reads well due to the values in both hue and contrast amid the blue distortion. And with the other characters colored in their normal, or local color, there's a separation that allows those characters to remain in focus and not look like they're about to be eaten by the giants behind them.

Monochromatic Doesn't Mean Monotonous

A clear range of values and tints fools the reader's eye into thinking that colors are different than they appear. We see a figure hanging upside down. The smoke and color indicate that he's hanging over some kind of heat source and that it's not comfortable. We can tell he's a Caucasian male. We can tell this even with his red skin because it's all relative. The whites of his eyes aren't really white. They seem white because it's the lightest value on the panel. And the lightest value on the panel draws the reader's eye to the face, which is the most important aspect of the panel. His skin isn't that peachy color we're used to seeing on Caucasians. It's a light red with oranges and yellows in the highlights and purples mixed into the shadows. Because of the values of the skin in relation to everything else, it reads as though it were that peachy color. The red palette is defined by the heat source that's off panel. By exploiting the red light, I'm helping to drive home the urgency of the scene and hold the reader's interest. Because of the value range, everything reads as though it's correctly colored even though I used an analogous color scheme of purple, red, orange and yellow to hammer home the dramatic tension.

***Defenders* #5, page 2: ©2008 Marvel Characters, Inc. Used with permission.**

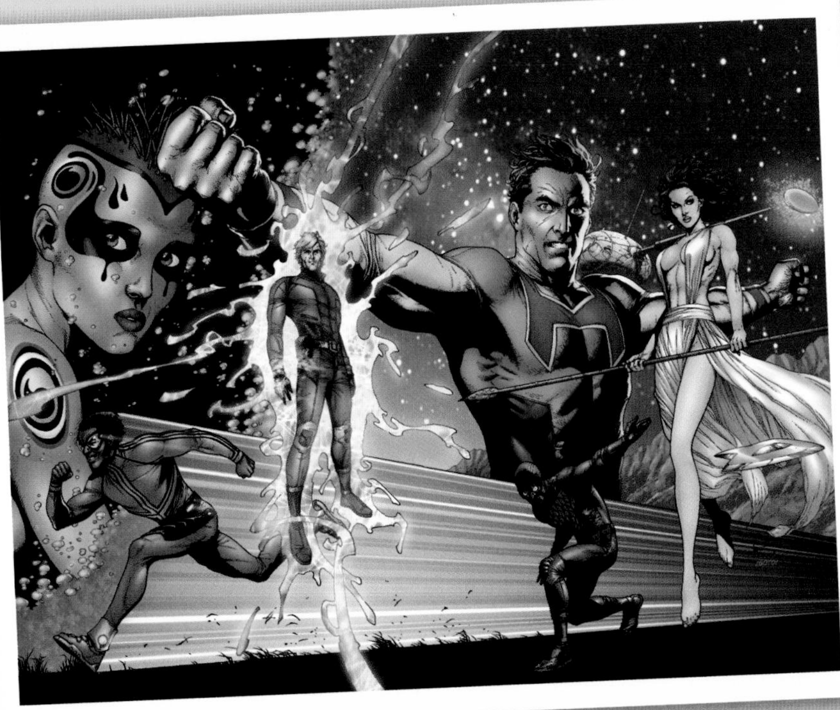

Coloring Thematically

From Chris Sotomayor

Another area in which colorists take some liberties is when coloring thematically.

When taking this approach, the colorist has to consider a different level of elements. Remember that using specific colors will elicit certain reactions and moods from the reader. So we have to take this into account, not only when coloring a specific scene, but when coloring a certain location or character or object. Let's try a very basic example to make the point a little easier to understand: Spider-Man.

SPIDER-MAN BATTLES EVIL SECONDARY COLORS

Spider-Man is dressed in red and blue, right? Primary colors. His archenemy, the Green Goblin, is dressed in green and purple. Secondary colors. The Vulture, Sandman and Mysterio: all in secondary colors. Superman is in red, blue and yellow. You can't get more primary than that. When Lex Luthor puts on his battle armor, it's green and purple. Even kryptonite is green. Secondary colors. If you want to convey that something or someone is evil, using secondary colors is the way to go. Lots of times, green by itself is considered evil.

Using color to convey a larger concept is a great way to move the reader through a story. It worked pretty well in the *Star Wars* movies. The Empire was always cued up in bleak black and white colors, with the occasional accent color, while the Rebellion would always have some kind of warm hopeful color around them, from the pilots' orange jumpsuits to the warm earthy landscape of Tatooine. As soon as the scenes cut from one to the next, you always knew which side you were looking at. And it was no accident. It was set up like that with the specific purpose of guiding the viewer through the story.

In order to effectively pull off thematic coloring, we can apply the rules of color theory. Like the Spider-Man example, primary colors can be used for positive things—like heroes. Secondary colors can be used for opposing elements—like villains. Particularly greens (which is also a favorite among horror stories to try to convey something spooky or supernatural). There are, of course, other combinations. If we wanted to convey a certain environment as having a feeling of despair, we would use lots of cool grays in different values. If we're looking to convey hope, oranges and yellows are probably where we'll want to go. Once we grasp color theory, it's not hard to come up with good color choices to get the message across.

Everyone always wants to know how to master 3-D modeling and rendering on the 2-D printed page. Now, I don't usually use any 3-D software; matter of fact, I pretty much stick to Adobe Photoshop, and not much else. Also, rendering doesn't necessarily mean to try to obtain photorealism on every panel of every page. I don't think it would be very creative if comic art were always photorealistic. So, this will all be done with painting techniques. After all, the computer is simply another tool in the artist's stable, not the be all and end all. There is no color button that we push to automatically color everything perfectly.

Keeping painting in mind, this is where we'll apply values and contrast. There are some rules to keep in mind with this also.

- Lighter values will most likely bring the reader in, especially if it's a point of high contrast.
- As values get closer together, visual elements will flatten out and fall on the periphery of the reader's attention.

These rules are important to master, if only so we can break them later. It's just as important to know what the rules are as it is to know when and how to break them.

DECIDE ON A FOCAL POINT

First and foremost, we must decide what the focal point will be. Not only will the focal point get the most attention and time, but everything plays off of it. It's not always the case that what's closest to the reader is what he should be focusing on, so we want to make sure that the clearest and most intense point of color and contrast is where we want the reader to look.

CONSIDER DETAILS

What time of day is it, and how will that affect light and color temperature? Using some hints in the drawing, we can figure out where the light source is, how intense it is and if it's defined by a particular color or family of colors (this can also come into play when trying to define the mood of the scene).

CHOOSE COLORS

The light color must be chosen, along with a complementary shadow color. As a general rule, warm light will deliver cool shadows; conversely, cool light will often deliver warm shadow colors. Now, that's not a hard-and-fast rule. Something else we can do is to use a color that appears in the background (usually a dark area of sky) and add a little of that color into the shadows. This helps to unify the page so we get the sense that everything on the page exists together in the scene at the same time. It's equally important to use the same temperature of light to highlight the entire scene, building up the intensity of things as it gets closer to the reader's eye, or the focal point.

RENDERING

When rendering a page, I usually like to start out with a basic shadow color and build my highlights from there. Often after defining the highlights, I'll go back into the shadow areas and add a bit of a glaze of some background color into the areas, usually something that complements the temperature of the highlight color.

Once we've clearly defined and rendered the focal point of the page or panel or whatever, we can then try to push the depth of certain elements around by adding color and/or darkening certain values. The same way we'd add a little glaze of color into the shadow areas of the image, we can also use glazes of color to push the depth.

Now, as far as rendering goes, I always suggest a slow buildup of highlights, starting from either a midtone or a shadow color. Picking the area to work on, we can quickly lay in some basic idea of where the light will fall. We have to consider how light will fall onto the area and how different things react to light (skin reacts much differently to light than metal). I suggest keeping skin tones fairly soft, and metals should have harsh highlights with some reflected color from nearby objects. Other surfaces have different textures and should be rendered accordingly—like spandex with a slow build of highlight color and a harsh spot of bright highlight. Leather often has harsher-edged highlights. It takes some experimentation, but we can most likely figure out these things by looking at nature.

Atmospheric Perspective

Often, adding a glaze of the far background color over certain elements of the background will push it back even further into the background and allow the focal point to pop more.

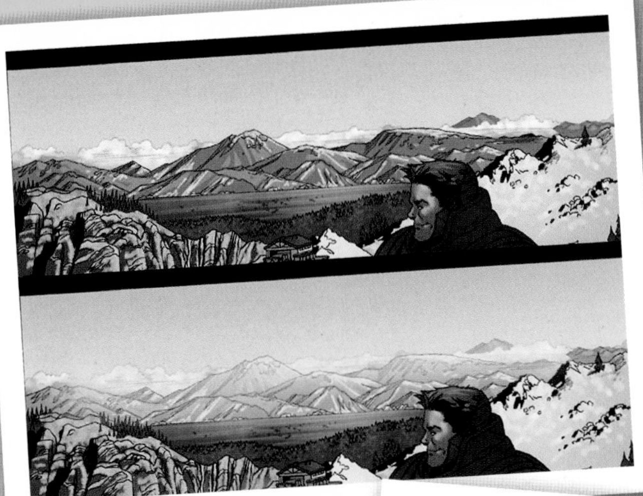

Before and After

Adding a slight haze of background sky color over part of the background image will bring the elements closer together and push the background farther into the distance.

***Marvel Adventures Hulk* #4, page 1: ©2008 Marvel Characters, Inc. Used with permission.**

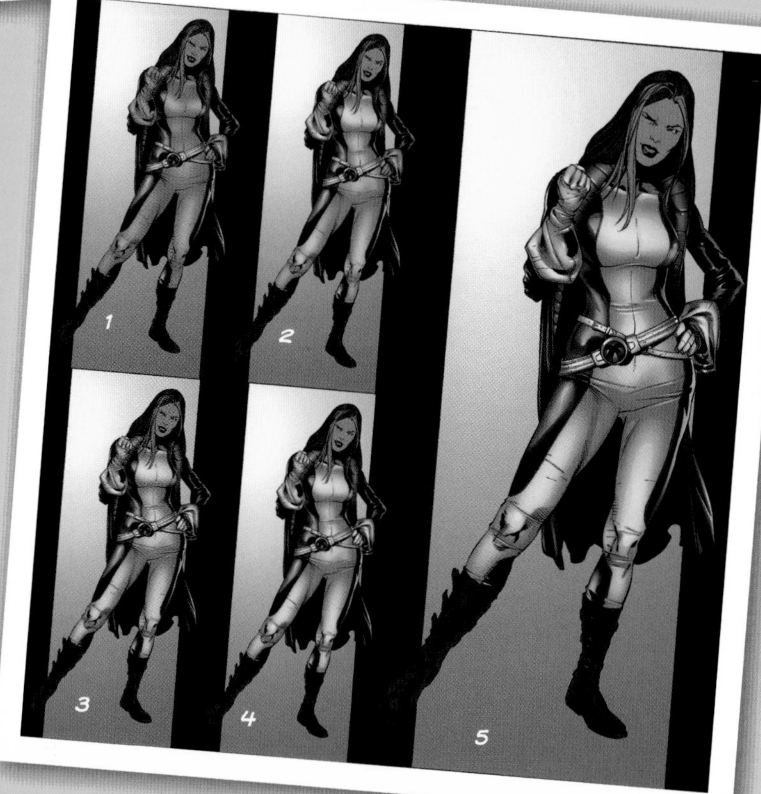

Slowly Build Highlights

Slowly build the light sources up from a darker base color. Details can be added and the shadow colors fine-tuned.

Rogue, *Ms. Marvel* #8, page 22: ©2008 Marvel Characters, Inc. Used with permission.

Lighting and Depth

From Chris Sotomayor

Rendering gives the illusion of mass and volume to elements. In order to do that, we need to be able to adjust values in hue and contrast. This also comes in handy with lighting and depth.

As you saw on page 143, atmospheric perspective is an excellent way to add depth. Considering that objects lose detail as they recede into the distance, they must gain detail, as well as saturation and brightness (strength of color), the closer they come to the reader. This is the basis of how to convey depth. Anything close to the reader's eye will be clearer with more contrast, whereas the farther things are in the background, the values will be closer together and result in a kind of haze effect. But, of course, that's not the only way to create depth. The composition of any given panel can also be manipulated.

With something as complex as multi-layered depth, basic compositional values define spatial relationships. We must think about the different planes with light, middle and dark values, or white, gray and black.

Composition and Value

You can see how the different elements break down into values and thus allow each element its own place in the depth of the panel.

This is pretty much what it becomes in terms of composition: The face in the front is dark. And since he's looking off into the distance and doesn't seem to have much dialogue, I can get away with it. His face can still be seen clearly. But the focus becomes the figure behind him who's gesturing enough to give me an indication that he's probably got more dialogue in the panel.

Because I've accented the basic composition with my color choices and values, everything exists in a different space, giving the reader the sense that one person is in the front and the other is in the back. If the figures were closer in value, it would look like one giant person and one tiny person standing next to each other.

This doesn't mean that every time someone is in the extreme foreground, he should be dark. As long as each element has its own compositional value, and the point of highest contrast is where the reader's eye is drawn to, everything is in fine shape.

***Defenders* #3, page 20: ©2008 Marvel Characters, Inc. Used with permission.**

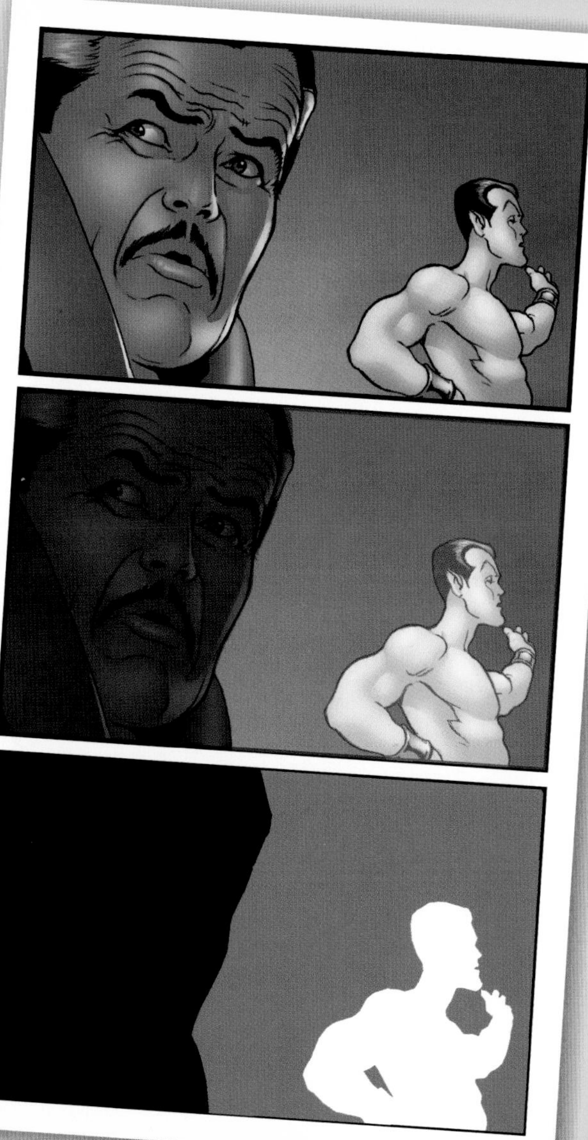

INSIDER VOICE

John Byrne on the Case for Collaboration

The best thing about the collaborative process, of course, is having another voice in the mix. Co-plotting *The Uncanny X-Men* with Chris Claremont, my function often as not was to say, "No." (When I left the book, Chris did everything I had said "No" to, in order!) But, on the other hand, if the talent is really on the ball, the other voice can come from within one's own head, pushing to take everything one step, two steps, three steps further.

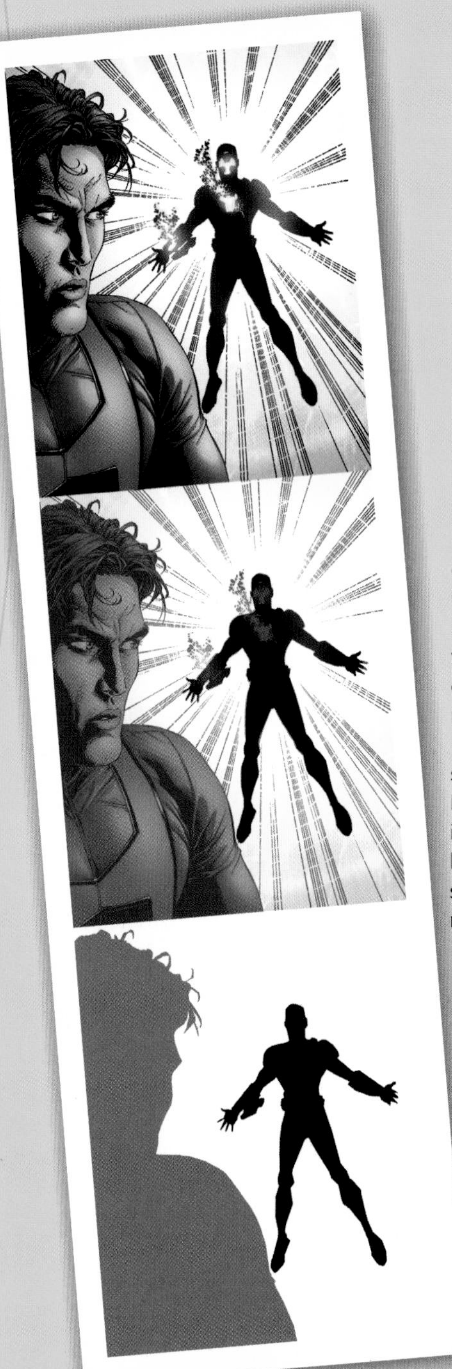

Light Sources and Contrast

A value breakdown for this panel shows how the highest point of contrast works with the white.

The obvious point of highest contrast is between the darkest value and the lightest value. So, why did I choose the gray value to be the character in the foreground? Besides the fact that the drawing indicates that the far background character will be the darkest value no matter what I do, and is radiating light, it's very important for the reader to notice and spend a little time on the reaction of the man in front. Because both figures have different overall values, they can be easily recognized as existing in different places in the same scene.

As for lighting, depending on how open the drawing is or how it's lit, we can have some real fun playing with lighting direction, color and intensity. But as important as it is to be creative, we also have to be reasonable. Light sources cannot be created out of thin air for our convenience.

Lighting a face from underneath will make someone look evil and give him a lot of presence. It never fails to make something look way more interesting than it would be otherwise. Harsher lights cast longer and wider shadows. Those long shadows can add a lot of sadness or, with the right color choices to back it up, tension. And shadows must be added to give light sources balance and realism.

As long as light sources are consistent, they add a lot of dramatic effect to different objects to help move the story and keep the reader's interest. And that's really what is needed for great storytelling.

***Squadron Supreme* #3, page 3: ©2008 Marvel Characters, Inc. Used with permission.**

Much like the letterer or even an inker, the better the colorist, the more he blends in.

The colorist's role is a contribution, a part of a greater whole. The artwork should maintain a level of cohesion and have a certain flow about it. As much as we all want to leave our marks and stand out, we can't do it at the risk of everyone else's work. Fighting the inked drawing with overdone color risks pulling the reader out of the reading experience and ruining not just the pacing of the story but the story itself. So it's important to be able to accurately judge just what a particular story or penciller needs to complement the rest of the work and the tone of the story. Some pencillers will require a lighter touch—simple coloring with a somewhat limited palette. A more graphic style can really benefit from something like that. A book like *Hellboy* would suffer from reader distraction if it were over-rendered, given not just the artistic style but the subject matter. But then, some pencillers thrive on allowing their color artist to help "fill in the blanks," thus leaving many things open for interpretation. We must use our creative judgment to decide what's best for the project. How far to go. What kind of techniques to use. Use the opportunity to problem solve, and look at what some other people are doing. There may be many different ways to accomplish one particular thing. One of the best tools in our problem-solving arsenal is to examine nature. Most of the answers can be found there, and our interpretations can lead to fresh ideas, which is really where creativity starts.

INSIDER VOICE
Neal Adams on Teaching and Learning

A person is not taught; a person learns. As a teacher I've had these experiences: You can go into a classroom with the assumption that you're going to teach people something. Well, that isn't going to happen. People can only be taught what they are willing to learn. And if they want to learn, they can suck things out of you that you might not otherwise give them. So the concept of teaching is almost a ridiculous concept. The concept of learning is the important concept. You can't teach people who don't want to learn. But you can easily teach people who want to learn by just making the information available.

10

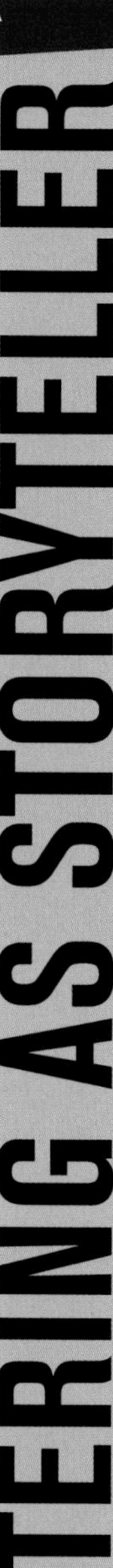

Every part of creating a comic can improve or detract from storytelling. Lettering is no different. To most people, lettering is just a matter of slapping type on a page to tell what characters are saying and avoiding covering a character's head. While that's part of it, it can be a useful tool in telling a story and in some cases can be the only thing that can tell the story. Many of the tools in the letterer's toolbox effectively impart to the reader what the writer and artist are trying to show. For example, a character is fighting a bad guy in a scene, and the text calls for the protagonist to say, "Take this, evildoer!" Now, if that were done in a large, bold and open-faced font with a starburst around it, it would convey the good guy being heroic and standing up to his nemesis. But what if the type were small and the balloon were normal-sized with a lot of white space around the text? It might convey to the reader that maybe the good guy is unsure of himself and doesn't believe he means what he says.

Another large part of storytelling that the letterer must deal with is leading the reader through a page. That is usually done by placement of balloons on a page, in order, reading from left to right and up to down. This sounds simple, but sometimes letterers have to make up for storytelling mistakes made by the artist. And poor placement of balloons can ruin good storytelling by covering up vital parts of a panel—the head of a character, an important focal point of the story or maybe even the character speaking. I've seen it happen and it's not pretty.

Another way that lettering helps in the storytelling starts right at the choice of font for a book. Years ago, when books were hand-lettered, the look of a book was pretty much dictated by who you got to letter it. Nowadays, with the availability of so many comic book fonts, the choice of font to use on a book has much more impact. There are scary-looking fonts, high-tech fonts, scratchy fonts—you want it, someone has created a font. The choice of font can also be chosen to match stylistically with the artist on a book. All these decisions will impact the storytelling in a comic almost as much as the choice of artist on a book. And the choice of font for sound effects is vital. A big craggy font would work well with an earth-shattering explosion, but not so much for a character falling into the ocean. The right choice can enhance the scene and sometimes make it much more important and powerful.

The other basic focus is on balloon shapes, styles and colors. Rough balloons, square balloons, oval balloons: All tell the reader something about the story. Some balloons have a long history and have become a "language" for comics. A burst

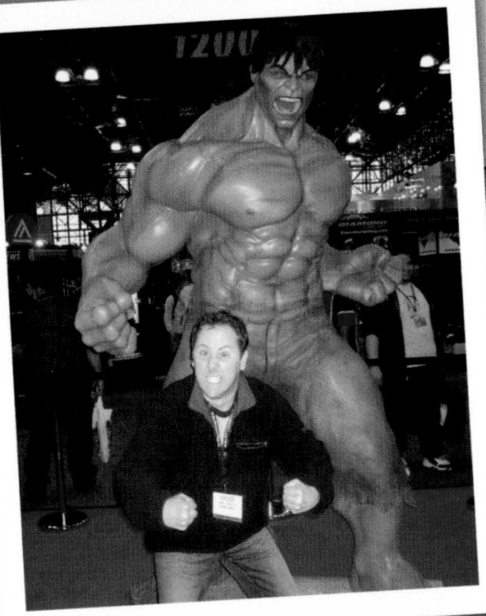

iNSidER PROFiLE

Chris Eliopoulos

OCCUPATION: Cartoonist/letterer

DATE OF BIRTH: September 30, 1967

FIRST PUBLISHED WORK: No clue.

INFLUENCES: Charles Schulz, Berkeley Breathed, Walt Kelly, Bill Watterson, Bill Oakley, Jim Novak

LONGEST RUN ON A BOOK: *Savage Dragon,* 106 issues

BEST KNOWN FOR: Lettering way too many books.

FAVORITE CHARACTER WORKED ON: Savage Dragon

DREAM PROJECT: My own comic strip.

MOST PERSONAL WORK: My webcomic, *Misery Loves Sherman.*

ART TRAINING: BFA from the Fashion Institute of Technology.

BEST ADVICE RECEIVED WHEN STARTING OUT: A type instructor in college told me to do the best you can in the time you're given.

CHRIS ELIOPOULOS is a fine cartoonist in his own right—check out his *Desperate Times* strip—but he has spent the majority of his time lettering other people's comics. He started his own company, Virtual Calligraphy, and quickly caught the eye of Marvel Comics where he snagged an unprecedented deal for his company to letter the majority of Marvel's publications. Chris himself oversees the quality of the lettering from his staff, trains them and continues to letter projects himself to this day. No other letterer has managed to train as successful and professional a staff of letterers as Chris.

balloon with sharp angles usually indicates shouting. A wavy balloon may indicate weakness while a dashed balloon indicates a whisper. A bubbly balloon has stood for someone's thoughts for many years and recently has started making a comeback on comics' pages. These are all tools that can help the reader really get into a story or boost the art and story to another level.

All lettering can help with storytelling or pull the reader right out of a story if not done right. In theory, if a letterer is doing his job properly, you won't notice the work. It should blend effortlessly with the art and story so that it's not something the reader focuses on.

Again, I've turned to an expert in the field. Chris Eliopoulos, owner of Virtual Calligraphy and letterer on *The Ultimates*, *Ultimate Spider-Man*, *Civil War* and hundreds more comics, will lead us through the lettering process.

Mechanics of Lettering

From Chris Eliopoulos

In the past, comics were lettered by hand using quill pens and a thing called an Ames guide. It took years to learn and perfect the craft of hand lettering for a professional to get the consistency and skill needed to be good. These days, with the advent of computers, the lengthy learning process of training your hand is no longer needed. All you need now is a credit card, a computer, software and fonts. That's the easy part. Learning how to use them takes more time, maybe not as much as hand lettering, but definitely a while if you want to be good. Since today, most books are lettered on the computer, I'll stick with those mechanics.

Most comics are lettered in Adobe Illustrator. The other important things are fonts. There a number of places online to buy fonts or download them for free. Artists also make their own fonts using programs such as Fontlab and Fontographer.

THE SCRIPT

The script is usually done in a word processing program, but Adobe Illustrator can open it. Once it's open, letterers can select all the type and change it to

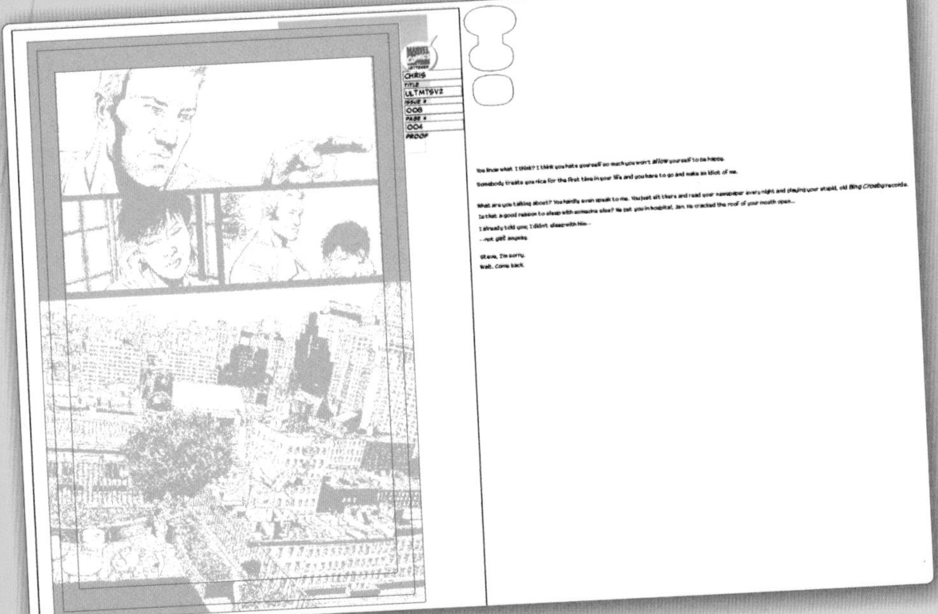

Setup

Here is what the letterer's screen looks like on the computer. The art file is on the left, and the script is on the right.

***The Ultimates* #8, page 4: ©2008 Marvel Characters, Inc. Used with permission.**

the font and size they like. Usually, at print size, most fonts are good at 6 points with a leading of 6.5 points. (*Leading* refers to the amount of vertical spacing between two lines of type.) Then they cut and paste individual balloon dialogue for each page.

BREAKING TYPE

After all the balloon text is broken up into individual type lines, it's broken up into smaller lines that look good in a balloon. I usually leave the type flush left and just insert the type tool and hit return at key spots to make sure that when I'm done, there's a slight bow in the middle. After that, I select all and, using the paragraph palette (or command-shift-c), center the type.

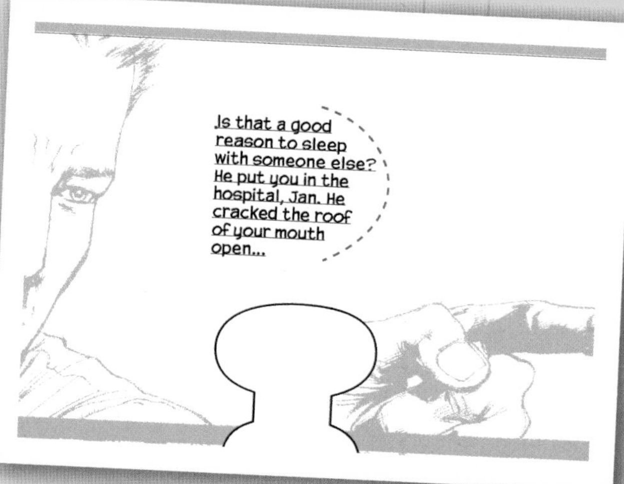

Typebreaks

There should be a slight bow in the middle of a block of text.

***The Ultimates* #8, page 4: ©2008 Marvel Characters, Inc. Used with permission.**

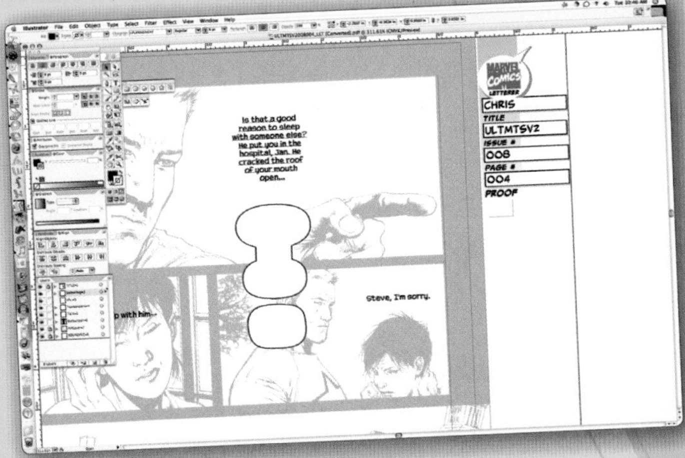

Type Centering

After the typebreaks are inserted, the type can be centered.

***The Ultimates* #8, page 4: ©2008 Marvel Characters, Inc. Used with permission.**

THE BALLOONS

Now, the balloons go around the type. To make things simple, I make all balloons with a white fill and a black stroke set at .75 points. Sets of balloons can be pre-made, also, to keep things simple. They're a little more squat than a pure oval, which I prefer, but the ellipse tool will always work. I choose among my balloons to find one that I think will fit around the text nicely, leaving as little dead space as possible.

Then I use the scale tool to increase or decrease the balloon to go all around the type. It's important to make sure the balloon shape isn't too big or too tight around the text. My rule of thumb is to have about a letter's space from the edge of the type to the line of the balloon.

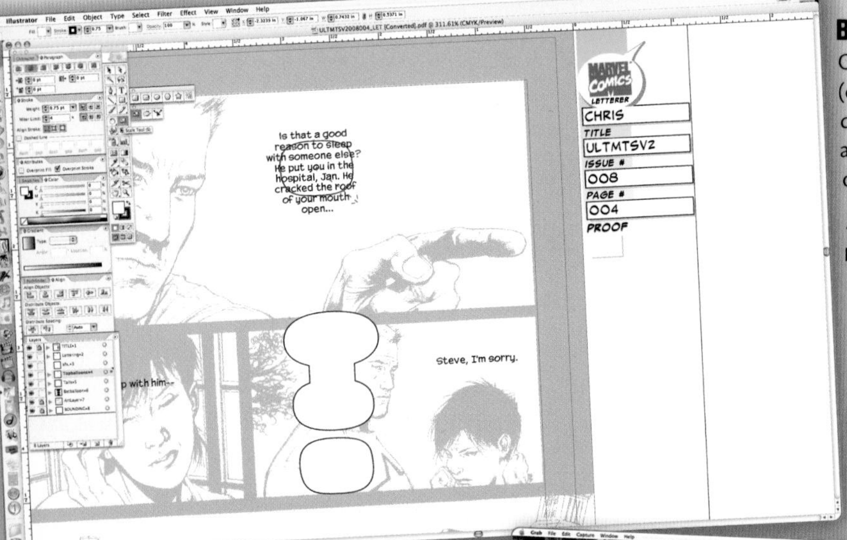

Balloon Shape

Once I choose a balloon, I copy it (click and hold down the option key, drag it where I want and release) and drag it centered, approximately, on the type.

***The Ultimates* #8, page 4: ©2008 Marvel Characters, Inc. Used with permission.**

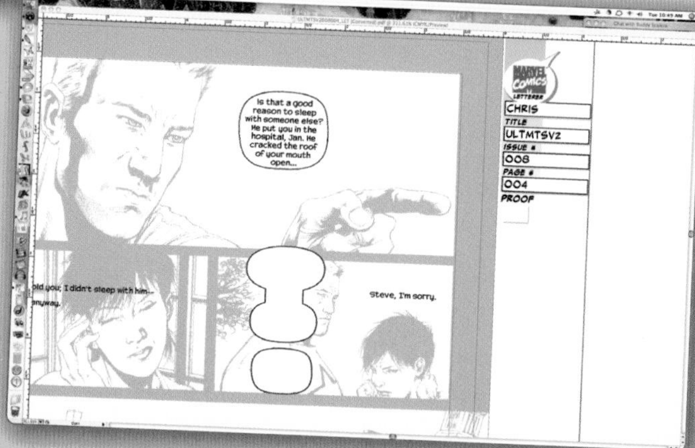

Centering the Balloon

The scale tool allows me to fit the balloon around the type.

***The Ultimates* #8, page 4: ©2008 Marvel Characters, Inc. Used with permission.**

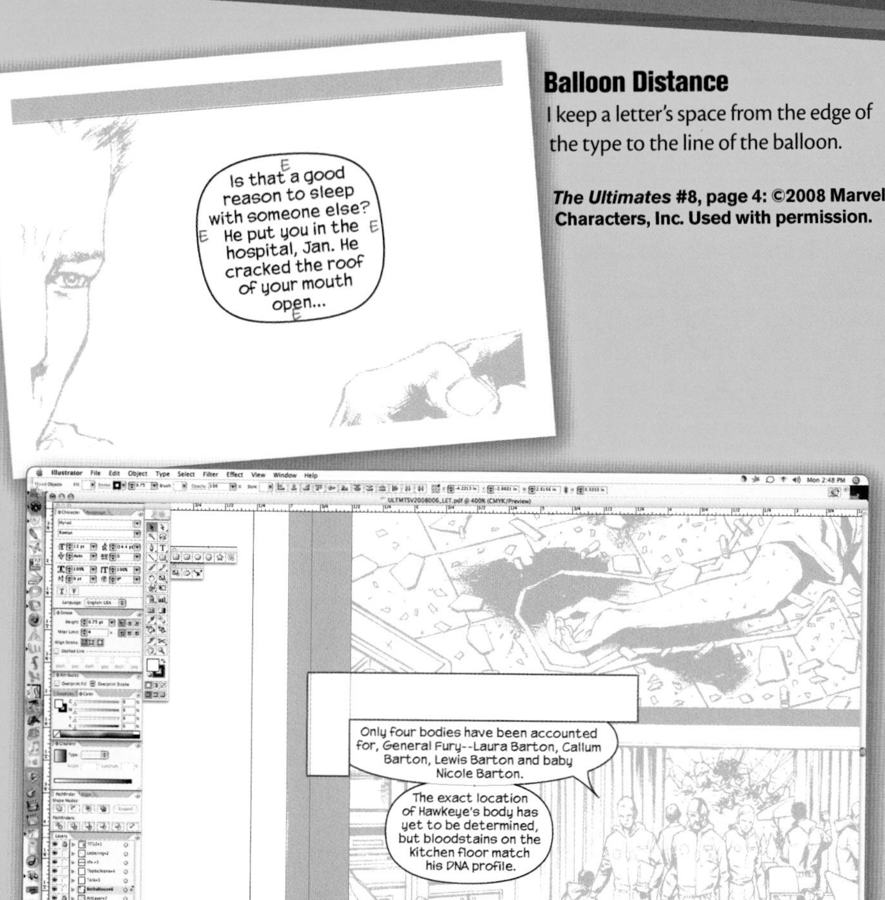

Balloon Distance

I keep a letter's space from the edge of the type to the line of the balloon.

***The Ultimates* #8, page 4: ©2008 Marvel Characters, Inc. Used with permission.**

Border Balloons

For balloons that butt up against a border, I ensure that the balloon is more spaced out on that side, make a rectangle along the borderline, select the two objects, and using the pathfinder palette, use minus front.

***The Ultimates* #8, page 4: ©2008 Marvel Characters, Inc. Used with permission.**

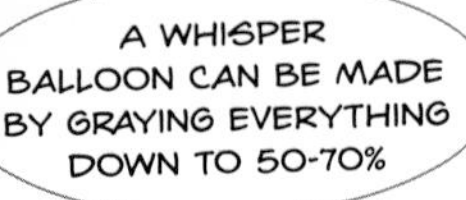

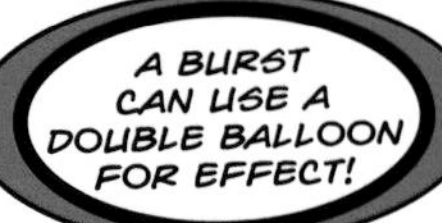

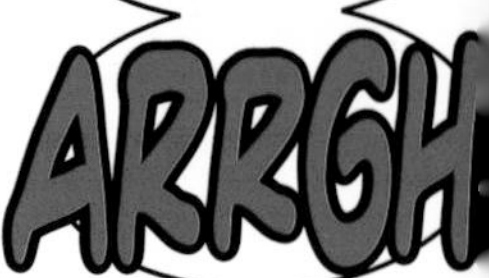

Style

Here are some tricks I use with my balloon styles.

Whispers: Gray everything down to 50 to 70% or use dashed edges.

Thoughts: Premade balloons or made with anchor points and using Pucker and Bloat in the Distort filter.

Bursts: Double balloons or bursts with sharp points.

Weakness: Reduce the type size, use the Roughen filter with the size set at 19, and the points smooth.

Television, radio or speakers: Add anchor points and use the Pucker and Bloat filter set at -11 or make special versions, making sure the text is italic.

Shouts: Burst out of the balloon.

STYLIN'

There are a number of effects you can use to present meaning in context of the story. The rules still apply in distance and spacing.

THE TAILS

Tails can be premade to save time, but I usually do mine for each balloon using the pen tool. Tails should always point at the face of the character that's talking, generally, and at their mouth, specifically.

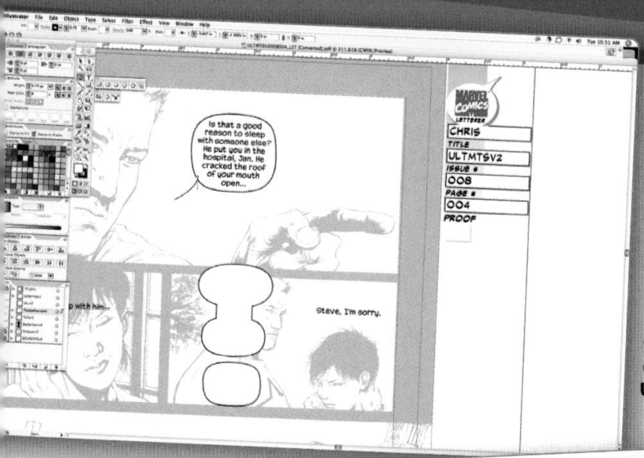

Tails

Using the pen tool, I click somewhere inside the balloon and, while still clicking, drag out to another point that aims toward the mouth, then release.

***The Ultimates* #8, page 4: ©2008 Marvel Characters, Inc. Used with permission.**

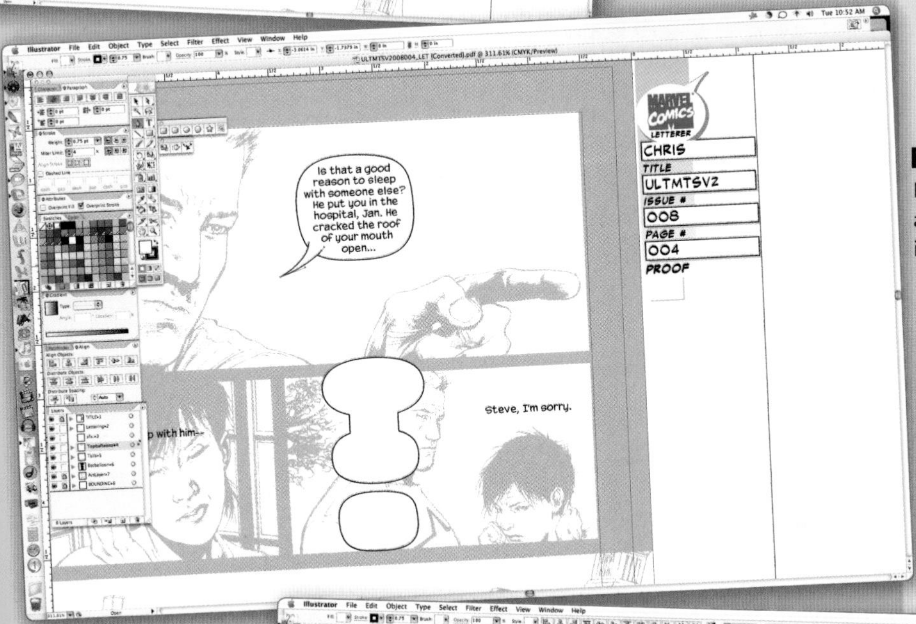

Repeat in Reverse

Repeat the same action from "Tails" in reverse, trying to give at least a letter's distance from the first point.

***The Ultimates* #8, page 4: ©2008 Marvel Characters, Inc. Used with permission.**

Unite

Then select both the balloon and tail and, using the pathfinder palette, unite them.

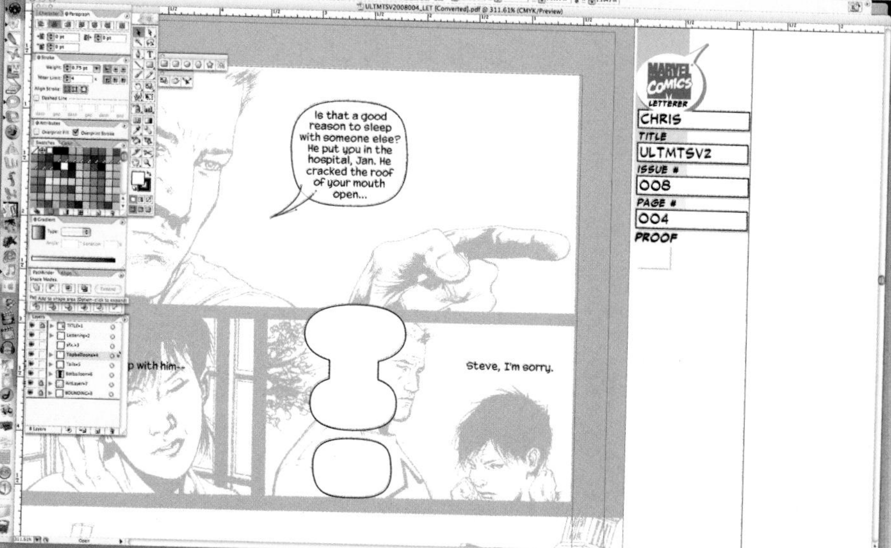

***The Ultimates* #8, page 4: ©2008 Marvel Characters, Inc. Used with permission.**

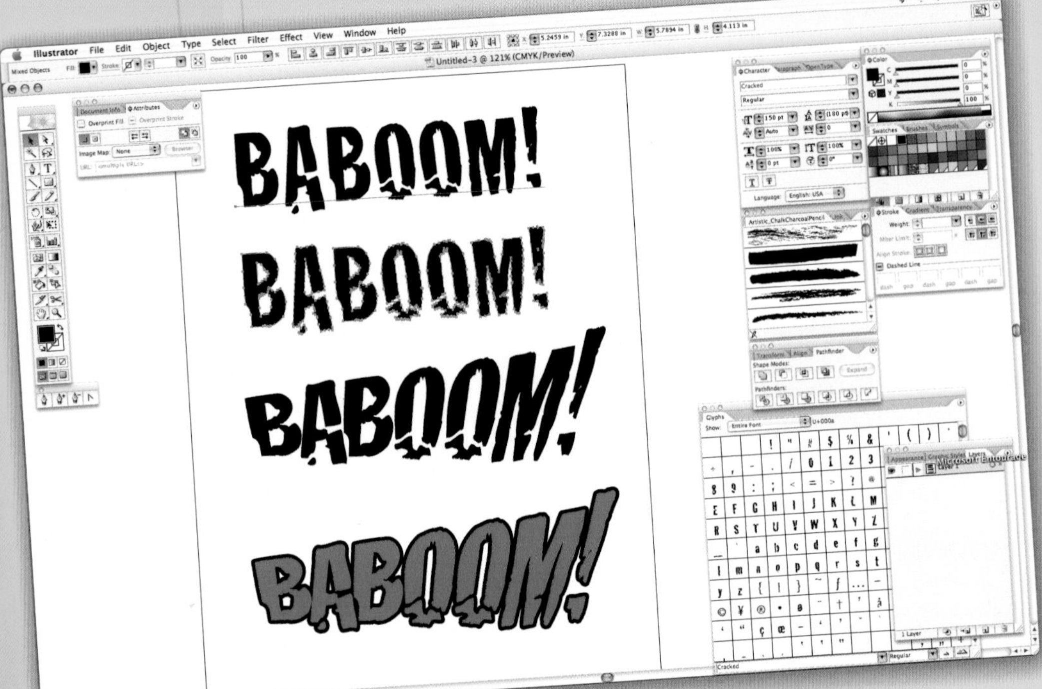

Sound Effects

A sound effect can be transformed from its original form in a basic sound effect font to a more developed "baboom!" in only a few steps.

INSIDER VOICE

John Byrne on the Case Against Collaboration

There are some good things that can come out of collaboration, but complete vision is usually the better product. Assuming you have someone with the chops to pull it off, that is!

Sound Effects

Creating sound effects looks complex, but it can be really simple. Just type in the word you want to use—like "baboom!"—then convert it to a sound effect font you own and create outlines and ungroup. The skew and scale tools help to vary the size of each letter (it's good not to vary *too* much from letter to letter). Then select the sound effect and copy it and paste behind it (command-b). Then increase the point size to the size that works. Pretty simple, eh?

Balloon Placement

From Chris Eliopoulos

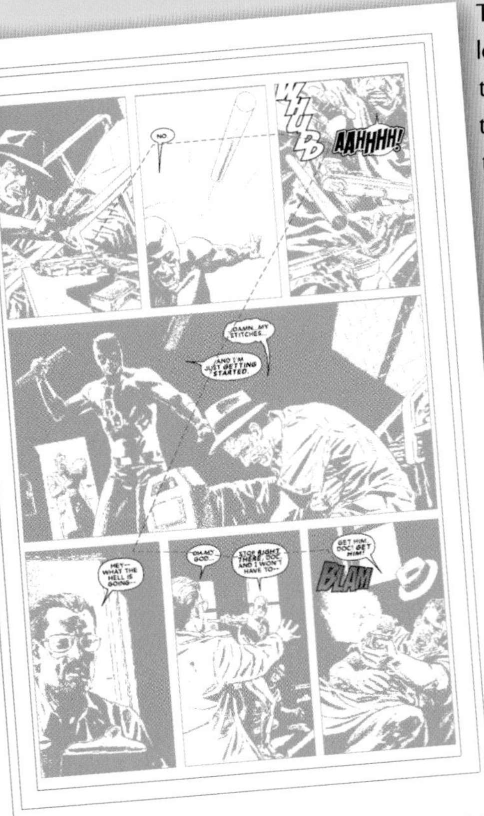

Balloon Placement

Comics read the same as everything else in the English language—left to right, down, then left to right again.

***Daredevil* #103, page 13: ©2008 Marvel Characters, Inc. Used with permission.**

The deceptive craft of balloon placement looks relatively easy, but can be difficult at times. The thing to remember is that, in the English language anyway, we read left to right, skip down and then read left to right again. Comics follow the same rule, from the text inside a balloon to the balloons in a panel to the panels on a page. That logic should be followed when placing balloons.

The big thing beyond order of balloons is not covering important things like heads, figures, faces of the character speaking and the person that character is speaking to. Also, it's important not to cover anything that is important to a story. For example, in a panel two people are talking about a box on the floor, and in the next panel, the box blows up. The letterer has to make sure not to cover the box in the first panel.

INSIDER VOICE

John Romita Jr. on Conversation Scenes

If it's a generic conversation in the middle of a park, and the writer wants a lighthearted conversation and you break away to show a couple of birds in a tree, you know you can pull back a little bit, you don't have to leave room for a rapid-fire conversation. You know, there's so much that goes into it. It's what I do. I spend a day or two thumbnailing out the whole story. And then I do it, and I pace it in a way that I like and that I know works.

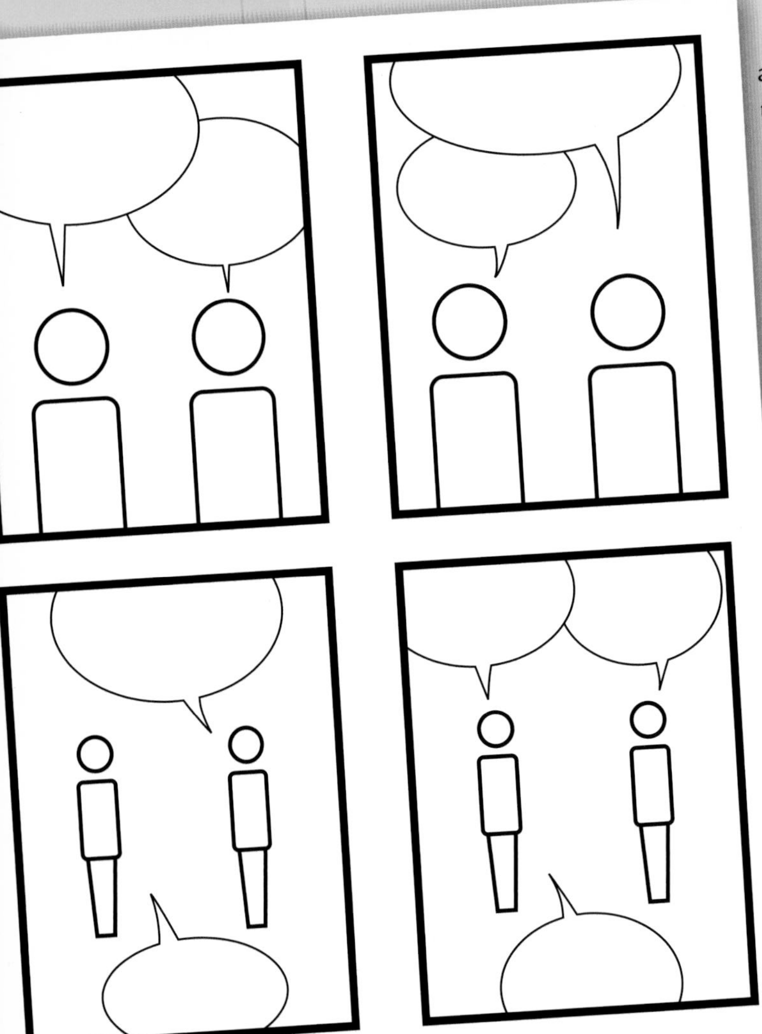

The lettering can also lead the eye around a page and help guide the reader to the next panel when it may be unclear. A simple solution is to overlap two panels with a balloon. That acts as a bridge between panels and helps to gently bring the reader along without having a big arrow pointing to the next panel.

A big mistake I see in novice letterers is crowding the characters in a panel. The balloons don't need to be right on top of characters. They can use a little breathing room. This goes for overlapping figures as well. A balloon can cut behind a figure as long as it doesn't overlap another figure that is at an equal distance or closer to the reader than the person overlapping the balloon—it can throw off the imagined distance in the art.

Finally, balloons must go in the order in which they should be read even if the artist has drawn the first character speaking on the right side of the panel. These are the big things to keep aware of when placing balloons.

Balloon Placement Options

In this image, there are four possibilities of balloon placement. Panel 1 shows ideally want you want to do. Panels 2 and 3 are ways to get around the fact that the person speaking first is on the right. Panel 4 is an example of how to fit balloons into a panel and not cover over the characters.

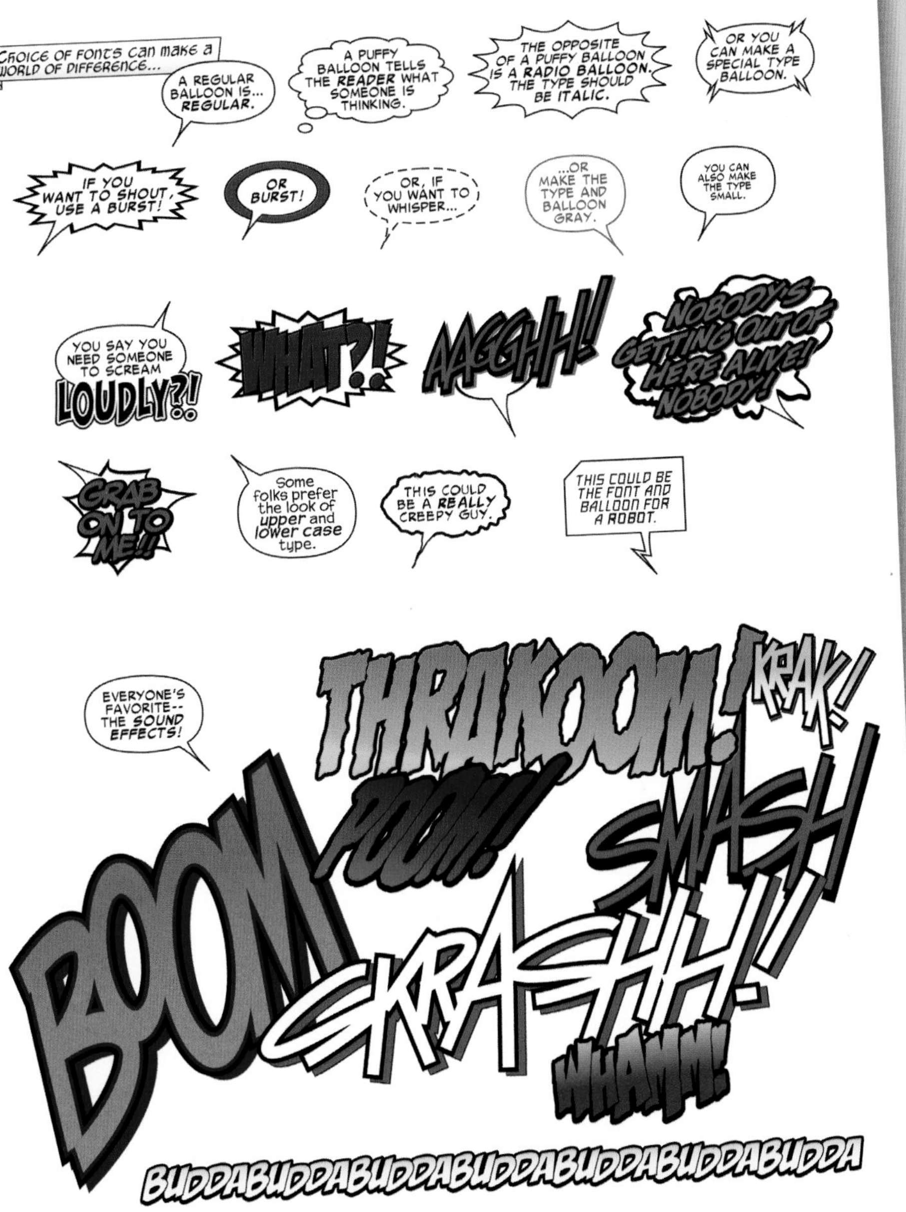

Variations

Creating a balloon effect is not an exact science. There is plenty of room for creative instinct. It's up to you to choose the right balloon and font style for your project.

Getting started in the comics industry isn't easy, but it's not as confusing and mystifying as many would have you believe. Like most industries, a lot of your success will come from connections you make, friendships you forge and being in the right place at the right time. All these are factors you have some control over. I have three rules of thumb for connecting in the comics industry.

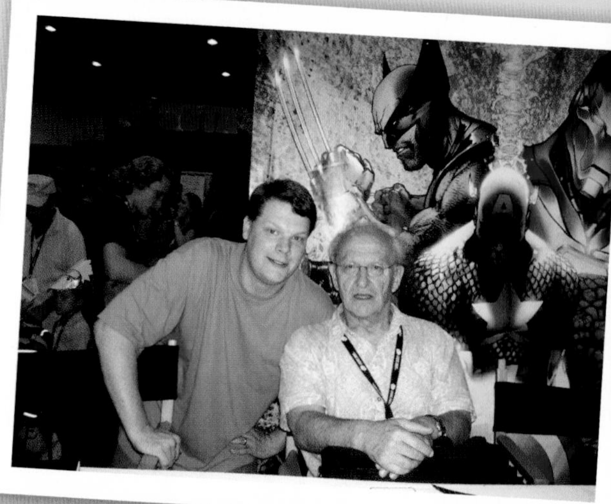

Moebius and Me at San Diego Comic-Con

The convention circuit is a fantastic place to meet other creators, editors, publishers, agents and fans. Heck, you even meet legends from time to time.

BE CONFIDENT

The first is be confident. Don't go overboard to the point where you're arrogant, but speak from a place of success. "Did you draw these pages?" "Yes, I did. You'll notice that I opted for an ink wash here to emphasize the growing storm…" That's a good answer. "Yes, I did. I'm new at this, so they're pretty weak, but I'm working on it…" is not a great answer. How you carry yourself and how you present your work means a lot to fans, editors and publishers.

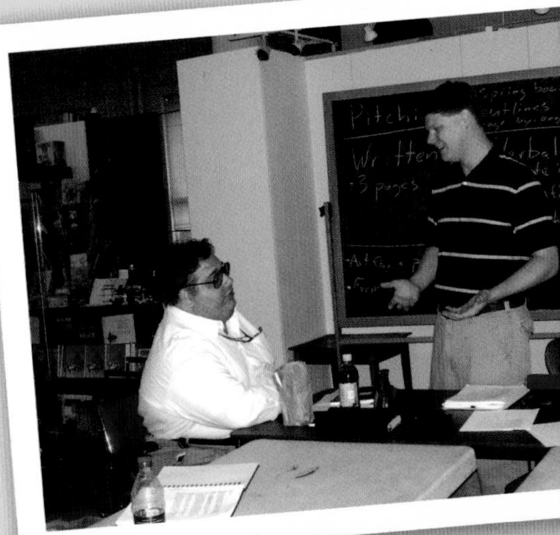

Comics Education

There are schools with courses in comics illustration and design. My business is called Comics Experience and you can find it at www.comicsexperience.com, where I offer courses on art and writing for comics as well as seminars on various other topics. The Joe Kubert School of Cartoon and Graphic Art has a long history of training artists to work in the comics industry. And many, many colleges and art schools offer courses on comics.

GET OUT THERE

Go to conventions if you can, meet up with people on the Internet, email and call on the phone to get people to notice you. Most of this won't produce direct results, but you're getting your name and your work in front of people, and that means you're starting to have a conversation with the industry, as I like to put it. You're saying to the industry, "Here I am. I'm ready to take you on, and I'm not going anywhere." And staying in the industry eye carries weight. The longer your name keeps floating around, the more likely you are to start picking up work.

BE NICE

Lastly, be nice. It's really as simple as that. When you meet people, be respectful of their time and thank them for talking with you. They're under no obligation to speak with you or look at your work. Take any critique you get with a smile and really try to see what the person is saying to you. Opinions may vary and it's up to you to decide who is right and who is wrong, but if you think you're right all the time and everyone else is wrong, you might want to look again—but I digress. Be nice to people. Editors and publishers don't like working with jerks.

INSIDER VOICE

Neal Adams on Freelance Fee Negotiation

You're gonna go for a job and show your work and they say, "We'd like to use you." Now, the question is what are they going to pay you? The first scenario is: They tell you how much they're going to pay you, "We pay this for this." Nine times out of ten that's not what happens. What happens is they say: "We want to use you, how much do you charge?" You have to be smart. You could say something really stupid like, "What do you want to pay me?" or "What can I get?" or name some low price in hopes that they'll say "Yes." Don't do that.

What you do is: Think about the number you would like to get, not the number you would be satisfied to get. Let's say you would be satisfied to get $600, but you'd like to get $2,000 dollars.

What you say is, "The last time I did a job like this I got $4,000"–double the number you would like to get–"I got $4,000. But I want to work on this job so I'd like find out what you guys are willing to pay or what's in your budget."

Now, what's gonna happen as a result of that? First of all, they can't pay you $4,000 dollars. The question is what could they pay you, what's in their budget? They have some idea what they can pay, so they will either say to you, "OK" or "Oh golly, that's kind of steep for us, I wasn't thinking of anything more than like $2,500," or "I'll pay you $1,000." You say "I want to work with you, that's fine."

The guarantee is your fee will never be $600.

Networking

From C.B. Cebulski

The old adage "It's not what you know, it's who you know" can be applied to almost any aspect of life, especially in the business world. There's nowhere it's more true, though, than in the business of comic books. And yes, no matter how hard we try to deny or ignore it, this is still a business!

Comic books are about people who LOVE what they do! Which in turn means that there's nothing more important when breaking into comics than networking. Every comic creator I've ever met has his or her own story about breaking in, and 99 percent of those stories are simply about being in the right place at the right time. About having met the right person. All it takes is one person to open that magical door that leads you to a paying gig in this biz. So basically, all you have to do is meet the right people. And in this day and age, modern technology makes it so much easier. Or does it?

It seems we have so many more advantages today than comic book wannabes had even ten years ago. Long gone are the days of typewriters and faxes and mailing in letters of inquiry. The Internet makes everything so much simpler. You'd think in this wondrous, new, wired world of scanners and JPEGs and email, networking should be a breeze. Never has it been easier to find and contact the actual people who can hire you to write and draw comics. The editorial staffs of each and every comic book publisher are just a few clicks of your mouse away. You can have your pitches and sample pages in their inboxes in an instant. So you'd think the doors would open that much faster, right?

Wrong.

If you ask me, technology's only made it harder to break in to comics. Keep in mind that everyone else has access to those exact same online outlets now as well. And everyone else is using them just like you are. They call it the World Wide Web for a reason! Every editor is being flooded with writing and art samples on a daily basis. To them, you're simply a name with an attachment. There's a darn good chance you'll be deleted along with every other unsolicited inquiry, which means you have to work harder to get the attention you think your work deserves. You have to make a name for yourself first. You have to make yourself unique and make them know who you are! And in that regard, there are ways where the Internet can be your biggest boon.

Sure, you can join MySpace or Facebook or LinkedIn. They are social networking sites after all, right? And truth be told, I've met some of the people I currently work with on those exact sites. But again, in joining one of these networks, you're just becoming a cell phone picture and digital friend along with the thousands of others who are visiting a creator's or an editor's profile and leaving comments or messages. You've gotta start smaller and think bigger. What I recommend doing is starting a blog.

CREATING A BLOG

In my opinion, blogs are the best way to establish a foothold for yourself on the Internet. Whether you're a writer or an artist, a blog is the best way to showcase who you are and what you do. It's easy to create, easy to post and easy to update. It will become your own personal social network, where you are in control and you can do whatever you like with it. And speaking from the editor's side of the desk here, the blog format makes it extremely

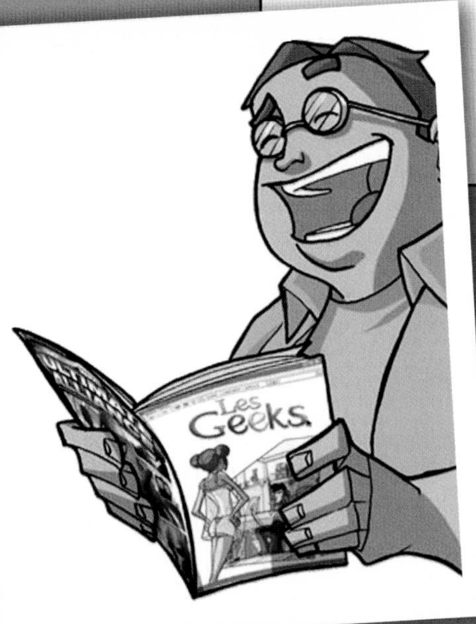

The most connected man I know, **C.B.** has worked at several comics publishers over his career but has spent the most time at Marvel, where he was an editor for several years before starting the Talent Management Department there. Essentially, his job became what he already was—a friendly face. He helps artists ensure that they always have projects to work on, helps recruit new artists and generally helps freelancers out however he can (within legal limits).

Art by Thomas Labourot and Christian Lerolle.

iNSidER PROFiLE

C.B. Cebulski

OCCUPATION: Writer/consultant

DATE OF BIRTH: February 17, 1971

FIRST PUBLISHED WORK: *Mythography* #7

INFLUENCES: George Lucas, Chris Claremont, John Hughes, Akira Kurosawa, Jim Morrison

LONGEST RUN ON A BOOK: Not all that long.

BEST KNOWN FOR: *Loners*, *Wonderlost*

FAVORITE CHARACTER WORKED ON: Medusa of the Inhumans

DREAM PROJECT: An original New Mutants Reunion.

MOST PERSONAL WORK: *Wonderlost*, my autobiographical anthology.

ART TRAINING: I can't draw to save my life!

BEST ADVICE RECEIVED WHEN STARTING OUT: It came a bit after I'd started writing, but Joe Michael Straczynski once advised me that when you write, you should write with only two people in mind: yourself and one other reader. If you're happy with the story you've written and one other person read and enjoyed it, you've done your job as a storyteller.

easy to visit, read and review...much more so than other options you have out there, even personal websites. Remember, editors are very busy people, and having to click through numerous links for each art gallery and every sample page will make their eyes glaze over before too long. A blog offers everything at one touch of a button. All an editor has to do is click the link to your blog to find a simple and cleanly formatted page, where all he needs to do is scroll down to see what you're all about. I can tell you from experience that it's much more convenient than any other format online, and a better way to present yourself and your work in a professional manner. Much better than using DeviantART, Flickr, ComicSpace or other sites that generate revenue through click-throughs and page views. On a personal blog, the only thing you're selling is yourself!

Once you have a blog and have it all loaded up with whatever presentation you feel like putting out into the world, it's time to spread the news. Now, here's where larger social networking sites like MySpace and Facebook can come in very handy as they have built-in ways of communicating information to larger groups of people, like Bulletins and Updates. This is where you can use these more far-reaching network services to get the word out and drive traffic and eyeballs back to your newly created personal blog.

Update your blog regularly, encourage commenting, always respond promptly to inquiries and keep things professional. Remember that your blog will pretty much become your résumé and you should always keep things focused on your work. If you wanna talk about the newest *Star Wars* news or comment on Spider-Man and Mary Jane's relationship, create a different blog for it.

DEVELOP A PRESENCE

And don't stop there! Develop a personal presence on popular comic book community message boards and forums. Brand yourself in these online communities. Make friends, talk about your shared love of the medium, and always keep promoting your own work and your own blog. Keep your name in the public eye. Popular sites I would recommend visiting the message boards and forums on are: news sites like Newsarama, Comic Book Resources and Alvaro's ComicBoards; sites dedicated to the sharing of ideas and art like Digital Webbing, Gutterzombie and eatpoo; and the sites of popular comic creators with large Web followings, like Brian Michael Bendis's Jinxworld, Mark Millar's Millarworld, Warren Ellis's Whitechapel and the Comic Bloc group site. All these sites usually have lively Creative sections where you can share your work with other up-and-comers as well as current professionals for feedback, recommendations and...networking, of course! Build a buzz around yourself.

PUT YOUR BEST FOOT FORWARD

Always put your best foot forward. That's advice I suggest you follow when you start contacting editors and sending out the link to your new blog. Always title your email in a way that gets right to the point: New Art (or Writing) Samples for (Editor's Name), then include a short message introducing yourself or reminding the editor who you are, explain what you do and direct him to where he should look at your work. One little piece of advice I often give: Do not include attachments unless requested in a reply from the editor. It only slows things down and seems pushy out of the gate. Another piece of advice: While being professional and polite, also try and be natural and humorous. Editors are guys and gals just like you and me who love comics and work long hours. Sometimes a little levity and a couple laughs can go a long way in getting them to click on your link and may even help them remember your name.

RESPONSE TIMES

Now if you don't get an immediate response, which you most likely will not, don't fret. It's just how the game is played. I always tell people to wait at least four to six weeks. If you haven't received a reply in that amount of time, then you should follow up with a polite reminder. Which now brings me to my "Rule of Four Ps." This is a little mnemonic device I always tell folks who ask me about networking, put in print for the first time here:

Be Professional and be Persistent. Don't be Pushy or a Pain-in-the-ass.

I don't think I need to explain that much more, do I? They are words to live by when trying to break into comics, be it online, during portfolio reviews or over beers in the bar at a show. By sending in your work and presenting yourself to an editor for a position writing or drawing comics, you're basically going in for a job interview. People forget that. Yes, we're all fans at heart and most editors I know don't wear suits to the office, but they're the people with the power to get you a job and should be treated with courtesy and respect. Remember that they're getting hundreds of emails just like yours and can't always get back to you right away. Yes, you are enthusiastic about your proposal and/or pages and you want immediate feedback, but so does everyone else. Don't keep sending out pesky follow-up emails, shooting over new samples and demanding responses. All you'll serve to do is annoy the editor, which is something no one wants to do. Just be cool.

There are no guaranteed ways or easy answers about breaking into comics, but it really does all start with people. Like I said at the beginning, it's all about getting your name out there, getting your work noticed, and becoming someone people know. And once they know you, you know them, and then you join the ranks of the "who's who" working professionally in the comic book medium.

Best Place to Meet Editors

Bars are the best places at conventions to network face-to-face with editors and other creators. Buying someone a beer guarantees you have his attention for at least a couple minutes and is always something you can use later in follow-up with him. Someone is always sure to open an email that reads: The Beers We Shared at the Hyatt. However, I would advise artists to not bring portfolios to the bar. It just seems desperate and people will avoid you. And also, don't get drunk as you don't want to become the joke of the con. Yes, that makes an impression, but not the kind an up-and-coming young creator needs hanging over him. Watch the editors get drunk instead.

It doesn't matter if you don't live in a city with comic book publishers. These days, with the online community, you've got plenty of resources streaming into your home through your modem. The resources tend to fall into a few categories.

NEWS WEBSITES

These are the most common and most frequented of comics-related websites. Stay in touch with the latest news and artwork in the industry by plugging into the comics news websites. You'll get the latest release information, comic reviews, first looks at artwork, interviews with creators, and all kinds of goodies that help you stay in touch with the industry that you love. Some of the more popular news websites are Comic Book Resources (www.comicbookresources.com), Newsarama (www.newsarama.com), Comics Bulletin (www.comicsbulletin.com), Wizard Universe (www.wizarduniverse.com), and Pulse (www.comicon.com/pulse).

PROFESSIONAL PRODUCTS AND INSTRUMENTS

These provide your basic supplies. They range from your standard art supply stores, to stores to get comic boxes and bags, to places where you can get comic book art board delivered to your door. Blue Line Pro (www.bluelinepro.com) is one of the more common places to go for comic book industry-specific art supplies.

NETWORKING WEBSITES

Networking is a lot like the joke about the tree falling in the forest. If you're the greatest comic book artist of all time, but no one ever sees your work, do you have a job? There are new websites set up every month to help comic creators and hopefuls meet each other and maybe even meet publishers or editors as well. Some of these come and go and some have places for actual job postings. Some of the more popular places for artists to go are Digital Webbing (www.digitalwebbing.com), Penciljack (www.penciljack.com), and ConceptArt (www.conceptart.org). All these sites allow you to show off your stuff and look at the competition. DeviantART accounts can give you a place to showcase your artwork as well. And much like MySpace, there is a ComicSpace where you can find many creators, editors and publishers mingling from time to time.

INDIVIDUAL CREATOR WEBSITES

Hey, Brian Michael Bendis has one, so should you! If you like a particular creator, there's a pretty good chance that he or she has a website. If so, that's a great place to go to start talking with him. If you're thinking of becoming a comics artist, I recommend that you have your own website if you can. It doesn't mean anything in particular, but it gives you a good place to focus your energies when you're not working on paying gigs and it allows people to find you easily on the Web, which is good when they have money they want to give to you!

PUBLISHER WEBSITES

The last major category is the publishers themselves. Almost all of them have websites of their own. If you have a question about how to submit samples or a pitch, check out the website for guidelines. If you're not sure what kind of comics they publish, you'll probably get a good idea from their website. Take a look around and see what's out there. Figure out where you are likely to fit in and concentrate your efforts there.

Conventions are still the best place to network for comics. They are also a lot of fun. This can be a bit of a problem if you let it. Excessive drinking, partying, yelling and even touching can lead to big problems for your potential career. So it's important to stay focused. Your goal is to impress colleagues and professionals, and that does not mean leave any impression, just a good one. There are only two things you need to remember to do.

WHAT TO DO AT CONVENTIONS

1 **Research before you go**. Go to the convention website and find out which publishers and creators are going to be there. If you are not already familiar with the publishers or creators, research them so you know who you're going to try to talk with and ensure that you can speak intelligently with them about their needs. Find out what editors from a publisher are going to a convention and research their work. This way, if you find yourself in a conversation with an editor, you can speak about his projects—finding something nice to say is usually a plus. Don't stop at just publishers. Make sure to meet as many creators as you can while at the convention. The more you can find out about how they work and what working in the industry is like for them, the better prepared you're going to be for the start of your own career. Remember, at the end of the day, if you're looking for paying work, you're trying to help them get what they want, not the other way around.

2 **Know where you're going.** Most conventions offer maps online, but even if they don't, you should get one at the door. Take a few minutes at the beginning of your day (or the night before if the map is online) to figure out where you want to go, who you want to see and in what order. Conventions are crazy busy, so you'll miss something the first time around. Plan for time to go back and check out things you wanted to see but missed.

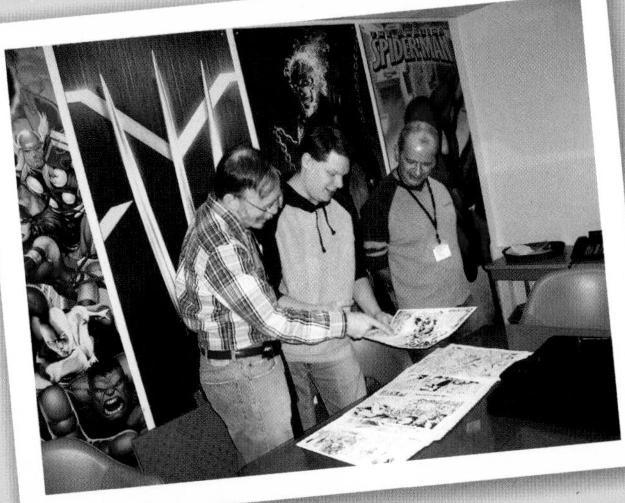

Art Reviews at Cons

While at a convention, many publishers offer art or portfolio reviews free of charge. Here, I'm standing with Walt Simonson and Klaus Janson, reviewing their work.

INSIDER VOICE

Gene Ha on Conventions

Comic conventions are great because I can see how everyone else is doing their job. It's always nice seeing a beautifully inked page on Bristol. It's exciting seeing a page where you can't figure out how they did it. Eastern European artists like Esad Ribic and Adi Granov come to mind. Their artistic influences and techniques are so different than American ones.

Small Presses

I've spent most of my time talking about the two biggest American publishers, Marvel and DC Comics. They do primarily superhero comics. But that's far from all that's out there. The other publishers that have been growing over the past decade are IDW Publishing, BOOM! Studios, Image Comics, Dark Horse Comics and Oni Press. They offer unique comics with different spins on characters and genres. They all have websites and are worth looking into. You may find better success at one of them than the largest companies.

Beyond even those, it's great to look at even smaller publishers like Antarctic Press, Th3rd World Studios and many, many others. It's okay not to make a huge splash with your first published work, and it's probably for the best. You'll be learning so many new things about your art, telling a story, how to work with publishers and printers, that you'll look back on your first efforts with a sense of pride. But also it's good to cut your teeth on smaller projects instead of big ones. If you get too much exposure too soon, it can actually work against you. Often, what happens is the comics reading public doesn't think an artist has paid his dues and becomes unusually harsh on that artist's work. You can't predict when that's going to happen, but it's good to avoid that if you can.

The thing to remember about smaller press publishers is that they are in almost all cases having a difficult time making a living and a profit. So if you own your own idea or story, you'll want to be aware that you will most likely have to give up some of the rights for licensing. The number of people trying to rip you off is quite small, but that doesn't mean you shouldn't be careful. But be aware that the publishers will need to cover their costs somehow, and that probably means some sort of deal beyond just printing the comic.

Search on Google or even Wikipedia for comic book publishers to find out all the different ones out there. New publishers crop up and others shut their doors all the time, so be alert and stay on top of the publishers.

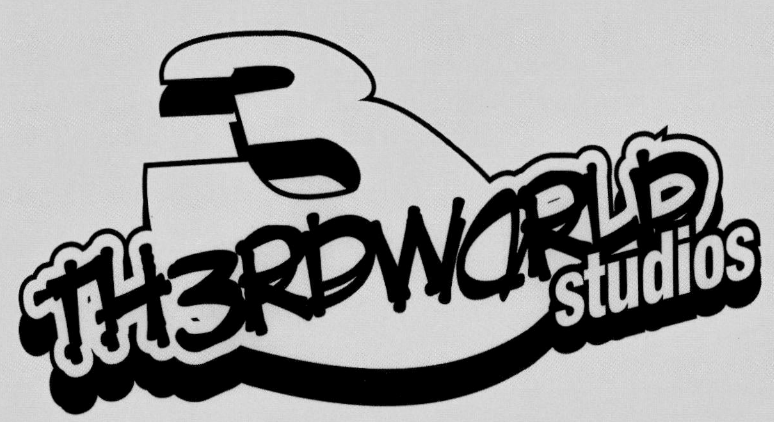

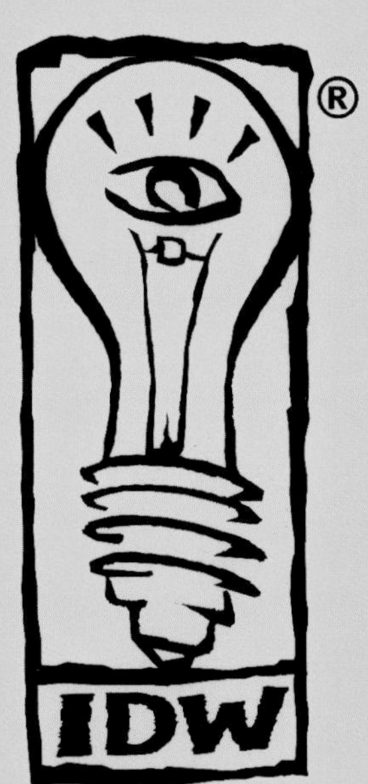

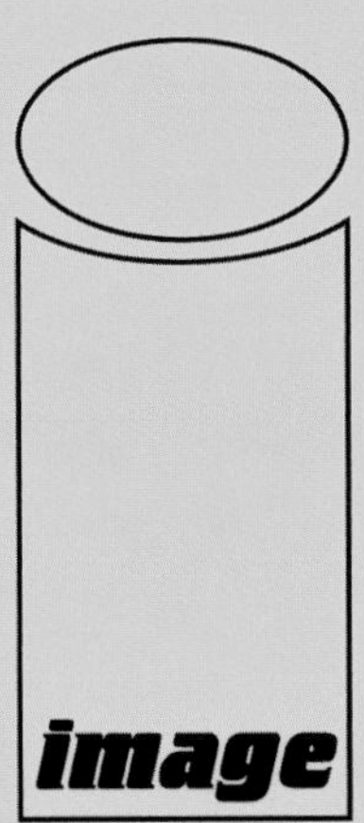

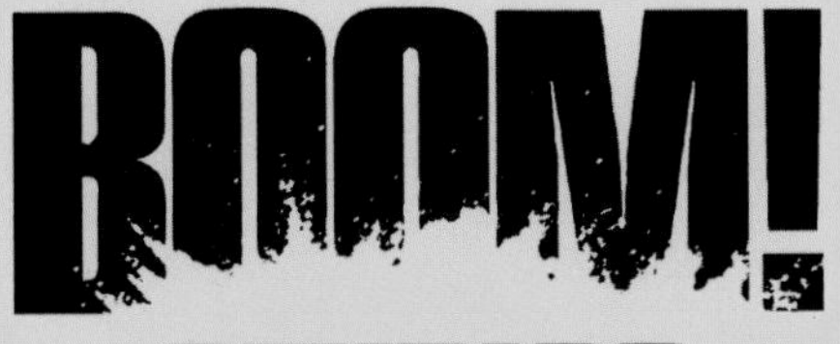

BOOM-STUDIOS.COM

I've seen it a thousand times. Creators who don't understand how to approach editors and publishers experience difficulty getting their careers off the ground. It's a cold reality that creators, writers, pencillers, inkers and colorists have to be able to sell themselves to editors and publishers. It's important to realize two things about approaching editors:

1 Why editors are there and what their goals are.

2 How to approach them.

WHAT EDITORS WANT

It's not always the same thing. Most of them are interested in putting together projects that interest them and that they can sell to their superiors within the company. What that means is this: Editors and publishers are not there to do you favors and they are not there because they owe you work. They are there (at a convention or in their own offices) to complete their jobs the best way possible. Take into account the editors' needs and focus on what you can do for them, rather than what work is "owed" to you or how great you are. Find in your own work or process how hiring you can benefit an editor and the publisher.

HOW YOU BENEFIT THE EDITOR OR PUBLISHER

There are a few ways you can benefit an editor or the publisher.

1 High-quality work.

2 Speed. If you can pencil four pages a week or more, you're in good standing. And that can help increase your value to a publisher.

3 The ability to get along and communicate clearly with your editor, and to listen to your editor, is also extremely helpful.

The last one is more difficult to prove, since an editor typically has to experience working with you to come to this conclusion. Present yourself as an easygoing professional who understands their pressures and obligations. You want them to know that your goal is to help them make their jobs easier.

APPROACHING EDITORS

Approaching editors can be daunting. It just can be. I sat on that side of the desk for over five years and now I'm on the other side and know the editors, and I still find it daunting at times. It's an intimidating process. Do your best not to let it intimidate you. The more natural you are, the better your conversation with an editor is going to go.

At conventions, don't approach an editor while he's clearly on a lunch break or walking the convention floor. That's usually him on his own time and it's not appropriate to hit him up at those times. After convention hours isn't a very good time either. But during convention hours, at the publisher's booth, is perfect. That's

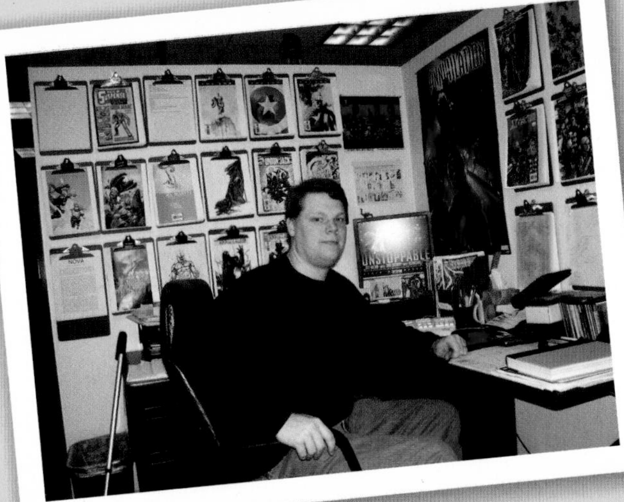

Me at My Desk at Marvel

why they are there—to talk with fans and professionals.

When approaching an editor, take into account that the editor is a human being. He is not a deposit box for your samples. He is not a microphone to record your verbal pitch. He is a human being. Be polite. Ask how he is doing. Inquire about what comics he has worked on or is currently working on. Find out about his job. Ask him to talk about himself a bit. It loosens up the editor, gives you some valuable information (maybe even something to talk about if he mentions something that interests you), and gives you time to become more comfortable.

You may be dying to show your pages, but don't back an editor into a corner. Simply ask if he would mind looking at your samples. If the answer is no, ask if you can leave him with a packet. But don't get pushy. That won't help you in the long run.

Pocket Tips for Approaching Comic Book Editors

- Remember, it's not about getting a job on the spot, it's about making that connection.
- Engage them at appropriate times.
- Be polite.
- Ask questions about what they do.
- Ask them to look at your work.

If you get that far, you've done really well.

END WITH THREE QUESTIONS

At the end of the conversation, ask three quick questions:

1. Ask for a business card. You want his contact information so you can follow up later.
2. Ask if it is okay to follow up with that editor (even if you don't get a business card).
3. Ask if there are any editors that this person would recommend you speak with. If you get more contact information, that's a huge success. You won't get any of those things if you don't ask, so be sure to ask. You've got nothing to lose.

COMICS & SEQUENTIAL ART, BY WILL EISNER

Will Eisner is the grandmaster of American comics, and lucky for the rest of us, he's also a great teacher. This is the first and classic text on how to draw and create comics by the industry's most beloved creator.

THE DC COMICS GUIDE TO PENCILLING COMICS, BY KLAUS JANSON

DC Comics recently put out their own book on pencilling by comics great Klaus Janson. His book is an amazing wealth of information and theory all combined into practical lessons. This text focuses less on superhero stories in particular and more on how to tell great stories. But let's be honest, you can't be a great superhero artist without being a great storyteller.

THE DC COMICS GUIDE TO COLORING AND LETTERING COMICS, BY MARK CHIARELLO AND TODD KLEIN

When you're ready to get into coloring and lettering, start here. Chiarello is DC Comics's art director and has been an influential force in the comics industry for twenty years. He absolutely knows everything he's talking about backwards and forwards. Klein is also one of the foremost letterers in the industry. Between him and Chris Eliopoulos, whom you read in this book, you'll have all there is to know about lettering technique and tips.

DYNAMIC FIGURE DRAWING, BY BURNE HOGARTH

There's not an artist out there who doesn't have trouble with anatomy from time to time. Hogarth's now classic book is the best book about how to draw the human anatomy I've ever read. This book teaches anatomy and drawing in an easy to understand and use way. It truly is amazing.

HOW TO DRAW COMICS THE MARVEL WAY, BY STAN LEE AND JOHN BUSCEMA

If you want to draw superhero comics, this is the place to do it. This book is harder to find nowadays, but it's the single best book on pencilling dynamic and exciting superhero stories you'll ever find.

UNDERSTANDING COMICS, BY SCOTT McCLOUD

This book is perfect for understanding the medium of comics. It covers how comics work and why people relate to them so easily. It's fascinating and is a staple of any comics enthusiast's collection.

WRITING FOR COMICS WITH PETER DAVID

Not only does Peter provide great advice for storytelling, but he also covers format and balloon placements. Most importantly, though, his book makes you think about how to tell your story in the best possible way.

Index

Look for these exciting titles!

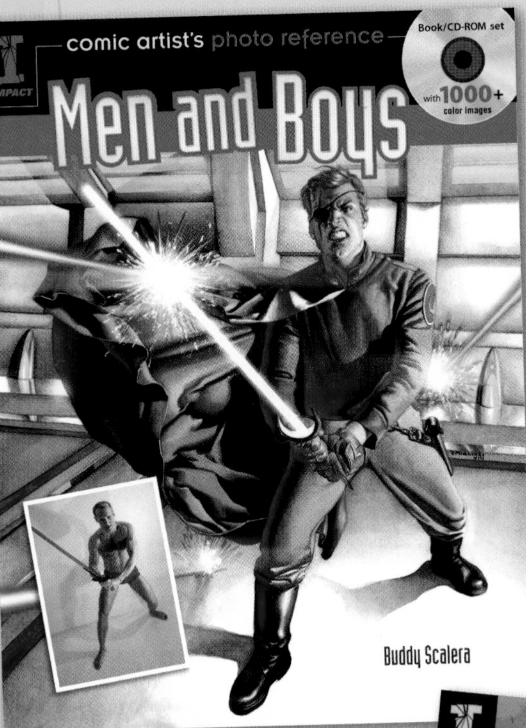

Whether the storyline calls for your character to perform incredible feats of strength, puts him in a shoot-out with the bad guys or hurls him across the page, *Comic Artist's Photo Reference: Men and Boys* will help you draw the perfect pose. With more than 1,000 high-quality photos to choose from, you'll find the inspiration you need to give your heroes, villains, studs and other characters attitude and authenticity.

ISBN-13: 978-1-60061-004-2
ISBN-10: 1-60061-004-8
PAPERBACK W/CD-ROM, 144 PAGES, #Z1000

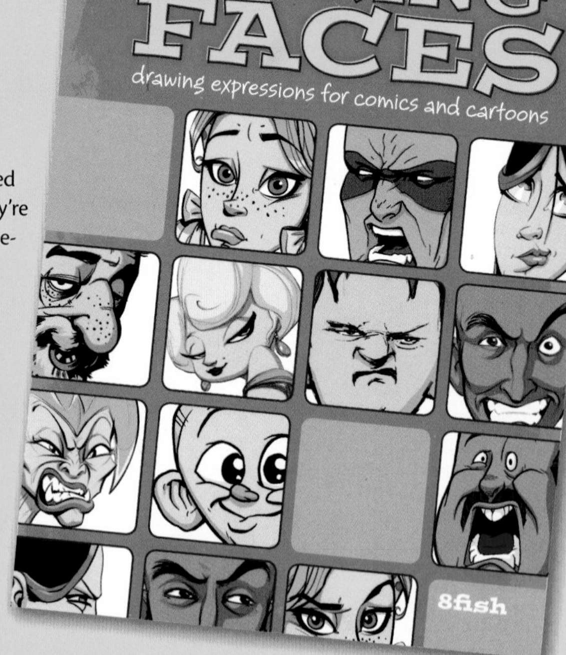

In order to give characters life, you need to know what they look like when they're about to sneeze, when they smell something stinky or when they're flirting, horrified or completely blotto. That's what this book is all about.

ISBN-13: 978-1-60061-049-3
ISBN-10: 0-60061-049-8
PAPERBACK, 176 PAGES, #Z1598

These other fantastic *IMPACT* titles are available at your local bookstore, art retailer or online supplier.

Get free tutorials at our website, www.impact-books.com.